Guy Maddin: Interviews

Conversations with Filmmakers Series
Peter Brunette, General Editor

Guy Maddin
INTERVIEWS

Edited by D. K. Holm

University Press of Mississippi / Jackson

www.upress.state.ms.us

The University Press of Mississippi is a member of the Association of American University Presses.

Copyright © 2010 by University Press of Mississippi
All rights reserved

First printing 2010

Library of Congress Cataloging-in-Publication Data

Maddin, Guy.
   Guy Maddin : interviews / edited by D. K. Holm.
      p. cm. — (Conversations with filmmakers series)
   Includes filmography and index.
   ISBN 978-1-60473-562-8 (cloth : alk. paper) — ISBN 978-1-60473-563-5 (pbk. : alk. paper)
 1. Maddin, Guy—Interviews. 2. Motion picture producers and directors—Canada—Interviews. I. Holm, D. K. II. Title.
   PN1998.3.M322A3 2010
   791.4302'33092—dc22
   [B]   2009044663

Contents

Introduction   ix

Chronology   xvii

Filmography   xxi

Far from the Maddin Crowd   3
    Robert Enright

Far from the Maddin Crowd: Guy Maddin Interviewed   19
    Alan Jones

Weird Art and Science: Guy Maddin's Primitive Genius   28
    David Chute

A Trip through Maddin's Videotape Collection   31
    Caelum Vatnsdal

"I may be straying into a minutiae that even *I'm* not interested in at the moment"   40
    Guy Maddin

"Well, maybe now's the moment"   42
    Guy Maddin and George Toles

Tales of Guy Maddin   45
    Mike White

"Now here we have . . ."   53
    Guy Maddin and George Toles

Purple Majesty: James Quandt Talks with Guy Maddin   57
   James Quandt

"Hi, I'm Guy. I made this thing"   67
   Guy Maddin

Guy Maddin Discusses His Film Career   70
   Terry Gross

The Reconfiguration of Film History: Guy Maddin   77
   Jonathan Marlow

Mr. Beaks Gets to the Root of Brilliance with Guy Maddin—
An Absolute Genius!   110
   Jeremy Smith

"I wanted to use as much Bram Stoker text as possible"   117
   Guy Maddin

The Pleasures of Melancholy: An Interview with Guy Maddin   119
   Marie Losier and Richard Porton

Dissecting the Branded Brain: An Interview with Guy Maddin   140
   David Church

When in Winnipeg   166
   José Teodoro

Interview with . . . Guy Maddin   172
   D. K. Holm

Talking with Winnipeg's Remarkably Well-Adjusted Guy Maddin   174
   Aaron Hillis

Interview with Guy Maddin, Director of *My Winnipeg*   176
   James Nadeau

"So, this was our first full talkie. And how"   182
   Guy Maddin and George Toles

Guy Maddin 185
   Isabella Rossellini

Index 197

Introduction

In an old joke about psychoanalysis, a patient reports to his analyst, "I had a dream last night, Doc," and goes on to recount a fantastical, surrealistic, and lurid nocturnal narrative. When the patient comes to the dream's end, the typically laconic psychoanalyst murmurs, "Ah, very interesting." But a little later, when the hour is up and the patient is about to leave, he turns to the therapist and says, "Doc, I gotta admit something to ya. That dream I told you? I lied. I made it all up." To which the psychoanalyst replies, "Ah, even *more* interesting."

This joke captures something of the response to Guy Maddin and to his persona and to the anecdotes he tells in interviews. It gradually dawns on the reader that, charming as he is, Maddin is a fantasist, a trickster, a bit of a practical joker. But the result is to make the director even more interesting, because his fantasias can be more instructive than straightforward fact.

For a filmmaker who likes to describe himself as a primitivist, a garage band filmmaker, and even an outsider artist, Guy Maddin proved from an early date in his career that he was adept at that dismal but necessary side of commercial filmmaking, promotion. From his earliest major interview, for *Border Crossings* magazine, the persona is already in place: ironically megalomaniacal, deferential, and blessed with a vast vocabulary of antique words. He says he was named by his older brother after actor Guy Madison as a form of pun on the family name. Interviewer Robert Enright's reaction is simply, "Is that true?"—and we're off on a two-decade-long journey through the hall of mirrors that is Maddin's interview persona.

Journalist and cartoonist Michael Russell has called the comic strip "the hardest form of writing to create the easiest form of reading," and the same could be said of the labor-intensive (lots of transcribing) entertainment interview. If historically the entertainment interview has been a form of easy virtue, one beholden on the one hand to studios and their publicity arms and on the other to the fickle attention span of the reader, the form also is a means by which the subject can burnish an image, test the waters concerning new projects, send veiled messages to studio chiefs, and subtly settle scores. But this forum is open not only to the masters of commercial cinema. Independent filmmakers can also use the vehicle of the interview to advance the cause of their art, albeit usually in lower circulation publications.

Canadian filmmaker Guy Maddin has proven to be a master of the image-enhancing, career-boosting interview. Cozy and warm, his interviews are memorable and quotable. In fact, they are at times even as readable as prose. Apart from his films themselves, the ostensible cause for their existence, his interviews are Maddin's enduring masterpieces. They contain at once the two facets of Maddin's public face, the shy, self-deprecating filmmaker who seemingly fell into all this moviemaking stuff by accident and is learning as he goes; and the erudite, cosmopolitan art maven with a deep knowledge of silent cinema, modernist artists, and novelists such as Bruno Schulz, Vladimir Nabokov, and Robert Walser, who speaks in seemingly perfectly publishable prose.

Overall, Maddin's films are characterized by a pursuit of the past, both autobiographically and aesthetically. He attempts to replicate the look if not the feel of older cinema styles, from the silent era, through the transitional part-talkies, to the robust explosion of activity in early sounds films, as well as "art house" styles such as Soviet propaganda films and the variety of stylistic approaches found in Dreyer's silent and his later sound films. Iris framing, intertitles, theatrical acting styles, and narrated montage sequences are among the terms in his cinematic vocabulary. In Maddin's "color period" he embraced first a style drained of the full color range, and then a lush, almost cartoony style. In more recent developments, Maddin's editing style has become "busy," with multiple cuts that flit in and out of a photographed subject, and with some "shots" lasting no more than a frame or two. The tone that Maddin brings to his work is also unusual. Melodrama fights tooth and jowl with humor, for simultaneous screen time. Though essentially a comic filmmaker, there is an underlying seriousness that takes as its subject matter such boundary-threatening topics as cannibalism and incest, spun with an antique probity. Within these elaborate constructs, Maddin addresses issues in his personal life, disguised under layers of obfuscation.

Guy Maddin was born in Winnipeg, Manitoba, Canada, on February

28, 1956. His father was Charles Maddin, the manager of the Winnipeg hockey team the Maroons, and his mother, the former Herdis Eyolfson, was a hairdresser. The unexpected last of four children, Maddin was by his own testimony a bit of a loner and a lazybones, content to watch a lot of television in the company of the family's pet Chihuahua, Toby. Maddin's older siblings were a successful lot; his sister Janet was an athlete, his brother Cameron a technical wizard who as a teenager was arrested for operating a pirate radio station. Though otherwise "normal" by most standards, Maddin's early life was punctuated by various exceptional moments, such as receiving a pony ride from a touring Bing Crosby, and significant crises, such as the death of his brother Cameron when Maddin was seven. Throughout his childhood, though, his family life was marked by tension and what he calls a lot of passive-aggressive behavior, as he recounts in some of the more recent interviews here. His father died of heart disease when Maddin was twenty-one.

Maddin attended the University of Winnipeg, graduating in economics in 1977. After a short stint in a bank, Maddin fell into house painting with a friend, John Harvie. At the same time, he began to socialize with a group of movie-mad young men dubbed the Drones, and became friends with University of Manitoba professors Stephen Snyder and George Toles (who later went on to co-write many of Maddin's movies). Maddin fell in love with silent cinema, and acquired the itch to make films. Inspired by the low budget but technically sophisticated work of filmmaker John Paizs of the Winnipeg Film Group, Maddin embarked on his own project, *The Dead Father*. The forty-minute black and white and essentially silent film cost $5,000 to make and three years to shoot, and before starting on the project, Maddin didn't even know how to operate a camera. "I got someone who agreed to be the cameraman," Maddin told Robert Enright of *Border Crossings*, "and then he didn't show up for the second shoot. I went over to his house and he showed me how to work the camera from his bed. I left him there, never saw him again, and was my own cameraman after that." The film made its debut in 1985.

Though he says he made *The Dead Father* for the amusement of friends and family, Maddin shortly thereafter formed his own film company with some friends, called Jumbo Pictures, quickly changed to Extra Large Pictures. As the director told Caelum Vatnsdal in that essential Maddin interview book, *Kino Delirium*, "We went over to the pizza joint in Gimli to celebrate this decision by ordering a jumbo pizza . . . all they had were extra large pizzas, so we had to order that, and change the name of our company as well."

His first project under this banner was *Tales of the Gimli Hospital*, based loosely on the book *Gimli Saga* published by a women's club in Winnipeg, as well as on lore heard from family members, and on discreet autobiographical elements. Shot in black and white, though with a few two-tone moments, and mostly silent with the exception of music culled from Maddin's collection of 78s, *Tales* further establishes some of the devices that would draw Maddin over the rest of his career: stories within stories, jeopardized children, outsized visual flourishes borrowed from silent cinema, surrealist humor, and taboo-breaking narrative cruxes. Though some critics have compared Maddin's interest in *Gimli* in pestilence and pustules to the early work of fellow Canadian filmmaker David Cronenberg, the older filmmaker's themes of identity and psychosis are in fact distant from Maddin's interest in warped, parodic nostalgia.

Tales acquired a certain cult status on the midnight movie circuit popular at the time, especially in New York City. It's popularity was enough for Maddin to proceed with his next project, *Archangel*, released in 1990. "I do like the part-talkie," Maddin told Marie Losier and Richard Porton years later, "for what it represents—when the camera couldn't have been as mobile as people would have liked. They had the option to have people talk or not talk." Though adding to his cult status, *Archangel* also confused some viewers. As Maddin notes on the audio commentary track of the film's DVD, among other problems people thought that two separate women characters were the same person.

The following few years were productive for Maddin. As well as several short films, Maddin made his first color film, *Careful*, which solidified his reputation as a fascinatingly eccentric filmmaker, a sort of Canadian David Lynch, although the two filmmakers share little if anything in style, subject matter, or politics. The film's florid visual style and ornate language were among the reasons that Maddin was awarded a lifetime achievement award at the 1995 Telluride Film Festival.

At this juncture, Maddin's career, in the best manner of a melodramatic Hollywood biopic, takes a downward dip. After the collapse of one feature, *The Dikemaster's Daughter*, his next project, 1997's *Twilight of the Ice Nymphs* was the equivalent, for Maddin, of a major production, with a large budget and produced by one of Canada's most high profile movie companies. Noam Gonick's documentary about the making of the film, *Waiting for Twilight*, unveils Maddin's anguish over a production fraught with tension and disappointments. In addition, Maddin directed a half-hour television production titled *The Hands of Ida*, which Maddin prefers to leave off his filmography. Thereafter followed a long absence from the screen. Though Maddin continued to make short films, as he had always done and continues to do, he contemplated giving up cinema, as he confided to Gonick.

Maddin's "comeback" occurred in 2000 when the Toronto Film Festival invited Maddin to join fellow filmmakers Cronenberg and Atom Egoyan to contribute a short film celebrating both the festival and one hundred years of cinema. The resultant film, *The Heart of the World*, proved to be one of the most popular films at that year's festival. A flurry of activity soon followed from a rejuvenated Maddin: *Dracula: Pages from a Virgin's Diary*, made from the Royal Winnipeg Ballet production; *Cowards Bend the Knee*, initially an art installation; *The Saddest Music in the World*, an attention grabbing musical melodrama; *Brand Upon the Brain!*, part nostalgia, part parodic boy's adventure, and then the award-winning *My Winnipeg*, his "docu-fantasia" about his ambivalent feelings toward his home town.

The interviews in this anthology chart Maddin's career highs and lows and his seemingly even-tempered attitude towards these unruly events. In language almost always eloquent, Maddin looks at his ambition and experiences as if from the outside, as curious about his luck and mishaps as we are. Alan Jones catches the young Maddin in the first full flush of creative activity and media attention. In those early days, Maddin exulted in proclaiming, "I've always liked the minimalist style."

David Chute, who profiled Maddin years later on the eve of a retrospective of his work in Los Angeles, finds Maddin in a optimistic mood about his work on *Twilight of the Ice Nymphs*. "I liked the idea of denying myself my usual cheapest prop, which is a shadow," he quips. Years later, however, Mike White of *Cashiers du Cinemart* finds Maddin castigating himself for the failure of *Twilight*. "Ultimately, I must accept all blame for the malaise that made it to screen. I was indecisive about what my next movie should be like—whether I should continue in the same primitive vein as I had been, or perhaps make a movie to modernize somewhat."

Just as his films are surprisingly autobiographical, Maddin is candid in interviews, but without the ornate machinery of his rococo tales. On Terry Gross's radio show *Fresh Air*, Maddin discusses the making of *Saddest Music in the World*, but also talks revealingly about some childhood traumas, significantly his brother's suicide. "I don't know how to make sense of what I thought of it." José Teodoro in *Stop Smiling* explores the autobiographical components in Maddin's later works, especially *Cowards Bend the Knee*. "All I can go by is what I myself would do in a certain situation."

Yet for all his forthrightness, Maddin can be cagey, and some critics became alert to this. James Quandt is the first interviewer to challenge Maddin on issues of fantasy and veracity—issues that will come up years later when Maddin releases *My Winnipeg*, whose blend of myth and memory intrigued viewers. Quandt alludes to Maddin's work as "manufactured biography." In response, Maddin replies, "The audacious fact is that I haven't camouflaged much of anything. I just try and put things into forms that will be fun, and if anything, it feels just too good to blurt out the truth. Also, I haven't done that much in my life." Aaron Hillis in the *Village Voice* also examines with Maddin the "line between autobiography and quasi-doc" in Maddin's films up through *My Winnipeg*, about which Maddin recounts that the documentary was "an assigned propaganda project, but I viewed it more as a documentary of my feelings, as ambiguous as they may be." James Nadeau in *Big Red Shiny* also questions the blurred lines between reality and fiction in *My Winnipeg*, inspiring Maddin to say, "mythic truth is more important that facts."

Many of Maddin's interrogators like to get down to brass tacks. David Church presses Maddin on some of the recurrent imagery in his films and compels him to sort out the shooting chronology and sources of many of his short films. He offers a filmological philosophy in return: "I've always thought of movies as another species of bedtime story or campfire story or tall tale or dream. There's no obligation to being literally realistic anywhere." In a brief interview for the book *Independent Cinema*, Maddin discusses budgets and film funding in Canada, the definition of independent cinema, and jokingly thinks out loud that an identity as a *"Regie maudit* would be romantic." Like many other interviewers, Jonathan Marlow of *Green Cine* explores Maddin's artistic relationship to David Lynch, and in return receives the most thorough account thus far. *Eraserhead*, he says, "always impressed me and emboldened me to just go after a story in a nonlinear way. I felt it was important to be true to the feelings I had and to get them up on the screen." Marie Losier and Richard Porton explore Maddin's interest in and defense of melodrama. "The first time I watched [Sirk's *Imitation of Life*] I was just delighted by it as a confection and thought it was rather funny, as well as a little bit moving. Now, it just wipes me out."

Maddin's quirkiness and openness bring out the confessional in his interlocutors. In an interview that mostly concerns *The Saddest Music in the World*, Mr. Beaks of *Ain't It Cool News* also commiserates with Maddin about the state of contemporary hockey, another one of Maddin's passions. In an appendix from the book *Kino Delirium*, Maddin walks author Vatnsdal, through his videotape collection, which ranges from Dreyer's *Vampyr* and Capra's *The Bitter Tea of General Yen* to the final game played in the World Hockey League. Maddin tells how he once ordered Joseph H. Lewis's *Terror in a Texas Town* in order to find a scene significant to his childhood, only to discover that the scene didn't exist—"So here," he says to the interviewer, "you take it."

In a charming and flirtatious exchange between Isabella Rossellini and Maddin for *Bomb* magazine, the two celebrities explore their differences and similarities in childhoods and attitudes toward their fathers. Maddin reflects on his life: "When I started out making movies I was in my late twenties and thought I was making really hip stuff. It was cheeky and looked underground. But, the more I think of it, I was writing stuff that would more naturally come out of a much older man, an elderly man contemplating all the things that had gone before which he can only revisit through sudden accesses of lucid memory, Proust-like."

In a facet unique to this anthology, at least so far, excerpts from several of Maddin's many audio commentary tracks are offered to the reader. In these tracks, Maddin is effortlessly eloquent (as is his frequent collaborator, George Toles), once again calling into question Maddin's pose as a kind of intellectual feral child who emerged into civilization only as an adult. For *Tales of the Gimli Hospital*, Maddin explains the roots of the comical tale in family lore. In the first of quotes from two different audio commentary tracks for *Careful*, Maddin and writing partner George Toles discuss Maddin's color and sound design, and the literary antecedents of the film. In regards to *Twilight of the Ice Nymphs*, Maddin and Toles discuss the evolution of the script, sing the praises of Frank Gorshin, and explore the ramifications of the difficult decision Maddin made (or at least consented to) of replacing the lead actor's voice with that of another actor. In excerpts from his track for *Dracula: Pages from a Virgin's Diary*, Maddin discusses his apprehensions about shooting a ballet and some of his strategies for doing so, as well as the source and meaning of the film's title. In an extract from Maddin's commentary for *Cowards Bend the Knee*, Maddin delineates the roots of the script in autobiographical and literary sources. And finally, in an extract from a second, recent *Careful* yak track, Maddin and Toles talk in more detail about literary influences and the film's color schemes.

Roger Ebert once wrote: "If you love movies in the very sinews of your imagination, you should experience the work of Guy Maddin." It is hoped that this collection of interviews will help viewers understand and better appreciate that experience.

As with other books in the Conversations with Filmmakers series, the interviews contained herein are reprinted as first published, unedited but to silently correct solecisms or factual errors. The reader will find inevitable repetition as Maddin discusses the same movie with different interviewers, but Maddin rarely says the same thing twice and cumulatively these discussions offer a rounded picture of the director's attitudes and experiences. Future Maddin scholars should find this span of interviews a convenient springboard to further research into his life and lore.

As with most books attributed to one author or editor, this one could not have come into existence with the support of otherwise invisible contributors. Let this brief paragraph salute their work. Among them are Christine Brandenburg, Mark Christensen, Maddin scholar David Church, Desiree French, Helaine Garren, Charles and Ingrid Gordon, Damon Houx, Shawn Levy, Deborah Lewis, Patti Lewis (crucial in making a mock up), Andrea Marsden, Cindy Mason, Gregg Morris, Becky Ohlsen (for well-timed editorial advice), Greg Reese, Michael Russell, Dr. Charles Schwenk (a great scholar and a great human being), Larry N. Smith (for bringing my attention to a key Maddin interview), the various rightsholders who generously allowed the work contained herein to be published, as well as such institutions as the Multnomah County Library, Portland State University Library, the Pro version of the Internet Movie Data Base, and the numerous transitory or one hopes permanent websites that feature Maddin. Recognition is also due to Leila Salisbury of the University Press of Mississippi, who has been generous with her enthusiasm and time. In addition, I'd like to show my appreciation to Mr. Guy Maddin for the gift of his time and attention at crucial moments. Finally, there is Britta Gordon, who was steadfast through both the creation of this book and through various personal ordeals, to whom this book is dedicated with love and affection. And I want to hail Jodi Nemeth Bergstrom, for her love and laughter.

DKH

Chronology

1956 Guy Maddin is born in Winnipeg, Manitoba, Canada, on February 28. His father is Charles Maddin, by day a grain clerk and by night the general manager of the Winnipeg Maroons hockey team; his mother Herdis is a hairdresser. The Maddins live in the upstairs apartment over the hairdressing shop owned by Maddin's Aunt Lil. At the time of his birth, Maddin has three older siblings, Ross (b. 1944), Cameron (b. 1946), and Janet (b. 1949).

1959–1967 Maddin attends Greenway Elementary through the sixth grade in the Canadian educational system. For grades seven through nine, attends General Wolfe school, and for grades ten through twelve, the Daniel McIntyire Collegiate Institute.

1961 Maddin receives a horseback ride from Bing Crosby.

1963 Maddin's brother Cameron takes his own life.

1970 Works as a delivery boy for a local drugstore.

1973–1977 Maddin attends the University of Winnipeg, studying economics.

1976 After a brief stint working in a bank, Maddin begins a career as a housepainter. He continues in this job until 1990. During this time, Maddin falls in with film professor Steve Snyder, viewing and discussing films with him and others.

1977 Charles Maddin dies in the summer of 1977. Maddin marries Martha Jane Waugh. The marriage ends in 1979.

1978 January 25: Birth of Maddin's daughter Jilian.

1981 Maddin begins associating with a group of like-minded and inspirational friends, loosely gathered under the sobriquet The Drones. The Drones era comes to an end in 1985.

1982 Begins shooting *The Dead Father*. Also appears in John Paizs's short film *Oak, Ivy, and Other Dead Elms*.

1983	Appears in John Paizs's short film *The International Style*.
1984–1988	Maddin works as a photo archivist at the Western Canada Pictorial Index.
1985	*The Dead Father* premieres.
1988	*Tales from the Gimli Hospital* premieres.
1989	Directs the short films *Mauve Decade* and *BBB*.
1990	Maddin's *Archangel* is released. Maddin also directs the short film *Tyro*. During the making of *Archangel*, Maddin contracts a rare neurological ailment, called myoclonus, in which he suffers the sensation of unexpectedly being touched.
1991	Wins U.S. National Society of Film Critics Award for Best Experimental Film of 1991 for *Archangel*. Directs the short documentary film *Indigo High-Hatters*.
1992	Releases his first color feature film, *Careful*. *Careful* goes on to win the Sudbury Cinéfest award for Best Canadian Film.
1993	Directs the short film *The Pomps of Satan*.
1994	Directs the short film *Sea Beggars*.
1995	Maddin receives the Telluride Film Festival's Lifetime Achievement Award. Directs the (later repudiated) TV film *The Hands of Ida*, and the short film *Odilon Redon or The Eye Like a Strange Balloon Mounts Toward Infinity* as well as the first version of *Sissy-Boy Slap-Party*. *Odilon Redon* goes on to win the Best Canadian Short Film award at the Toronto International Film Festival. Maddin marries Elise Moore; the marriage ends in 1997.
1996	Directs the short film *Imperial Orgies*.
1997	Directs *Twilight of the Ice Nymphs*; in addition, friend and fellow filmmaker Noam Gonick profiles Maddin and the making of *Twilight* in his film, *Waiting for Twilight*.
1998	Maddin directs the short films *The Cock Crew*, *The Hoyden*, and *Maldoror: Tygers*. He appears as a party guest in Caelum Vatnsdal's film *Black as Hell, Strong as Death, Sweet as Love*.
1999	Maddin compiles *Hospital Fragment*. In addition, he appears in the documentary, *And So to Bed*, as himself, along with George Toles, a college professor and a frequent collaborator on Maddin's screenplays. In late April he enjoys a retrospective of his work, *Silver Apples of the Moon: The Films*

	of Guy Maddin mounted by the American Cinematheque at the Egyptian Theater in Hollywood, California.
2000	Directs the short film, *Fleshpots of Antiquity*. The Toronto International Film Festival invites Maddin as one of several directors to make a short film celebrating the anniversary of the birth of cinema. Maddin's contribution is *The Heart of the World*. The short goes on to win six awards, including a Genie. In addition, Maddin has a small part in Tibor Takacs's suspense film *Nostradamus*. He also appears in Alan Zweig's documentary *Vinyl*.
2001	Maddin directs *It's A Wonderful Life*.
2002	Directs *Dracula: Pages from a Virgin's Diary*. Maddin also directs the short film *Fancy, Fancy Being Rich*. In addition, Maddin appears in the documentary *Celluloid Dreams*.
2003	*Dracula: Pages from a Virgin's Diary* wins a Blizzard award for art direction, an International Emmy for Arts Programming, Gemini Awards for Best Canadian Performing Arts Show and Best Direction, first prize at the Golden Prague Television Festival, and the Stiges Catalonian International Film Festival award for Best Film. Directs *Cowards Bend the Knee*, which starts out as an installation piece in the Power Plant Gallery in Toronto. Shortly thereafter, he directs *The Saddest Music in the World*, which goes on to win six awards, including three Genies. A compilation of Maddin's diaries and reviews, *From the Atelier Tovar: Selected Writings* is published by Coach House Books, Toronto. There is also a book version of *Cowards Bend the Knee* published by The Power Plant Gallery.
2004	Directs the short films *A Trip to the Orphanage* and *Sombra Dolorosa*, and revises his earlier 1995 short film *Sissy-Boy Slap-Party*. Appears in Jill Sharpe's documentary *Weird Sex and Snowshoes: A Trek through the Canadian Cinematic Psyche*.
2005	In January Maddin enjoys a second retrospective of his work at the American Cinematheque in Los Angeles. Maddin directs *The Brand Upon the Brain!* in Seattle. He also collaborates with Isabella Rossellini on the short film, *My Dad Is 100 Years Old*.

2006 — Directs the short film *Nude Caboose*. Receives the Persistence of Vision award at the 49th annual San Francisco International Film Festival. Maddin marries Kyra Rogers. The marriage ends the following year.

2007 — Directs the quasi-documentary feature, *My Winnipeg*, which goes on to win the Best Canadian Feature Film award at the Toronto International Film Festival, among other awards. Also directs the short film *Odin's Shield Maiden*. Maddin is appointed the first artist-curator for the UCLA Film and Television Archive. In autumn, Maddin begins a stint teaching at the University of Manitoba.

2008 — Begins a collaboration with poet John Ashbery on *Keyhole*, a project that, as described at this time, blends cinema and internet broadcasting; directs the short film *Spanky: To the Pier and Back* and the video short *Footsteps*. *My Dad Is 100 Years Old* appears as one of the entries in the compilation *Cinema 16: World Short Films*.

2009 — Maddin's installation piece *Send Me to the 'Lectric Chair*, made in collaboration with Isabella Rossellini, makes its debut at the Rotterdam Film Festival in January. In February, gives a lecture at the University of Manitoba's St. John College on "Stripper Ghosts and Sofa Traumas: The Theft of Infancy's Lucent Promise." In April attends the 11th Annual EbertFest in Champaign-Urbana, introducing *My Winnipeg*. On May 12, publishes the annotated script to *My Winnipeg*; on the same day, Maddin is awarded, along with eleven others, the Order of Manitoba, for "a unique mark on this province and its people with achievements that both impress and inspire." From late July to early August, the Era New Horizons film festival in Wroclaw, Poland, mounts a retrospective of Maddin's films.

Filmography

1985
THE DEAD FATHER
Canada
Production: Extra Large Productions
Producer: **GUY MADDIN**
Direction: **GUY MADDIN**
Screenplay: **GUY MADDIN**
Photography: **GUY MADDIN**
Editing: **GUY MADDIN**
Music: From archival 78 RPM records
Art Director: Jeff Solylo
Sound: Wayne Finucan
Story Consultant: George Toles
Cast: The Son (John Harvie), The Dead Father (Dr. D. P. Snidal), The Widow (Margaret Anne MacLeod), The Daughter (Angela Heck), Little Girl I (Rachel Toles), Little Girl II (Jill Maddin), Cesar (W. Steve Snyder)
Black and white
30 minutes (a preferred director's cut is 21 minutes)

1988
TALES FROM THE GIMLI HOSPITAL
Canada
Production: Extra Large Productions
Producers: Greg Klymkiw, Steve Snyder
Distribution: Cinephile; Circle Films
Direction: **GUY MADDIN**
Screenplay: **GUY MADDIN**
Photography: **GUY MADDIN**
Editing: **GUY MADDIN**
Assistant Director: Kyle McCulloch

Music: From archival 78 RPM records
Art Director: Jeff Solylo
Model Maker: Rick Atkinson
Costume Design: Donna Szöke
Make Up: Donna Szöke
Sound Editor: Laurence Mardon
Story Consultant: George Toles
Cast: Einar the Lonely/Minstrel (Kyle McCulloch), Gunnar (Michael Gottli), Snjófridur (Angela Heck), Amma (Margaret Anne MacLeod), Granddaughter (Heather Neale), Grandson (David Neale), John Ramsay (Don Hewak), Pastor Osbaldison/Patient (Ronald Eyolfson), Lord Dufferin (Chris Johnson), Fish Princess (Donna Szöke), Gunnar's Strolling Companion/Gimli Maiden (Tiffany Taylor), Dying Mother (Linda Schinkel), Angry Husband (Jeff Solylo), Angel (Randy Kray), Angel With Mustache (George Toles), Sigvalda Sigurdsdottír (Carmen Snidal), Valdimar/Gimli Manfolk (Brent Neale), Gravedigger I (Greg Klymkiw), Gravedigger II/Highlander (Ian Handford), Elfa Egilsdóttir/Nurse/Gimli Maiden (Caroline Bonner), Gimli Manfolk/Bleeding Patient/Highlander (Steve Snyder), Patient (Herdis Maddin), Child/Dancer (Jilian Maddin), Child (Rachel Toles), Doctor (**GUY MADDIN**)
Black and white
72 minutes

1989
MAUVE DECADE
Canada
Direction: **GUY MADDIN**
Screenplay: **GUY MADDIN**
Photography: **GUY MADDIN**
Editing: **GUY MADDIN**
Cast: Earle (Steve Snyder), Wilton (Kyle McCulloch), Fecus (Ian Handford), Truck Driver (George Toles), Waldorf (Tynee Ralston)
Black and white
7 minutes

BBB
Canada
Direction: **GUY MADDIN**
Screenplay: **GUY MADDIN**

Photography: **GUY MADDIN**
Editing: **GUY MADDIN**
Cast: Narrator (Steve Snyder), Herdis Maddin
Black and white
12 minutes, documentary

1990
ARCHANGEL
Canada
Production: Cinephile
Producers: Andre Bennett, Greg Klymkiw
Distribution: Zeitgeist Films
Direction: **GUY MADDIN**
Screenplay: **GUY MADDIN** and George Toles, from a story suggestion by John B. Harvie
Photography: **GUY MADDIN**
Editing: **GUY MADDIN**
Production Design: Dennis W. Smith
Art Directors: **GUY MADDIN**, Jeff Solylo
Costume Design: Donna Szöke
Cast: Lt. John Boles (Kyle McCulloch), Jannings (Michael Gottli), Geza (David Falkenburg), Doctor (Michael O'Sullivan), Baba (Margaret Anne MacLeod), Philbin (Ari Cohen), Danchuk (Sarah Neville), Veronkha (Kathy Marykuca), Sea Captain (Victor Cowie), Monk (Ihor Procak), Kaiser Wilhelm II (Robert Lougheed), Stage Kaiser (Steve Snyder), Young Philbin (Sam Toles), Worshipper (John Harvie), Worshipper/Home Woman (Donna Szöke), Worshipper (Herdis Maddin), Hun (Greg Klymkiw), Home Woman (Tiffany Taylor), Russian Soldier (Angela Heck), Allied Soldier (Ian Handford), Allied Soldier (Jeff Solylo)
Black and white
90 minutes

TYRO
Canada
Direction: **GUY MADDIN**
Screenplay: **GUY MADDIN**
Photography: **GUY MADDIN**
Editing: **GUY MADDIN**
Cast: Boy (David Neale), Father (Brent Neale), Prater Impressario (John

Harvie)
Black and white
4 minutes

1991
INDIGO HIGH-HATTERS
Canada
Direction: **GUY MADDIN**
Screenplay: **GUY MADDIN**
Photography: **GUY MADDIN**
Editing: **GUY MADDIN**
Music: The Indigo High-Hatters
Cast: Ian Handford, Don Hewak, Ron Eyolfson, John Harvie, Zenaida Cramden
Black and white
34 minutes, documentary

1992
CAREFUL
Canada
Production: The Canadian Council, The Canadian Manitoba Cultural Industries Development Office, The Manitoba Arts Council, The Greg and Tracy Film Ministry
Producers: Andre Bennett, Greg Klymkiw, Tracy Traeger
Distribution: Zeitgeist
Direction: **GUY MADDIN**
Screenplay: **GUY MADDIN** and George Toles
Photography: **GUY MADDIN**
Editing: **GUY MADDIN**
Music: John McCulloch
Production Designer: **GUY MADDIN**
Art Director: Jeff Solylo
Costume Design: Donna Szöke
Sound Editor: **GUY MADDIN**
Cast: Grigorss (Kyle McCulloch), Zenaida (Gosia Dobrowolska), Klara (Sarah Neville), Count Knotkers (Paul Cox), Johann (Brent Neale), Herr Trotta (Victor Cowie), Blind Ghost (Michael O'Sullivan), Sigleinde (Katya Gardner), Franz (Vince Rimmer), Frau Teacher (Jackie Burroughs), Chief Steward (Ross McMillan), Butler Blore (Leith Clark),

Butler Schrammel (Glen Hubich), Mortician (Brendan Carruthers), Countess Knotkers (George Toles), Shower Meister (Greg Klymkiw), Gerda the Mountain Girl (Kelli Shinfield), Townsperson (Dora Sigurdson), Townsperson (Jillian Maddin), Butler Student (Matt Holm), Butler Student (Jeff Solylo), Butler Student (Ian Handford), Butler Student (Caelum Vatnsdal)
Color
100 minutes

1993
THE POMPS OF SATAN
(Also known as THROUGH A MAN'S EYEGLASS)
Canada
Direction: **GUY MADDIN**
Screenplay: **GUY MADDIN**
Photography: Terry Reimer
Editing: **GUY MADDIN**
Cast: Roulette Ruby (Margaret Anne MacLeod), Trader (Jim Keller), Aviator (John Harvie)
Black and white
5 minutes

1994
SEA BEGGARS, OR THE WEAKER SEX
Canada
Direction: **GUY MADDIN**
Screenplay: George Toles
Photography: **GUY MADDIN**
Editing: **GUY MADDIN**
Cast: Sea Beggar (Kyle McCulloch), Wife (Alice Krige), Parson (Jim Keller)
Color
7 minutes

1995
THE HANDS OF IDA
Canada
Production: Marble Island Pictures
Producer: Ritchard Findlay

Direction: **GUY MADDIN**
Screenplay: Gerry Atwell
Photography: Michael Marshall
Editing: K. George Godwin
Art Directors: Réjean Labrie, Gordon Wilding
Cast: Adam (John Bekavac), Jason (Paul Anthony), Witness (Jennifer Joseph), Woman (Joyce Krenz), Pamela Sinha
Color
30 minutes

ODILON REDON OR THE EYE LIKE A STRANGE BALLOON MOUNTS TOWARDS INFINITY
Canada
Production: BBC
Producers: Keith Alexander, Diane Freeman, Keith Griffiths, Rodney Wilson
Direction: **GUY MADDIN**
Screenplay: **GUY MADDIN**
Photography: Tammy Jones
Music: Roger White
Art Director: Jeff Solylo
Costume Design: Wanda Farian
Cast: Keller (James Keller), Berenice (Brandy Bayes), Caelum (Caelum Vatnsdal), Lil' Caelum (Evan Richards), Zeppelin Pilot (John Teunissen), Pastor Osbaldison (Ron Eyolfson)
Black and white
5 minutes

SISSY-BOY SLAP-PARTY
(Also known as THE COMING TERROR)
Canada
Production: **GUY MADDIN**
Direction: **GUY MADDIN**
Screenplay: **GUY MADDIN**
Photography: **GUY MADDIN**
Editing: **GUY MADDIN**
Black and white
2 minutes
1996

IMPERIAL ORGIES, OR THE RABBI OF BACHARACH
Canada
Direction: **GUY MADDIN**
Screenplay: **GUY MADDIN**
Photography: **GUY MADDIN**
Editing: **GUY MADDIN**
Cast: Rabbi Finkleberg (Noam Gonick)
Black and white
3 minutes

1997
TWILIGHT OF THE ICE NYMPHS
Canada
Production: Marble Island Pictures
Producers: Ritchard Findlay, Derek Mazur, Charlotte Mickie
Distribution: Zeitgeist Films
Direction: **GUY MADDIN**
Screenplay: George Toles, from the novel *Pan* by Knut Hamsun
Photography: Michael Marshall
Editing: Reginald Harkema
Music: John McCulloch
Art Director: Ian Handford
Costume Design: Donna Szöke
Costume Supervisor: Wanda Farian
Miniatures: Conrad Percheson
Cast: Juliana Kossel (Pascale Bussiéres), Amelia Glahn (Shelley Duvall), Cain Ball (Frank Gorshin), Zephyr Eccles (Alice Krige), Dr. Issac Solti (R. H. Thomson), Matthew Eccles (Ross McMillan, voiced by Peter Glahn), Man in Black (Frank Kowalski), Baby (Breanne Dowhan), Peter Glahn (Nigel Whitmey)
Color
91 minutes

CHIMNEY WORKBOOK
Director: **GUY MADDIN**

ZOOKEEPER WORKBOOK
Director: **GUY MADDIN**

ROOSTER WORKBOOK
Director: **GUY MADDIN**

1998
THE HOYDEN
(also known as IDYLLS OF WOMANHOOD)
Canada
Direction: **GUY MADDIN**
Screenplay: **GUY MADDIN**, from the Dawn Powell play, *Walking Down Broadway* and the Erich von Stroheim film of the same title
Photography: **GUY MADDIN**
Editing: **GUY MADDIN**
Cast: Ross McMillan, Vince Rimmer, Jilian Maddin
Black and white
4 minutes

THE COCK CREW, OR LOVE-CHAUNT OF THE CHIMNEY
Canada
Direction: **GUY MADDIN**
Screenplay: **GUY MADDIN**, George Toles, based on Herman Melville's *I and My Chimney*
Photography: Caelum Vatnsdal
Editing: **GUY MADDIN**
Costume Design: Wanda Farian
Cast: Ari (Darcy Fehr), Taryn (Megan McIvor), Care-Giving Woman (Krista Morrison), Sybill (Micheline Marchildon), Windy (Rachel Toles), Helen (Michael Powell)
Color
5 minutes

MALDOROR: TYGERS
Canada
Direction: **GUY MADDIN**
Screenplay: **GUY MADDIN**
Photography: **GUY MADDIN**
Editing: **GUY MADDIN**
Special Effects Make Up: Simon Hughes, Caelum Vatnsdal
Cast: Delmas (Kyle McCulloch), Dol (Alyssa Szöke), Uncle Scrotus (Caelum Vatnsdal)

Black and white and color
4 minutes

1999
HOSPITAL FRAGMENT
Canada
Direction: **GUY MADDIN**
Screenplay: **GUY MADDIN**
Photography: **GUY MADDIN**
Editing: **GUY MADDIN**
Cast: Male Lead (Darcy Fehr), Gunnar (Michael Gottli), Snjofridur (Angela Heck), Brent Neale (Valdimar), Deborah Axelrod
Black and white
3 minutes

2000
FLESHPOTS OF ANTIQUITY (also known as GAS III)
Canada
Direction: **GUY MADDIN**
Screenplay: **GUY MADDIN**
Photography: **GUY MADDIN**
Editing: **GUY MADDIN**
Cast: Selma Kaiser (Leslie Bais), Boles Harvie (Mark Pomrenke), Wife (Linda Danchak), Happy Jack (Ian Handford)
Black and white
3 minutes

THE HEART OF THE WORLD
Canada
Production: Astral Media
Producers: Niv Fichman, Jody Shapiro, Jennifer Weiss
Distribution: Zeitgeist Video
Direction: **GUY MADDIN**
Screenplay: **GUY MADDIN**
Photography: **GUY MADDIN**
Editing: **GUY MADDIN**, with Deco Dawson
Music: "Time, Forward" by Georgi Sviridov, from the film *Vremya, vperyod!*
Art Director: Olaf Dux

Production Design: Réjean Labrie
Costume Design: Meg McMillan
Cast: Anna (Leslie Bais), Osip (Caelum Vatnsdal), Nikolai (Shaun Balbar), Akmatov (Hryhory Yulyanovitch Klymkyiev), Mary Magdalene (Tammy Gillis), Centurion (Carson Nattrass)
Black and white
6 minutes

2001
SPARKLEHORSE: IT'S A WONDERFUL LIFE
Canada
Production: The Sundance Channel, "Sonic Cinema" series
Direction: **GUY MADDIN**
Screenplay: **GUY MADDIN**
Photography: **GUY MADDIN**
Editing: **GUY MADDIN**
Music: Sparklehorse
Cast: Brent Neale
Black and white
3 minutes

2002
DRACULA: PAGES FROM A VIRGIN'S DIARY
Canada
Production: Vonnie Von Helmolt Film, Canadian Broadcasting Company, Royal Winnipeg Ballet
Producers: Vonnie Von Helmolt, Robert Sherrin, Danishka Esterhazy, Lesley Oswald
Distribution: Domino Film & Television International
Direction: **GUY MADDIN**
Screenplay: Mark Godden, from the novel Dracula by Bram Stoker
Photography: Paul Suderman
Editing: Deco Dawson
Music: Derived from Mahler's Symphonies Nos. 1 and 2
Production Designer and Art Director: Deanne Rohde
Costume Design: Paul Daigle
Cast: Dracula (Zhang Wei-Qiang), Lucy Westernra (Tara Birtwhistle), Dr. Van Helsing (David Moroni), Mina (CindyMarie Small), Jonathon Harker (Johnny Wright), Arthur Holmwood (Stephane Leonard),

Jack Seward (Matthew Johnson), Quincy Morris (Keir Knight), Renfield (Brent Neale), Mrs. Westernra (Stephanie Ballard), Maid/Nun/Vampiress (Sarah Murphy-Dyson), Maid/Nun (Carrie Broda), Maid/Vampiress (Gail Stefanek), Maid/Nun (Janet Sartore), Gargoyle/Nun (Jennifer Welsman), Gargoyle/Nun (Emily Grizzell), Gargoyle/Nun (Chalnessa Eames), Gargoyle/Nun (Vanessa Lawson), Nun (Michelle Lack), Vampiress (Kerrie Souster)
Black and white
73 minutes

FANCY, FANCY BEING RICH
Canada
Production: Koshka Productions
Producers: Danishka Esterhazy and Rebecca Sandulak
Distribution: Koshka Productions
Direction: **GUY MADDIN**
Photography: **GUY MADDIN**
Editing: Deco Dawson
Production Design: Ricardo Alms
Set Decoration: Ricardo Alms
Cast: The Lonely Housemaid (Valdine Anderson), Chief Labourer (David Stuart Evans), Wife (Shelley Kern), Twig Lady (Shannon Slater), Boy (Matthew Stefanson), Wealthy Husband (Geoff Trubiak), Drowned Man (Kristopher Turner), Michael Larocque
Black and white
6 minutes

2003
COWARDS BEND THE KNEE
Canada
Production: The Power Plant
Producer: Philip Monk
Distribution: Zeitgeist Films
Direction: **GUY MADDIN**
Screenplay: **GUY MADDIN**
Photography: **GUY MADDIN**
Editing: John Gurdebeke
Production Designer: Shawna Conner
Art Director: Craig Aftanas

Costume Design: Meg McMillan
Cast: **GUY MADDIN** (Darcy Fehr), Meta (Melissa Dionisio), Veronica (Amy Stewart), Liliom (Tara Birtwhistle), Dr. Fusi (Louis Negin), Mo Mott (Mike Bell), Shaky (David Stuart Evans), Chas (Henry Mogatas), Maddin Sr. (Victor Cowie), Grandma (Herdis Maddin), Mrs. Maddin (Marion Martin), Baby (Aurum McBride), Stickboy (Bernard Lesk), Customer/Stylist (Erin Hershberg), Customer (Erika Rintoul), Customer (Charlene Van Buekenhout), Customer (Sherrill Hershberg), Customer (Kathryn Stuart), Customer (Lauren Ritz), Customer (Rebecca Sandulak), Customer (Kirstin Ward), Customer (Billy Dee Knight), Customer (Erica Smith), Hockey Player (Ricardo Alms), Hockey Player (Craig Aftanas), Hockey Player (Jim Crawford), Hockey Player (Mike Silver), Hockey Player (Bob Unger), Hockey Player/Cop (Mark Yuill), Hockey Player (Caelum Vatnsdal), Hockey Player (Matt Holm), Stylist (Meghan Greenlay), Stylist (Erin McKenzie), Wax Maroon (Richard Orlandini), Wax Maroon (Don Hewak), Wax Maroon (Stan Lesk), Wax Maroon (Ted Avent), Wax Maroon (Ted Wynne), Wax Maroon/Cop (Ian Yorski), Wax Maroon (Dave McDonald), Cop (Steve Burke), Cop (Robert Enright), Cop (Spencer Maybee), Cop (Bradley Jonasson), Audience Member (Shauna Evans), Audience Member (Tracy McBride), Audience Member (Rodney LaTourelle), Audience Member (Alex Khizder), Toby (Moses)
Black and white
60 minutes

THE SADDEST MUSIC IN THE WORLD
Canada
Production: IFC Productions
Producers: Atom Egoyan, Jody Shapiro, Niv Fichman, Daniel Iron, Phyllis Laing, Sheena Macdonald, Barbara Willis Sweete, Larry Weinstein
Distribution: IFC Productions
Direction: **GUY MADDIN**
Screenplay: George Toles and **GUY MADDIN**, adapted from a text by Kazuo Ishiguro
Photography: Luc Montpellier (also **GUY MADDIN**, Mark McKinney, and Isabella Rossellini)
Editing: David Wharmsby

Music: Christopher Dedrick
Production Designer: Matthew Davies
Art Director: Réjean Labrie
Costume Design: Meg McMillan
Cast: Chester Kent (Mark McKinney), Lady Helen Port-Huntley (Isabella Rossellini), Narcissa (Maria de Medeiros), Fyodor Kent (David Fox), Roderick Kent/Gravillo the Great (Ross McMillan), Blind Seer (Louis Negin), Teddy (Darcy Fehr), Duncan Elksworth (Claude Dorge), Mary (Talia Pura), Young Chester (Jeff Sutton), Young Roderick (Graeme Valentin), Chester's Mother (Maggie Nagle), Man in Bar (Victor Cowie), Lady's Secretary (Jessica Burleson), Boardmember (Wayne Nicklas), American Mother (Nancy Drake), American Father (David Gillies), Widow (Daphne Korol), Agnes (Adriana O'Neil), Reverend (Jeff Skinner), Old Sleepwalker (Craig Aftanas), Guard (Miles Boiselle), Roderick's Son (Brock MacGregor), Amputee Double (Daniel Hawkins), Orphan (Erik J. Berg), Boy #3 (Matthew J. Kok), Polish Pianist (Brent Neale), Orphan Girl (Jessica Smith), Extra (Arthur McKinnon), Africa—Zani Drummers (Emile Bisseck, Marol Jal, Binasio Wani), India—Manochar Sitar Player (Joshua Stanton), India—Manochars (Sharmela Parboji, Alan Parboji, Nalini Reddy, Veena Goel, Aasttha Khajuria, Mohyna Dookun, Lena Shah, Shyamala Dakshinamurti, Usha Sharma, Sunayana Gupta), Mexico—Mini Mariachi (Jesus Paz Sr., Jesus Paz Jr., Isaac Paz, David Paz, Johanna Paz, Richard Escaffi), Scotland—Winnipeg—Heather-Belle Ladies Pipe Band (Daron Baxter, Crystal Hay, Gail Hay, Gwen Court, Sara Leclair, Diane Leclair, Shona Munroe, Catherine Russell, Shannon Baxter, Jessica Locke, Corie Johnston, Shawna Turner), Spain—Flamenco Ensemble (Claire Marchand, Jim Shewchuk, Sheila Ghosh), Siam Musician (Xio Nan Wang), and Members of the Winnipeg Folk Arts Group
Black and white and color
100 minutes

2004
A TRIP TO THE ORPHANAGE
Canada
Production: IFC Productions
Producers: IFC Productions
Distribution: IFC Productions; TVA Films

Direction: **GUY MADDIN**
Screenplay: **GUY MADDIN**
Photography: **GUY MADDIN**
Editing: **GUY MADDIN**
Special Effects: Ricardo Alms
Cast: Opera Singer (Sarah Constible), Maria de Medeiros
Color
4 minutes

SISSY-BOY SLAP-PARTY
(An remake of the 1995 short film)
Canada
Production: IFC Productions
Distribution: IFC Productions
Direction: **GUY MADDIN**
Screenplay: **GUY MADDIN**
Photography: **GUY MADDIN**
Editing: **GUY MADDIN**
Cast: Noam Gonick, Caelum Vatnsdal, Simon Hughes, Michael Powell, John K. Samson, Leith Clark, David Lewis, Don Hewak, Louis Negin
Black and white
6 minutes

SOMBRA DOLOROSA
Canada
Production: IFC Productions
Distribution: TVA Films
Direction: **GUY MADDIN**
Screenplay: **GUY MADDIN**
Photography: **GUY MADDIN**
Editing: **GUY MADDIN**
Music: Song lyric by **GUY MADDIN**
Art Director: Olaf Dux
Special Effects: Ricardo Alms
Cast: Mother (Talia Pura), Dolores (CindyMarie Small), Mexican Samaritan (Johnny A. Wright)
Color
4 minutes

2005
BRAND UPON THE BRAIN!
United States
Production: The Film Company
Producers: Jody Shapiro, Philip Wohlstetter, A. J. Epstein, Joy Fairfield, Jaime Hook, Amy Jacobson, Gregg Lachow
Distribution: The Film Company, Vitagraph Pictures
Direction: **GUY MADDIN**
Screenplay: **GUY MADDIN**, George Toles
Photography: Benjamin Kasulke
Editing: John Gurdebeke
Music: Jason Staczek
Production Designer: Tania Kupczak
Art Directors: Noel Paul, Apryl Richards
Cast: Narrator (Isabella Rossellini), Mother (Gretchen Krich), Young Guy Maddin (Sullivan Brown), Sis (Maya Lawson), Chance Hale/Wendy Hale (Katherine E. Scharhon), Father (Todd Moore), Savage Tom (Andrew Loviska), Neddie (Kellan Larson), Older Guy Maddin (Erik Steffen Maahs), Young Mother (Cathleen O'Malley), Old Father (Clayton Corzatte), Old Mother (Susan Corzatte), Murderous Sister (Megan Murphy), Murderous Sister (Annette Toutonghi), Oarsman (David Lobo), Oarsman (Eric Lobo), Adopting Couple (Sarah Harlett, Dan Tierney), Orphans (David Armo, Erica Badgely, Riley Calcagno, Jesa Chiro, Munya Chiro, Bailey Gibart, Frank Hughes, AnnieRose Kafer, Emma Kelley, Eleanor Kopf, Sam Kopf, Charlie Lachow, Sam Lachow, Maia Lee, Emma Mercer, Lucia Moser, Madeleine Moser, Eli Pruzan, Connor Russell, Electra Fire Scott, Vincent Scott, Iris Seiwerath, Ruby Seiwerath, Olivia Spokoiny, Maya Sugarman, Augustine Vanden Brulle, Anna Wichman), Baby Mother (Clara Grace Svenson)
Black and white
95 minutes

MY DAD IS 100 YEARS OLD
Canada
Production: Spanky Productions, Inc.
Producers: Michael Burns, Niv Fichman, Phyllis Laing, Jody Shapiro
Distribution: Documentary Channel
Direction: **GUY MADDIN**
Screenplay: Isabella Rossellini

Photography: Len Peterson
Editing: John Gurdebeke
Production Designer: Réjean Labrie
Art Director: Larry Spittle
Costume Design: Meg McMIllan
Special Effects: Ricardo Alms
Cast: Isabella Rossellini, The Belly of Roberto Rossellini (Isaac Paz Sr.)
Black and white
16 minutes

FUSEBOY
Canada
Director: **GUY MADDIN**
Direction: **GUY MADDIN**, Jody Shapiro
Photography: **GUY MADDIN**, Jody Shapiro
Editing: John Gurdebeke
Cast: Louis Negin, David Stuart Evans, Darcy Fehr, Mike Bell
Black and white
4 minutes

2006
NUDE CABOOSE
Canada
Production: Marble Media
Producers: Silva Basmajian, Mark J. W. Bishop, Judy Gladstone, Matt Hornburg, Jody Shapiro
Direction: **GUY MADDIN**
Screenplay: Ian Handford, **GUY MADDIN**, Jody Shapiro, George Toles
Photography: **GUY MADDIN**, Jody Shapiro
Editing: John Gurdebeke
Production Coordinator: Lindsay Hamel
Music: Jono Grant
Cast: Conga Line (Darren Anderson), Conga Line (Jim Bell), Conductor (Mike Bell), Conga Line (Deborah Carlson), Nude Caboose (Janet Hamel), Conga Line (Scott Hamel), Conga Line (Chandra Mayor), Conga Line (Sarah Myers), Conga Line (Terry O'Sullivan), Conga Line (Janice Sawka), Conga Line (Dawn Swirsky), Conga Line (James Swirsky)
Color
2 minutes

2007
ODIN'S SHIELD MAIDEN
Canada
Producer: Lindsay Hemel
Direction: **GUY MADDIN**
Screenplay: **GUY MADDIN**
Photography: **GUY MADDIN**
Editing: John Gurdebeke
Cast: Darcy Fehr, Ana Cabral, Ekaterina Chtchelkanova, Natalia Fioroni, Kate Yacula, Jacelyn Lobay
Black and white
5 minutes

MY WINNIPEG
Canada
Production: Buffalo Gals Pictures
Producers: Michael Burns, Phyllis Laing, **GUY MADDIN**, Jody Shapiro
Distribution: IFC Films
Direction: **GUY MADDIN**
Screenplay: **GUY MADDIN**, George Toles
Photography: Jody Shapiro
Editing: John Gurdebeke
Music: Jason Staczek, Sergei Prokofiev, The Bells
Production Designer: Réjean Labrie
Art Director: Katharina Stieffenhofer
Costume Design: Meg McMillan
Animator: Andy Smetanka
Cast: Narrator (**GUY MADDIN**), Mother (Ann Savage), Mayor Cornish (Louis Negin), Janet Maddin (Amy Stewart), Guy Maddin (Darcy Fehr), Cameron Maddin (Brendan Cade), Ross Maddin (Wesley Cade), Citizen Girl (Kate Yacula), Gwenyth Lloyd (Jacelyn Lobay), Viscount Gort (Eric Nipp), Althea Cornish (Jennifer Palichuk), Sleepwalker (Kalyn Bomback), Russian Bolshevik (Cory Cassidy), If Day Nazi (Aaron Hughes), Auntie (Joyce Krenz), Girl At The Paddlewheel (Bronwyn Ring), Con Johanesson (Will Woytowich), Lou Profeta, Fred Dunsmore, Deborah Carlson, Kevin Harris, Scott Hamel, Wayne Hamel, Althea Cornish, Olie Alto, Jeremy Dangerfield, Daniel Hussey, Tim Kiriluk, Lee Major, Roy Trumpour, Chris Turyk, John Warkentin, Brett Donahue
Black and white and color
80 minutes

MANUELLE LABOR
Canada
Production: Gaumont Franco-Film Aubert
Direction: **GUY MADDIN**, Marie Losier
Photography: Mary Billyou
Cast: Juliana Francis, Marie Losier, Bob Carey, Jean Barberis, Jason David Brown, Stefany Anne Golbers, Sebastien Santamaria, Geraldine Longueville, Mark Geffriaud, François Leloup
Black and white
10 minutes

2008
SPANKY: TO THE PIER AND BACK
Canada
Direction: **GUY MADDIN**
Photography: **GUY MADDIN**
Editing: **GUY MADDIN**
Music: Matthew Patton
Cast: Spanky, Maddin's girlfriend's pet pug
Black and white
4 minutes

FOOTSTEPS
Canada
Production: The Criterion Collection
Distribution: The Criterion Collection
Direction: **GUY MADDIN**
Photography: Benjamin Kasulke, Jennifer Piazza, Jody Shapiro, **GUY MADDIN**
Editing: John Gurdebeke
Music: Jason Staczek
Cast: Goro Koyama, Caomhe Doyle, Marilee Yorston, Andy Malcolm, Jenna Dalla Riva, Anna Malkin, Don White, Vanessa Marshak, Elektra Goncharova
Black and white and color
9 minutes

IT'S MY MOTHER'S BIRTHDAY TODAY
Canada
Production: The Criterion Collection
Producer: Lindsay Hamel
Distribution: The Criterion Collection
Direction: **GUY MADDIN**
Screenplay: George Toles
Photography: **GUY MADDIN**
Editing: John Gurdebeke
Music: Song "It's My Mother's Birthday Today," sung by Arthur Tracey with additional voice work by Stacey Nattrass
Cast: Dov Houle [Dan Tierney], uncredited children
Black and white and color
5 minutes

BERLIN
Director: **GUY MADDIN**
1 minute

GLORIOUS
Director: **GUY MADDIN**
12 minutes

2009
NIGHT MAYOR
Canada
Production: National Film Board of Canada
Producer: Joseph MacDonald and Lindsay Hamel
Distribution: National Film Board of Canada
Direction: **GUY MADDIN**
Screenplay: **GUY MADDIN**
Photography: Benjamin Kasulke
Editing: John Gurdebeke
Cast: Nihad Ademi, Mike Bell, Timna Ben Ari, Darcy Fehr, Audrey Neale, Shalini Sharma, Jenny Redzetodic
Black and white
14 minutes

SEND ME TO THE 'LECTRIC CHAIR
Producers: Simon Field, Keith Griffiths, Lindsay Hamel
Direction: **GUY MADDIN** and Isabella Rossellini
Scenario: George Toles, **GUY MADDIN**
Photography: W. James Meagher, **GUY MADDIN**
Editor: John Gurdebeke
Art design: Ricardo Alms, Rick Gilbert, Andy Byers
Starring: Isabella Rossellini, Louis Negin, Darcy Fehr, Brent Neale, David Stuart Evans, Jesse Fraser, Rei Hotoda, Michelle Henderson, Stephanie Graham, Timna Ben
Black and white
7 minutes

Guy Maddin: Interviews

Far from the Maddin Crowd

Robert Enright/1990

From *Border Crossings*, Summer, 1990, pages 33–41. Reprinted by permission of the author.

Guy Maddin is a thirty-four-year-old Winnipegger who, if fate arranges itself in some happy configuration with talent, may well go on to become one of the best filmmakers in North America. By best I don't mean the most polished, the most coherent, or the most profound. I mean the artist capable of making the most strangely compelling and disorienting films, characteristics shared by *The Dead Father* (1985), *Tales from the Gimli Hospital* (1988) and *Archangel* (1990). These three films centre on loss, jealousy, amnesia, and a collection of similarly disquieting conditions, all of which create an irresistibly elegiac tone. Still, an unmistakable cushion of innocence surrounds Maddin's films. It's a balloon that hasn't yet burst around him.

Maddin's narratives are often confused in the telling but gorgeous in the seeing. Watching his films is an exercise in frustration because you constantly want to stop them in order to savour single images. Maddin admits to no particular gift for photography but his shots are wonderfully composed. They look out of time in that they seem to prophesy a future that has already gone by. He is the laureate of Futurepast.

Maddin would no doubt appreciate the absurdity of this timelessness; his sense of humour is witty, self-deprecating, and unconsciously wicked. So are his films: their self-consciousness is a strength, their weirdness comforting. There's no question that Guy Maddin still has a lot to learn about filmmaking but in a way that I accept—and can't explain—he has already showed me the workings of an alchemy that transforms the strange, the curious, and even the disgusting into a world of beautiful bewilderment.

Archangel, Guy Maddin's latest film, premiered June 26 at the Munich

International Film Festival. It will also be shown this summer at the Montreal World Film Festival, the Toronto Festival of Festivals, and on a bedsheet in Gimli, Manitoba. The following interview was conducted in the offices of The Winnipeg Film Group in December, 1989.

GM: I was born at the old Grace Hospital on Portage and Arlington, delivered by Dr. Cuthbert Hanford and named by my twelve-year-old brother after Guy Madison, the B-movie western star.
BC: Is that true?
GM: Believe me, it's true. It's a stupid pun my brother came up with. I never really gave movies another thought, other than all the crummy horror movies I loved going to at the Lyceum Theatre. Then I just watched a lot of television.
BC: So you went to a lot of movies as a kid?
GM: Mostly horror movies. They had to have some sort of macabre bent. Then I went on a long movie hiatus. I don't think I watched a movie for about ten or fifteen years. I remember in 1978 the only one I saw was *Saturday Night Fever*. I caught up with it about the eleventh month of its run.
BC: But you indiscriminately watched television?
GM: Yes, I memorized the TV schedule. There were only seven stations, so you couldn't watch that much. Then I sort of grew out of television and by the age of sixteen or so I think I'd watched too much. And I haven't really watched it since.
BC: What was life like at home? I know your father was a sometime manager of Canada's national hockey team.
GM: He was and my mother was a hairdresser. I grew up in a beauty salon on Ellice Avenue. It was one of those storefront homes. My mom and my aunt ran it together and when they retired I turned the beauty salon into the studio where I made *Tales from the Gimli Hospital*. Then my mom sold that place so I had to rent another studio, also coincidentally on Ellice Avenue, in which I filmed *Archangel*.
BC: Did you hang around your mom's hairdressing business a lot?
GM: I was a fixture. If someone spilled a bottle of peroxide or something, I'd be called in to mop it up. The kids at school would make fun of me because I smelled like perm lotion all the time. It was a smell in the house that I didn't even notice. And there was always the hum of hairdryers, about twenty of them in a row.
BC: Was this an anxious childhood for you?

GM: No, I loved my childhood. It was great. Just the other day a kid I haven't seen since grade one came up to me and said, "Hi, Guy, I'm Jeff from grade one. Remember me?" Of course I remembered him, even though it was twenty-six years ago that I'd last seen him. I used to spend years looking at my grade one photo and pining for those days.

BC: Would you describe yourself as nostalgic?

GM: I'm getting less so now. I don't lie on my bed any more wishing I was in the first grade. But I really thought for the longest time that my goal as a filmmaker was to create in the viewer the feeling that I used to get when thinking of my childhood. I know a lot of filmmakers try to do that but I thought maybe I could intensify those feelings, make them not seem secondhand. I guess I wanted to do the work of poetry and actually create inexplicable feelings in the viewer that were equivalent to the myth-making feelings that you get as a child. Unfortunately, I've felt myself maturing a little bit lately and I don't know if I have those feelings any more. It's kind of sad.

BC: A couple of interesting things come out of what you've just said about childhood. In *Archangel* are the bogeymen Huns committing the consummate sin in your moral universe when they attack children?

GM: In a way the idea of a child being that frightened is a joke. That a bogeyman would actually come in, put a sack on a child's head and chew on its nipples, just the idea of that kind of terror, even though it works out in the end, fascinated me. I hope it's nervously funny. Like in the movie *Poltergeist*—movie quality aside—there's a pretty good scene where a tree just shoots through a window and takes this already terrified kid in its grasp and pulls him out. Now it's one thing to be scared of a tree—and that fear is real for most children—but when the tree actually grabs you and takes you away it's so ridiculously terrifying that it's pretty funny. I remember laughing like a lunatic during that scene.

BC: Let's let humour go for the moment. I have a feeling we'll get back to it. Do you have an informing mythology that is recognizable in your films?

GM: Mythology? I don't know. At times I'm a little vague on what it is. I guess when I think of myth I think of taking the first few things that happen in one's childhood and trying to create a cause and effect relationship out of them. Spring comes because you hang your laundry out—that sort of thing. So quite often it's the myths of early childhood that are most intriguing because they're not in the common parlance. The myths are wrong.

BC: Wrong because the cause and effect sequence is misread? Spring doesn't come because you put the laundry out, you put the laundry out because spring has come?

GM: Yes. But what intrigues me most are the early myths where you're really trying to make sense of something through trial and error. So I'm more interested in the rejected myths. I call them rotten myths. They're models of the universe that are constructed and then have to be disposed of because they don't work. The rotten myths are more intriguing because they tell you more about the way your mind works.

BC: Is myth-making and storytelling the same thing for you?

GM: I'm more interested in myth-making. Storytelling is something that if it's told well then it keeps people awake while you're throwing these rotten myths at them. When they're forced to reject them, they may recreate the feelings of childhood. Because that's what you're doing as a child, rejecting and sorting. That's my strategy for creating feelings.

BC: But feelings are treacherous. I don't know how to react to a film like *Gimli Hospital*. At times it's hilarious and absurd; at other times it's terrifying. The viewer never knows quite how he or she should be responding.

GM: That's the feeling I was hoping to get because I feel it's not just children who are constructing myths. As you encounter new phenomena you have to somehow make sense of them. When you get older, there's sex and death and all that stuff. I've never been very good at making sense of anything, so for me that's where the real joy of storytelling is. As an example, the protagonists in my first two movies attempted to sort out events by just sitting there and receiving them. The narrative was a bit passive, so I tried to design a story where people were actively trying to sort out their worlds. Even total slugs try to do something now and then.

BC: What made you start making films?

GM: I had nothing else to do. I had worked at a bank for a little while as a Branch Administration Manager, and it wasn't great. So I quit and started watching movies. At the university I dropped in on George Toles's class, and then I saw a John Paizs movie. I was totally thrilled that somebody from Winnipeg could make a great movie at an affordable price. I guess I first saw *The Obsession of Billie Botski*, and it was a moment of inspiration. I think his films are really good. John told me it cost $5,000, and I immediately thought if I had the same amount I'd spend it on a movie. At the time I only had $300, but it was enough to

start. I ran out after two days and then submitted what I had shot to the Manitoba Arts Council and received the money I needed to make *The Dead Father*, which I guess cost about $5,000.
BC: Did you have any idea what you were doing? Other than being a filmophile did you have any filmmaking experience?
GM: No. I got someone who agreed to be the cameraman and then he didn't show up for the second shoot. I went over to his house, and he showed me how to work the camera from his bed. I left him there, never saw him again, and was my own cameraman after that.
BC: Tell me about your camera work.
GM: I'm not an accomplished cameraman. I don't have the ability to plan everything and quite often I don't actually know what I want someone to do until I've looked through the camera. They'll be doing something, just kibitzing around while I'm trying to adjust the focus, and I'll see what they've done accidentally and I'll like it better. I wish I could be better organized, but I just never get around to planning things well enough, so I realized rather early that I would have to be behind the camera. When you're editing, you can get mad at yourself for taking bad shots, and then it's far easier to forgive yourself. I didn't want to spend a month cursing a cameraman for screwing up my idea of what the movie should look like. Still, I have to admit every now and then I look at a shot and I wonder why I positioned people that way.
BC: Are you good at explaining what it is you want?
GM: I just didn't want to spend all my time explaining. Movie-making is incredibly boring and slow, and when there's too much debate within the crew, it's even more boring. I knew it would take a lot of energy to make this movie, and I certainly didn't want to expend seven-eighths of it talking to my crew. So I got two of the most efficient and quiet crew members—Terry Reimer and Gerry Turchyn. And I don't think I heard them say more than three words in six weeks. Now and then I'd catch Gerry wiping Vaseline off the lens because he's a technical purist, so I'd have to scold him and put some Vaseline back on.
BC: Do you buy the notion that there is a Winnipeg or prairie sensibility in a number of the films that have been made here?
GM: I have no idea about it. People talked about isolation here, and I never really got a sense of it. What did they mean, I was isolated? I knew what it looked like in Hawaii without ever having gone there. But then I started travelling and I realized we *are* isolated? So maybe there is something geographical and demographic that makes people from

Winnipeg make the same kind of film. I have another theory, though. When you attend film festivals worldwide you realize there's a type of film that comes from an age group. There are films from Sweden and Denmark that remind you of films from Winnipeg. So this undercurrent is less geographical or cultural than chronological.

BC: You use a lot of appropriated images in your films, images that pay homage to earlier filmmakers.

GM: I'm just putting what I like in the films. It's just fun. I guess those old movies are my favourite worlds to be in.

BC: Let's talk about your first production, *The Dead Father*, the film that started with $300 and inspiration from John Paizs.

GM: I'm half proud of that movie. I think it's a bit too slow—or a lot too slow—but there's nothing phoney about it. Everything I put in there I put in for a reason.

BC: Where did the idea for it come from?

GM: It came out of the most persistent of all the stories I had bouncing around in my head. It was this recurring dream where my dead father kept revisiting me; I also remembered my dog died when I was little and it used to make cute little dream visits back to my lap. It left me with really strong residual feelings. I thought my only chance of making a short movie with any impact as a total beginner would be to zero in on one poetic feeling and maybe try to re-create that in the viewer.

BC: What about with *Gimli Hospital*? What was your informing idea in it?

GM: There wasn't as legitimate a source for that story. I wanted to make a second film, and there was a grant deadline coming up at 1:00 o'clock that afternoon. I was painting houses for the summer with a friend, and one rainy day we were writing little sketches about the pathetically tragic history of the Icelandic settlers in Gimli. The accumulation of tragedies was bizarre. They arrived with nets which were meant for ocean fish, and I think it was many years before they caught anything. I think Lord Dufferin offered five dollars to the first Icelander to catch a fish, and he died with the coin. Some hunting expedition went out on October 21st and returned on Christmas Eve with nothing. Then the poor souls got smallpox. It was just awful. I got all this information from a book called *Gimli Saga* which was put out in the '60s by a local women's guild. So, anyway, Kyle and I each wrote little skits which were kind of goofy and uncontrolled. They were more like Rowan & Martin's

Laugh-In skits. But for some reason one of them which got jotted down on a matchbook cover stuck in my head and I submitted that.
BC: So you met the deadline?
GM: Yeah, but I didn't win the competition. It was a Winnipeg Film Group script competition with a $20,000 prize. But at least the deadline made me type up the matchbook cover proposal, and I submitted it to the Manitoba Arts Council. I got the money from them.
BC: Do you know photography very well? I always want to stop your films because single images are so exquisitely composed.
GM: I am concerned about the way my films look. In the '70s I watched a lot of made-for-TV things on CBC and noticed that the images just weren't very interesting. So I made a pledge to give a little extra effort in each shot. Actually, the look of my films is something I take pride in because I'm *not* a visual person. I didn't even own a camera until after I'd finished my second movie, and I still can't take a snapshot for the life of me.
BC: Do you spend a lot of time planning a film; do you story-board it and work out each shot ahead of time?
GM: No, the whole spirit of filmmaking for me, possibly because I'm lazy, is to do it. I never spend more than a couple of seconds on any decision.
BC: But now that you have dialogue and a more complicated plot . . .
GM: I know, there's way more ways to go bad. That's why I overwrite now But I still try not to spend too much time on it. The script for *Archangel* was written with my friend George Toles in three sessions and we just blitzed through it.
BC: Do you still have a suspicion that dialogue is optional?
GM: No, unfortunately it's a little more essential.
BC: Why unfortunately?
GM: Because I like to make movies where the dialogue is just trimming but in *Archangel* the dialogue has an expository duty to perform. I have a narrator who reads ominous requiem-type things from cenotaphs. He's like someone reading "In Flander's Fields" at a Memorial Day Service.
BC: Is Archangel a real place?
GM: It is. A friend of mine—who is a World War I old movie and music buff—told me quite excitedly about this place where all the soldiers of the world gathered after World War I just to continue the fun of fighting. People quit fighting the Germans and started fighting the Russians.

Everyone was sort of forgetful and after a while people were quite confused. Most of the countries were pretty tired of fighting at this point, so they would send special troops—elderly soldiers, with one leg and missing eyes. I've seen footage of the original *Archangel* and the Americans were still wearing their civil war uniforms. They look like Union soldiers with red caps fighting beneath onion domes in Russia. It was really odd.

BC: Do you mean original footage from the town of Archangel actually exists?

GM: Yes, I have some on videotape at home but it doesn't look anything like my movie.

BC: Does the film take its inspiration from this polyglot of loon bags who were there or does it stick to some historical narrative?

GM: I had absorbed the setting over a period of months by reading about these things and through discovering pictures from World War I. Unfortunately, all those story fragments just didn't add up to anything. They were really just a mishmash of things and so George Toles and I tried to pinpoint what makes the difference between a script and a pile of garbage, a distinction I hadn't bothered making before. I had to ask myself what really mattered to me and I realized that forgetfulness was the dominant tenor of my life; I forget the most painfully embarrassing things, important things about myself. I don't know if I should be very specific because you'd blush. Let's put it this way: I've noticed in other people tendencies to forget they're married or forget they have children or forget they have any responsibilities. I could fit rather snugly into all of those categories.

BC: By forget do you mean that people choose not to act upon responsibility?

GM: No, I honestly forget.

BC: Is it important to you to make films that are correct, politically or otherwise? I guess what I'm asking is, do you feel any restraints on what you do?

GM: I don't want to do anything that's absurd just for the sake of being an asshole, but I'm also not interested in saying anything that isn't true just to make it correct. I'm not interested in propagandizing or proselytizing. A lot of times I get the feeling that I'm being propagandized, that I'm not even being allowed to make conclusions for myself. Isn't it kind of insulting to have things given to you all sugarcoated?

BC: So *Archangel* isn't an answer to *Triumph of the Will*? It's not a deliberately nonpropaganda film in any way?
GM: Propaganda can be humorous. Like in those great Edward D. Wood antipornography movies—you know, show me a clam and I'll show you a dirty picture that caused it. They're so ludicrously unsophisticated in their attempts at manipulation that they're hilarious. To a lesser degree a lot of overly correct movies strike me as just as ludicrous. I like the idea of propaganda as humour so *Archangel* has propaganda in it. It's stupid.
BC: Terry Heath has argued that it's not realism that characterizes the prairie sensibility as much as surrealism.
GM: Well, there's an evolutionary aspect involved. When you're a novice filmmaker you can't make realist films. First films are often quite odd because that's what you can do best. You end up maturing into realism. But because I have this theory about novice filmmakers having to make surrealist films I thought I stood a chance of making a slightly watchable film if I kept in mind where a novice might most likely make errors—continuity, lapses in plausibility, things like that. You just keep adapting as you work along.
BC: Did *The Dead Father* matter to you emotionally?
GM: By the time it was in the final editing stages there was nothing emotional to it, but when I jotted down the story idea there was something there. It wasn't about my actual father, it was more about the dreams I had that he was coming back. I wanted to re-create that feeling for viewers and I think it failed in that. As a matter of fact a lot of the feelings people have reported are a tingling of the buttocks, a sort of a numbness of the thighs. I honestly try to make these movies in the spirit of prose poetry. The prose part comes in the story, but I really want the feeling. I'll just keep trying.
BC: I like the prose poet idea because you must recognize there are moments of astonishing visual lyricism in your films.
GM: I'd like them to be there. I don't quite have the hubris to admit that I've succeeded to the degree that I want yet. Little moments, yeah. But I'd like the whole gosh darn thing to blow people out of the water.
BC: Have you been influenced by film noir?
GM: I don't like police movies that much for some reason, although there's some Fritz Lang movies that I like quite a bit. And I'm fond of those wet asphalt movies like *The Sweet Smell of Success*. It's great.
BC: But you go back to the earlier sources of that tradition in German and Russian film rather than through the American variation of it?

GM: That's right, I guess I've seen so much of it now. It doesn't give me goose bumps like it used to. But I just like what shadows can do in those German Expressionist films. If you're a low-budget filmmaker then shadows are the cheapest prop you can lay your hands on; if you can't afford real sets you can start unplugging lights and adding sound effects. I think of it as Darwinian: I had to have sets and lighting like that because I couldn't afford real ones.

BC: I think *Archangel*'s going to be a successful follow-up to *Gimli Hospital*. Are you worried about moving too fast?

GM: I have to watch out. A couple of people—one from Toronto and one from L.A.—have offered to hire me as film director, and I had to turn them down. I wouldn't know what I was doing with a real film and a real budget. The money was really tempting, but I felt quite noble turning them down. Anyway, they would have found me out within three hours on the set. I'd yell into the wrong end of the megaphone on the first day or something. What I have to watch out for is going too far beyond my meagre . . . instead of meagre, we'll call them nascent . . . abilities. So even with *Archangel* I fear sometimes that by going to a talkie I've already gone too far.

BC: You used the term "cannibalizing" the last time we talked to describe the way you borrow from other filmmakers. How much of that do you do?

GM: I guess first of all I have to say I'm not against cannibalism. The reason I have a clear conscience is I use it as part of my vocabulary the way other people use words. If people initially find it quirky and then ultimately find it derivative, then that's too bad. I'm not using it for those effects; I'm using it for my storytelling style.

BC: You said that you were proud of *The Dead Father* because there was nothing in it that was phoney, that everything you included you wanted there. When you use film references, are they there to both take advantage of their previous meaning and the meaning in the context of your film, or are they included for more playful reasons than that? How much latitude do you give yourself in the way the images work?

GM: Ultimately I just put in what I feel like. Sometimes they're included to surprise a friend who might see it.

BC: Filmmaking is still extremely personal for you, then.

GM: I've noticed around the Film Group that when a lot of people start making films they immediately speak in terms of winning Oscars. I think I was realistic in knowing that I'd be lucky if a hundred people saw my first film before it disintegrated totally. I thought, if I can't even please two or three close friends who enjoy movies then there's no point in even making a film. So in that regard it was pretty personal. I made the second film that way too. Because I fully intended it to be seen only by the same number of people who saw *The Dead Father*—which was pretty small. I feel it's only by a miraculous stroke of luck that anyone outside Winnipeg has seen any of my films because I certainly didn't make them with any distribution in mind.

BC: Were you surprised by the success of *Gimli Hospital*?

GM: I'm not surprised because there's evidently no ceiling to my inner arrogance. Pleased though. It's funny, even though I made it fully intending it to be seen by only a handful of people, I guess like all the other dreamers I was secretly hoping that it would win an Oscar. But I was also making sure that the top priority was getting it right for the people who mattered. I wasn't trying to fool the public or anything like that. Actually, I'm not so sure my few close personal friends did like it, so maybe that's why it found some success outside of town.

BC: "How Sweet to Die for One's Country" is the epitaph for *Archangel*. Is this film overflowing with irony or is it a prowar movie?

GM: Not prowar, let's just say it's about standing up and fighting about things that really matter.

BC: I want to come back to the question of forgetfulness. Do you want to talk a little bit more about memory disorders in *Archangel*? How much of a comment is that on your personal life, and how much is it a reflection on contemporary life?

GM: Forgetfulness is something I'm good at, but it makes little comment on anything out there. I'm not a social commentator or anything like that; I go straight to the sports page when I get the paper.

BC: But cultural amnesia is very much a condition of contemporary life. Your personal interest in forgetfulness happens to be a cultural metaphor as well.

GM: One reason I'm not a social commentator is I can never get past the first assumption on theories. I always assume that society hasn't changed in a thousand years, or maybe in 30,000 years. I take it for granted that there's an analogue in prehistoric civilizations for every social action today. I know that things I'm doing in my sleazy life have been done by cavemen, maybe exactly the same things as a matter of fact.

BC: You've said that you want to keep a lot of things submerged in your films. What do you mean?

GM: I hate it when after you've watched a film for the first time you think it's really good, and then after the second time it just doesn't feel like there's anything underneath. So I just try to take a basic story and then make it unrecognizable, piling on stuff. That's my strategy for submersion.

BC: So viewing your films is an act of witnessing the emergence of the layers that you've put into the work.

GM: If you don't do it correctly you obviously just bore people. If no one's paying attention, nothing's going to emerge. I'm aware of that risk.

BC: Let me ask you about some of the layers in *The Dead Father*.

GM: You have the scene where the deceased father is laid out on the breakfast table while the kids eat peanut butter and jam sandwiches around him. It's an hilarious scene at the same time that it's positively macabre, even disrespectful.

GM: I was worried that my mom would be offended by the movie. Unfortunately she didn't understand any of it. But I was also worried that it was more generally disrespectful and ultimately it really is. I think most people are now pretty inured to any kind of disrespect when you think of the kind of images that are bandied around. It's like jokes in a court room or a church; they're not as lewd as you really think. I thought these issues were really quite volatile when I was handling them but even eating from the dead father's stomach didn't seem to bother people that much.

BC: It's a weird scene though. Did it come out of the sensibility of horror films? It's a scene that is more horrific than any other except maybe the wrestling scene in *Gimli Hospital* where the two men glema wrestle and tear holes in each others' buttocks.

GM: I guess I figured if you're covered with pox and fissures you'd probably draw a little bit of blood in a fight like that. As far as the stomach-eating goes, the movie needed a climax. It needed a crisis to come to a head.

BC: So that after he eats the "dead father" their relationship changes dramatically.

GM: I think the narrator says, "I admit it was a night of great excess." He maybe felt he'd gone too far. So it was time to settle on an even keel.

BC: I read the whole relationship as a parody of vampirism. You eat of the father, and at the end of the film he's put in a trunk which is not unlike a coffin. I couldn't help but make associations with the whole Dracula story.

GM: I'm not really close to vampirism, other than those great décolleté shots in the Hammer films with that wonderful red blood. But in their purest Bram Stoker forms, vampire movies bore me for some reason.
BC: *Nosferatu* doesn't interest you?
GM: I watched it recently. It's my least favourite Murnau movie. Maybe because I watched a lot of horror movies as a kid I've just seen too many of them. So it doesn't have any mythological resonance for me because I've just assimilated it as a fact. In the same way I've noticed, much to my horror, some Walt Disney cartoons don't work on me any more either. It's disappointing because that was always a given. But I have to admit that *Bambi* worked on me. I saw it two years ago at the Gimli Theatre.
BC: There's an aspect of horror in *Gimli Hospital* too. The central tension in the movie comes out of an act of necrophilia. Did you have any reservations about including this incident, even at the level of comic suggestion?
GM: I keep forgetting it's in there, actually. It doesn't really have much to do with the movie. But necrophilia isn't common in films. I know there's a Nicholas Roeg film called *Bad Timing* in which we see Art Garfunkel's naked bum mounting what he thinks is a dead lover, but I didn't care for that. Maybe it's just Art Garfunkel's bum I don't care for. But I honestly keep forgetting that's in there; it doesn't even seem that significant to me. I just had to come up with an act that would really irk the former lover.
BC: How much of the film was shot with the full cast involved?
GM: Almost all of it was shot with two people at a time, me and one other person.
BC: So there were very few scenes where you actually had both participants in a dialogue in the same location at the same time?
GM: That's right. There'd be scenes with five or six people and they would never have met one another. It was just easier. Anyway, I wasn't ready to orchestrate twelve people together and do crowd scenes and things. I had to have a few of those, but I usually tried to get rid of people after an hour because I knew I wasn't emotionally strong enough to deal with people grumbling about how boring it was.
BC: The film has some unforgetable visual moments too. The nurses seemed to move almost as if they were joined together.
GM: Yes, the nurses' scenes I shot all in one day. It was originally going to be about three days, but the mother of two of the nurses was such a pain that we got things done quickly.

BC: You've got a lot of death in your films so far. Are you going to start dealing with sex more?

GM: I like suggested sex. I can't compete with Beinex and his ten-minute-long, single-shot copulation scenes. Jeez, ten minutes!

BC: You don't want to, or you can't?

GM: I don't want to. Just getting more and more explicit is a dead end. I go in the opposite direction.

BC: The little shadow play where the nurse undresses is quite nicely done. It's a tasteful invitation to voyeurism.

GM: That part is autobiographical. I've always been totally passive. My entire social life has consisted of sitting in a corner of a restaurant looking at people having fun.

BC: You've said that you use storytelling as a way of personally clarifying things.

GM: They're as clear as they'll ever get before I've made the film. Making the film then just becomes work and any therapeutic considerations disappear. If there's any therapy, it's the great feelings you get when the movie plays out of town. That's probably pretty bad for me.

BC: Why do you think that?

GM: It's a self-indulgent, ego thing. Every now and then I just stare at my poster and sigh.

BC: Were you raised funny or something? Why would you worry about success?

GM: I don't worry about it. I'd love to have success, but I want to be my own most critical judge. That way by the time I pronounce myself successful I'll be successful. That won't happen for a long time; I'm just trying to avoid smugness which I haven't successfully done. Believe me, I want everyone to love me.

BC: What do you do when you're not editing?

GM: I sit around with a nervous stomach, and I play a lot of ping pong with John Kozak, another filmmaker here. He beat me eighty-nine games in a row, and Dave Barber, who runs the Cinematheque, beat me something like ninety-two games in a row. But I've started to win. I actually beat Kozak two games in a row. As a matter of fact ping pong has supplanted editing for quite a while.

BC: Do you have your next film in mind?

GM: No, I was thinking of doing a Biblical epic or Guy Maddin's version of Gustave Flaubert's *Salammbo*, a book I enjoyed because it's so overripe. I took it to the laundromat one night and got to page five and had to reread page five four times because I was sleepy. I thought if I could even get through chapter one of the book then maybe I could adapt it. So I put it aside for a while. Maybe I just wasn't in the mood for it at the time. Then I started thinking of doing something smaller, maybe human movies with a room and one person in it. But that would drive me batty too. I have no idea what to do right now

BC: Has Gimli been a place that really matters to you?

GM: Yes, it's a place I dream of constantly. At least once a week I dream of swimming in Lake Winnipeg in the winter. I've been having that dream since I was four. I have ritualized the place to the extent that the act of swimming there is my church. I've swum in Lake Winnipeg ten out of the twelve months of the year now. Kyle and I went swimming on December 9th last year. It was pretty mild weather the day before when Kyle and I were sitting in the city and there was no snow. We said we're going to have to bring snow by swimming in Lake Winnipeg. So the next day a bunch of us drove to the lake. By the time we got there, it was night time and we expected the water to be open because it hadn't been that cold. Greg Klymkiw was the first person to see the lake, and he didn't have his glasses on. He remarked how calm the lake looked. It wasn't calm, it was frozen. But we'd all pledged that we were going to swim and we'd ritualized it in the ninety minutes it took us to drive out. We'd sung songs about swimming and how four went down and four went in. Of course none of us let on that we were absolutely convinced our hearts were going to stop. We drove by Gimli Hospital on the way, all silently knowing that one of us would soon be lying in there. So we stripped down and walked through the hoar-frosty grass. There was no snow, but the lake was frozen and there was this one open area. We took our shoes off at the last second, and Greg Klymkiw took pictures to prove that we went in. Unfortunately, he took his shoes off before he had a chance to get in and he froze his feet. Then he walked over a bunch of piled ice shards about three or four feet high and because he had no feeling the ice punched holes in the bottom of his feet and blood was pouring out. He didn't know. But we all felt good. Kyle earned his nickname "Two Swims McCulloch" by going in twice. It always seems to me that a trip to the lake isn't complete unless I've touched the water. Actually the night the movie premièred on April 16th we decided to seal the première by all going swimming. The lake had already started thawing, but at night it froze over again, just a razor-thin layer of ice, and when all five of us ran in we slowly realized it was cutting all the skin off our shins. So everyone was wearing little crimson socks of their own blood. I think seven of us crammed into a car, and only Angela Heck, the actress, didn't go in. She was the only one who wimped out. I have since learned that you can ice swim without any trouble. Snow baths are a Gimli tradition too. I was at a party last January in Gimli in a really cold caboose and I suddenly stripped to my boxer shorts and, hoping to impress everyone, I made a big snow angel outside. Instead, it just terrified them; they thought they were with a madman. It really wasn't the social gambit I thought it might be. I felt like Einar in *Gimli Hospital*.

BC: Are you interested in power?

GM: I don't think so. If I am, it's in a way that no one can figure out because I'm constantly trying to diffuse power. When I sense I have it over people, I notice I always try to undercut it, just so. I'm uncomfortable with the feeling of having any power over people. If I'm beating someone at ping pong, I try to get the game a little closer. I'll even lose. It's kind of odd, but then I suspect it's probably some sort of reverse psychology I'm using on myself to gain even more power over people. I don't trust my motives totally. I'm sure I would like nothing better than to control the entire world but do it with meekness.

Far from the Maddin Crowd: Guy Maddin Interviewed

Alan Jones/1991

From *Shock Xpress* No. 1 (London: Titan Books, August, 1991), pages 142–47. Reprinted by permission of the author.

He's been called the Canadian Jean Cocteau, David Lynch's bastard Russian son, and the new Buñuel by way of Eisenstein. Guy Maddin has only directed two and a half movies to date but his unclassifiable slices of tortured realism have made him the hottest name on America's Midnight Movie cult circuit. Words simply cannot do justice to this thirty-two-year-old's unique body of work. The half-hour short *The Dead Father* (1987), and his two twisted features, *Tales from the Gimli Hospital* (1988) and *Archangel* (1990), are "silence is golden" surreal tapestries of precisely pitched tableaux blending absurdist satire, warped horror, eccentric gore, and wrenching melodrama to fashion directional new forms of macabre intensity in the magical process.

Maddin's trademark brand of eerie silent movie nostalgia and expressionist symbolism, strained through a contemporary filter of '90s awareness, is very much an acquired taste. Apart from Lynch and Tim Burton, he's the sole purveyor of off-off-mainstream nonconformity at work in the industry today. A wilfully unconventional director, although he'll argue the contrary, Maddin's grudging destiny would seem to be shaking up the staleness the no-budget, low-rent amateur arena has slowly slid into since the advent of video. That Maddin is the most exciting individual to make weird and wonderful cinematic waves in over a decade is without question. So too is unshakeable global opinion that his stature and importance will keep growing. For each mind-boggling ball of confusion contains enough of his unique simplicity, chilling charm, dizzying dynamics, and brain-scorching imagery to make each lovingly wrought miniature an exquisitely hypnotic work of art. Fasten your seatbelts for a twin peek at Maddin's mad, mad, mad, mad world.

Tales from the Gimli Hospital

At a hospital in the small Canadian town of Gimli, an elderly woman tells a story to her grandchildren as they wait for their mother to die. It tells of two men, Gunnar (Michael Gottli) and Enair (Kyle McCulloch), affected by an unspecified epidemic at the turn of the century. Both men share the same hospital room and Gunnar tells Enair a dark secret about how he "murdered" his beautiful bride Snjofridur (Angela Heck) by passing her the deadly plague during their courtship. Enair has a tale to tell about Gunnar's wife too. But his shocking story will both unite them in grief and eventually make them sworn enemies.

SX: Did you purposely set out to make a cult movie?
GM: No, I just made it really. I shot it at weekends spread over a few months. Sometimes I got bored and didn't film for a while, and I was very relaxed and informal in my approach. It was the easiest film-making experience I'll probably ever have. I didn't have any market in mind as I come from Winnipeg where there's a tiny film community and, when I started making *Tales*, no homegrown films were being shown outside the city. So I had no intention of pushing it anywhere. I just wanted to make a home movie my friends could be in and see. People ask me if it's a massive put-on or a serious movie. All I can say is whenever I see a movie that amuses me, the more straight-faced it is, the better.
SX: *Tales* makes provocative use of necrophilia, Icelandic myths, AIDS, synchronised dance routines, anaesthesia by glove puppet, surgery by scythe, tinted black and white photography, and all manner of silent movie icon madness . . .
GM: I was always forced to spend teenage summers in Nordic communities to understand my heritage. I would attend speeches given by Icelandic elderly women elected as Festival maidens. *Tales* is my revenge on those people and so is the buttock wrestling. That's part of Icelandic culture and the object is to hoist your opponent up with all sorts of nimble foot movements required of the combatants. My actors couldn't do any of those so they just grabbed and hugged each other warmly. The movie ends with an Icelandic diplomat's speech about the evils of drink. Well I think that's what it is anyway! When I was scoring the movie I decided the only music I wanted for that scene was bagpipes. Don't ask

me why, I just felt in a Scottish mood! I got synchronised swimming out of my system the same way too, as I love going to swimming pools to watch teams practise. *Tales* was invited to the Reykjavik Film Festival. I've heard nothing since, but I'm probably excommunicated and my picture is a wanted poster at all Icelandic airports!
SX: What about the many references to fish?
GM: The actual town of Gimli in Manitoba is a good old middle-of-the-prairies fishing village. They are fish crazy and seafood is served with everything including Christmas dinner! I didn't go out of my way to include all the fish. It's part of the Gimli culture. In truth I tried to cut most of the fish references down but somehow they remain to the fore.
SX: Why did you decide on the silent movie form?
GM: I've always liked the minimalist style. My favourite kind of movie is the curious part-talkie genre. You know, the ones made in December 1927. *The Jazz Singer* opened in November and directors scrambled to add soundtracks to catch the new wave. I always liked dialogue in the form of quickly shot monologues. I'm charmed by the free movement back and forth between the, then, new and old mediums. It was a far simpler process for a beginner to handle too. I would have done exactly the same if I'd had a million dollars.
SX: *Tales* practically represents the whole history of cinema thrown into seventy-two minutes as a result.
GM: I'm not against modernism, I just found myself returning to the wonderful world of the past time and time again as I had access to this great film archive at Winnipeg University. I watched old movies constantly and *M, Birth of a Nation*, and D. W. Griffith homages are all included in *Tales*. I'm totally sick of modern cinema, and I just made what came naturally. Since I hadn't seen a colour movie for three years at the point I made *Tales*, the language and rhythm of silent black and white features came as second nature. I liked tinting the print to alter the mood indicating a change in emotion—a heavy influence from Griffith's *Broken Blossoms*. I'm glad the film looks about sixty years old. In many ways I wish it looked older. For some late night engagements the 16mm print has been blown up to 35mm. Funnily enough it works even better as it's scratchier and grainier. One reviewer said *Tales* looked like rotting images of past cinema. And, boy, in the 35mm version, does it look it!
SX: Kyle McCulloch plays a dual role in black face. Is that another nostalgic throwback to the past?
GM: I'm glad audiences are seeing it as nostalgia. It's an uncomfortable

convention, one I've always liked. I've never thought about it until now but I suppose it could be another connection to *The Jazz Singer*. Kyle insisted he wanted to play a part in black face as well as the Enair character. Just do it, he said, and then decide later if you want to keep it. So I did. It was a potentially touchy subject, but no one's ever complained.

SX: Have you had any formal film school training?

GM: No, I just worked in a bank one day and quit the next to fool around with a camera. I've been a film-maker for three and a half years now, but only recently could I look my Mom in the eye and say, "I'm a director." Now she won't talk to me!

SX: Another major *Tales* influence is your love of vintage music.

GM: I'm a huge buff. Old 78 rpm records are full of mysterious scratchy layers and often you can never get through them to actually hear the performers underneath. This creates a really strange world for me. When you're working with low budgets, you need all the help you can get to create an ethereal netherworld. I was happy to recruit it by proxy from my scratchy record library.

SX: You hint at there being many more *Tales from the Gimli Hospital* to tell.

GM: I actually hope it doesn't come to that, although I may get desperate. Certainly there are a million Icelandic myths to investigate. But with any luck you won't see them!

SX: You say you made the movie solely as a calling card to make new friends?

GM: And it worked! I made *Tales* in 1988 and Ben Bazenholtz saw it. He was the man who distributed *Eraserhead*, and he immediately put it into the Quad cinema in New York. It is still doing very well, and across America audiences keep growing. I'm pleased *Tales* has found any place at all in today's theatrical market. Let's be realistic—it hardly threatens *The Rocky Horror Picture Show* in terms of Midnight Movie greatness. Throwing fish at the screen is bound to upset the theatre owners! But I can still remember sitting all alone at the editing table dreaming of the best and worst possible things that could happen with *Tales*. And the best happened surpassing all my wildest dreams.

Archangel

During the Bolshevik Revolution in the Russian city of Archangel, the love lives of three people unfold whose senses have been afflicted by severe memory disorders due to mustard gas apoplexy. Dashing one-legged Canadian Lt. Boles (Kyle McCulloch) is in love with Iris. But she's dead, and when he meets Soviet nurse Veronkha (Kathy Marykuca) he assumes she's his late beloved. Unfortunately Veronkha is already married to Belgian pilot Philbin (Ari Cohen) who keeps forgetting this fact. And Veronkha, assuming Boles is Philbin, falls deeper in love with him. Then landlady Danchuk (Sarah Neville) falls for Boles too, so disgusted is she with the behaviour of her obese husband Jannings (Michael Gottli). Which woman does Boles love or lust after the most—Veronkha, Danchuk, or Iris? Guided by an ancient treasure map where X marks the spot for retro romance, Boles hopes his terminal catatonia will eventually defog to unearth the epic answer.

SX: As *Tales* slowly built late night word of mouth throughout the summer of 1989 you made *Archangel*. Was it easy to raise the money?
GM: Based on *Tales'* reception, very easy as it turned out. But whereas that cost only $22,000, and making a profit on such a sum obviously isn't hard, *Archangel* cost the Canadian tax payer $350,000. Telefilm Canada, formerly the Canadian Film Foundation, backers of David Cronenberg's early work, matched the independent money I raised from distributor advances and Arts Council grants. I suspect it won't make too much of its budget back though.
SX: *Tales* garnered you an instant cult reputation. Did you receive any Hollywood offers as a result?
GM: Loads and I turned them all down. I had no intention of nipping my career in the bud with such appalling lapses in taste. They were all along the lines of "Beverly Hillbillies from Outer Space" type movies. They'd say, "Here's a script just for you—you're weird and zany." Except they'd have discovered I was an impostor on the first day when I didn't know what end of a megaphone to yell into! Friends told me I should have directed under a pseudonym. But what's the point? They were diseased from the word go.
SX: What were the major differences between shooting *Tales* and *Archangel*?
GM: I shot *Archangel* in twenty-nine leisurely days and edited it during Fall 1989. It was the first time I'd made a movie on an actual shooting schedule. *Tales* was shot over a few months at weekends, or on Wednesday nights after the hockey game, at my mother's beauty salon where the interiors were hastily built. *Archangel* was all studio based in a huge

disused warehouse. We drew out a floor plan arranging each set like a jigsaw puzzle so they'd all fit in. Very cosy. I closed in the frame to make each set look cramped with stylised shadows curving in on top. Once more I had to rely solely on cleverness rather than budget.

SX: *Archangel* represents the return to a juvenile passion for you doesn't it?

GM: I often ask myself, do I have to account for my work in this way? But as a kid I loved the uniforms of World War One with their toy soldier quality. I still find it hard to believe anyone got killed in that war because they all look so toy-like. I would always imagine them curled up in the trenches getting ready for bed more than battle.

SX: *Archangel* is far more tongue-in-cheek than *Tales*.

GM: Is it? I honestly didn't know what I wanted half the time. The whole shoot was a blobby mass in truth. My directing style was a bit laid back, yet I'm pleased with the tone and feel I accidentally achieved. Because I was worried the actors' styles would be all over the place I decided to shoot the movie in sequence. Then if any feeling changed it would represent an onscreen evolution. I never really felt the performances were unified until we came to dub the picture. Because the studio sound was so crystal clear, the actors ended up whispering their lines in a relaxed Barry White sort of way. That's what brought the movie together. I didn't make the voices old, scratchy, or disembodied. I made them clean and upfront because I'm tired of being accused of simply imitating silent movie strategies.

SX: The publicity manual describes *Archangel* as "A tragedy of the Great War. A melancholy dreamlike world of long-ago lost love. A Goya war painting etched upon a child's window pane in frost." You say it's more a cross between *Dr. Zhivago* and *Battleship Potemkin*.

GM: *Archangel* utilises Soviet editing techniques and minimal camera movement—both Eisenstein influenced. But I don't copy anything intentionally, it's subconscious plagiarism. The silent era used a whole roster of similar phrases repeated in each film. I'm conversant with that vintage vocabulary as my visual experiences tripled weekly watching one great classic after another courtesy of the Winnipeg University archives. My style may have a familiar quality, but why should I go out of my way to correct it? To be honest I've used up all my cherished silent images now. I was wondering the other day what would be the feeling if I showed *Archangel* to anybody still alive from that golden heyday. I came to the conclusion that they'd be offended for certain.

SX: Why did you choose mustard gas as a narrative device?
GM: Because it serves a dual purpose. *Archangel* is about fogginess and forgetfulness. Mustard gas was a neat visual equivalent for the cloud of confusion the players find themselves in. I made it up for fairytale purposes to give the movie a folklore feel, hence the Iris, apple, and eye symbolism. Filigreeing on simplicity with careless boldness is the basic freedom a storyteller has. It's also an excuse for the story being more unfocused than I had initially hoped. There's a very complicated, very real narrative there which some people see while others don't. *Archangel*'s main failing is I don't give viewers a chance to get back on board if they get lost. There are no checkpoints anywhere to reenter the story. That's a major screw-up on my part. It's great I can rationalise that as an underground filmmaker by hiding behind all manner of artsy banners. But I'm honestly regretful that it's as unfocused as it is. There's no real punchline, yet I hope there's enough to engage the attention despite there not being quite the expected payoff.
SX: Rabbits stand in as metaphors for Bolsheviks who are "half man, half beast with great big eyes and great big claws." There's discreet cannibalism, enforced war medal eating and a strangulation by spilled intestine. The stylised gore is more upfront than in *Tales*.
GM: I strove for the artificiality of violence—like kids fighting in the back yard. I needed a savage punctuation mark and I wanted Michael Gottli to cram his guts back into his stomach to conquer his cowardice and shine better than the rest of the characters. I always welcome laughter in my entertainments. If audiences laugh or are puzzled by this false note, I think the sequence acquits itself once he forces his guts back in. Does it look convincing or fake? My rule of thumb is try your hardest, and you'll still end up with something that falls short. I had hired a makeup effects guy to sculpt an intestinal panel. He wanted to charge $1,500 and I could tell he'd be a problem. "Shit," I said, "let's get a pack of sausages and do it ourselves." We untied the links, smoothed them out, and it cost $30.
SX: You didn't actively pursue "rotting images of—past cinema" this time. You highlight Cecil B. DeMille–style judgemental intonations and signpost the narrative with deliberately wacko title cards instead.
GM: Don't forget the blotching that suddenly appears. That happened because the print laboratory accidentally water-spotted the negative. They were apologetic and didn't want to bill me but I told them to print it anyway. It suited me fine. Any time people tell me they've ruined

something, I get excited. It's almost always the best stuff! I shot *Archangel* on Kodak Plus X black and white negative because it gives a harsh, high key lighting effect. Some of the movie is speeded up too. That's another happy accident. I used my 16mm Bolex and because the spring is shot it kept adjusting to slow motion. I never clean it and abuse it all the time. I really must retire it soon! More confessions from a director whose art comes from calculated carelessness! My work ethic tends to infuriate the workers. But so what!

SX: How have the ultra-enthusiastic reviews of your movies affected your life?

GM: I'm a grade D celebrity back in my hometown. I'm getting mentioned in the local press enough to be resented now.

SX: What's your next project?

GM: It's a wholly studio based movie, titled *Careful*, set in the Swiss Alps which we've built in papier-maché. I'm aiming for a Michael Powell/*Black Narcissus* look. I'm filming in black and white again with the intention of computer colouring it for TV and video release because I'm tired of distributors whining about the noncommerciality of monochrome. If I'm in full control of the operation from the beginning, it will look like a hand-tinted picture. It's about an anxious Swiss community in the timeless '30s who are far too careful for their own good. They live in constant fear of avalanches and this over-caution insidiously infects every part of their lives. It's partly autobiographical. My family are infuriatingly cautious—like the whole of Canada. As with *Tales* and *Archangel* I've written the script, with George Toles again, from the standpoint it's an unsung opera set in that most neutral country of all, Switzerland. Heated passions come to the fore when an incest scandal seeps out through the commune's cracks. I have a one-and-a-half million dollar budget, meaning I can sign up higher profile actors alongside my repertory actor stable. I promise you it will still have the now expected, pretty cheesy Maddin quality to it.

SX: Are you sick of the constant comparisons to David Lynch?

GM: The only thing we have in common is we've both made a couple of monochrome pictures. I'm a gentle, quiet director who seeks viewer involvement. I'm working towards beauty, placidity, and exquisite strangeness. I don't think that's what Lynch is about at all. His work is far more contrived than mine.

SX: Looking back over your meteoric career rise what strikes you most in retrospect?

GM: That *Tales* and *Archangel* are an inventory of my movie-making mistakes so far. Now I want to sit back, take stock, and put everything I've learnt on this artistic collision course in dramatic perspective. My growing legion of admirers, and I still can't believe I have any, will see a development in the direction they like with *Careful*. The story is clear, yet peculiar. It's about people who love each other but who can't express their affection. They are tormented by Hamlet-style jealous passions, and it ends up poorly, very much like life itself. Hey, I've had some good times, but I'm not the only writer who thinks that way. Look at Chekhov. Anyway I like my characters being left the way I feel every morning!

SX: Will you ever "Go Hollywood"?

GM: I don't think so because my movies speak for themselves. I'm not a commercial film director. I have no passion for it. I couldn't make one if I tried, I'm not that versatile. I'm well aware my movies are considered strange, offbeat, and uncategorisable. But I'm proud of that. So I'll keep working in the areas that interest me and, who knows, maybe one day they'll stray into the commercial arena. But I doubt it!

Weird Art and Science: Guy Maddin's Primitive Genius

David Chute/1999

From the *L.A. Weekly*, April 30, 1999. Reprinted by permission of the author.

"I knew when I was starting out that I was a primitive," allows director Guy Maddin, speaking by phone from his home base in Winnipeg. "So the films would be primitive, and therefore I'd best choose a story that might benefit from being told primitively. All the elements have to evolve simultaneously. You have to make a film that has just the right number of flippers and fins and gills to survive."

No one will ever accuse Maddin of employing a conventional vocabulary. Now forty-three, he is one of the most uncompromisingly idiosyncratic filmmakers on Earth, working during one of the most homogeneous periods in movie history. His 1988 debut feature, the grisly smallpox farce *Tales from the Gimli Hospital*, played midnight shows and was compared to *Eraserhead*. But *Gimli* wasn't just a gross-out romp; it was a feverishly self-conscious art toy, a fake silent movie shot in grainy black and white, with elaborate retro title cards, iris-outs and stylized broad-brush acting that made a virtue out of sub-shoestring production resources and an admittedly rickety technique.

Maddin's subsequent features, the deliciously screwy *Archangel* (1990) and *Careful* (1992), have been more rigorous and sophisticated but no less willfully anachronistic. Set respectively in a remote Russian military outpost and in frozen alpine vistas, the films were studio fabrications that flaunted their artificiality, and were physically and hence emotionally snowbound. His new feature, *Twilight of the Ice Nymphs*, is all about heat and light: hot weather and hot blood. A complex love quadrangle set on a magical tropical island where the sun never sets, it betrays the influence of one of Maddin's favorite films, the 1935 Max Reinhardt/William Dieterle adaptation of *A Midsummer Night's Dream*.

"I liked the idea of denying myself my usual cheapest prop, which is a shadow," says Maddin. "And then I thought, 'What psychological tenor would impose itself in such a world?' It would have to be that people see things too clearly, as the paranoiac does. Things are almost magnified by an optical anomaly created by wavering wafts of heat." In Maddin's organic aesthetic of interrelationships, some of the work of motivation is always supplied by the setting, by the pressure of an extreme environment. In *Twilight*, he explains, "All the characters are intoxicated by seasonal adjustment disorder because the sun never sets."

A Canadian director might be expected to know a thing or two about the pressure of an extreme environment, and Maddin may be as distinctively Canadian, in this sense, as Atom Egoyan or David Cronenberg, typical only in his context-free singularity. He's not part of a movement, has no precursors or imitators. He's a dodo bird, a throwback, which is part of why he's so appealing: Maddin proves that it's still possible, even in today's bland and hypertrophied movie climate, for one weirdo to make feature films that couldn't have been made or even imagined by anybody else.

Maddin admits he'd enjoy reaching a wider audience outside the avant-garde ghetto of critics' awards and career achievement nods at Telluride, and his luscious visuals and effortless sense of fantasy could be applied to many kinds of genre material. But he has to talk production companies into giving him money, just like everybody else, and his rarefied, one-of-a-kind achievement is a tough sell. Even when he is able to raise some cash, as on *Twilight*, it inevitably comes with strings attached.

"I guess the way I was viewed in Canada was as an imaginative black sheep who needed to be taken to obedience school. The thought was that if I just had real actors and a real 35mm camera and a lot of discipline, I could produce a far more marketable film. So I made it in 35, even though I didn't want to, because it shows too much detail and costs $300,000 more than 16mm—so we had $300,000 less to put into the art department, but the film shows more."

It's still an open question whether a Guy Maddin movie can ever be domesticated, or "pass" commercially. His plans to make a musical, *The Dikemaster's Daughter*, and a docudrama about the '60s Canadian hockey scene fell by the wayside after the release of *Careful*. He wrote a script adapting the Victor Hugo novel *The Man Who Laughs*, but could not get producers to bite. ("It must have looked really expensive on the page. They didn't realize I was planning to make seventeenth-century England out of cardboard.") And he keeps busy making short films with wonderful titles like *Mauve Decade*, *The Pomps of Satan*, and *Sissy-Boy Slap-Party*. He doesn't know where his next feature will be coming from. Perhaps, like the others, it will simply sprout gills and emerge from the water someday soon, seemingly under its own power.

A Trip through Maddin's Videotape Collection

Caelum Vatnsdal/2000

From *Kino Delerium: The Films of Guy Maddin* (Winnipeg: Arbeiter Ring Publishing, 2000). Reprinted by permission of the author.

The following trek, by no means comprehensive, takes us through some of the many pictures which Maddin keeps on his shelves and close to his heart for one reason or another. One may take the mere mention of any of these titles as a firm recommendation to seek out and watch the movie.

Alibi (Roland West). "A really strange part-talkie."

Alice (Jan Svankmayer). "When I discovered the existence of this movie it made me very happy. The sheer density of ick is something to behold."

Autumn Leaves (Robert Aldrich). "Joan Crawford may be the Gordie Howe of film: she had many good decades strung together. She was a star in the twenties, thirties, forties, fifties, and even into the sixties from those Baby Jane movies. The most scared I've ever been from a movie, by the way, was seeing *Hush, Hush Sweet Charlotte* at the Gimli Theatre. That movie scarred me to this day."

The 1979 Avco Cup. "The very last game played in the WHA [World Hockey League]. The Jets versus the Oilers. Gretzky barely plays in that game, strangely enough. Anyway, the Jets won that."

Babes in Toyland (Gus Meins, Charles Rogers). "I love even the colorized version, which this is. I especially love the genuinely terrifying scenes in which the bogeymen steal children from their beds."

The Bitter Tea of General Yen (Frank Capra). "I like the look of this. It's the only movie from this era that looks as good as a von Sternberg movie. And it continues the strange tradition of getting a Swede, Nils Asther in this case, to play a Chinaman. Warner Oland did it too, of course. And there's a William Wellman movie called *The Hatchet Man* in which Edward G. Robinson plays a Chinese assassin, if you can believe it."

Blackmail (Alfred Hitchcock). "I love the part-talkie, as you know, and that has some great tropes in it that still seem super fresh."

The Blue Light (Leni Riefenstahl). "I like the idea of fables somehow being brought to film, and that's a pretty legendary one; and of course it's a mountain picture."

The Cameraman's Revenge (Wladyslaw Starewicz). "A pre-Soviet animated movie from 1912 starring nothing but dead bugs. It's pretty charming. It's a love triangle story in which a grasshopper is having an affair with a beetle, and the beetle's husband comes home and gets mad. But the grasshopper is a cameraman and gets revenge by filming the husband having a tryst of his own. It's really odd seeing a lurid love story enacted by dead bugs."

Cape Fear (J. Lee Thompson). "I love the score, and I love Bob Mitchum and the way he sucks in his gut."

Celebrations: Islendigudaggurun. "This tape belongs to my Uncle Ron, and I've been meaning to return it to him. It's a humdinger."

Chang (Merian C. Cooper, Ernest B. Schoedsack). "A drama of the wilderness by the King Kong boys, really quite wonderful."

La Chienne (Jean Renoir). "A movie I thought I should watch because John Harvie, Ian Handford, and I obsessed over *Scarlet Street*, which is the remake. We watched that movie eighty times over a weekend once. As far as *La Chienne* goes, there's no Dan Duryea; and though I love Michel Simon, especially in *L'Atalante*, he can't touch Edward G. Robinson as Chris Cross in *Scarlet Street*."

City Girl (F.W. Murnau). "An agricultural melodrama made right after *Sunrise* that Terrence Malick apparently watched fifty times just before making *Days of Heaven*."

Councillor At Law (William Wyler). "I just love John Barrymore."

The Days of Wine and Roses (John Frankenheimer). "This is the great Kinescope version with Cliff Robertson and Piper Laurie. I love that Kinescope look, with the ghosting quality and everything, and I've studied it to see if it's possible to re-create that look without using an actual Kinescope or some digital effects. But it isn't.

"Movies made in 1958 seem outrageously modern to me; I consider them contemporary. But television from that era makes it seem that Robertson or Gleason or Serling or whoever must have been rubbing shoulders with Meliés or the Lumière Brothers; the calendars get out of whack."

Design for Living (Ernst Lubitsch). "Even if Lubitsch is placed at the top of the list of movie titans, he still doesn't seem to be up high enough. Just the way he effortlessly mixes music and plot and charm. The pain he mixes in with the comedy in *Design for Living* is something that I really wish I could do. But Lubitsch fans, and even Herman G. Weinberg, who wrote *The Lubitsch Touch*, hate the movie for some reason."

Dirigible (Frank Capra). "I want it on record that I love *Dirigible*."

D.O.A. (Rudolph Mate). "I love the way Edmond O'Brien drops dead at the end, faster than gravity could possibly pull him down. They must have had bungee cords on him or something. Those are the kind of details I really like."

Dr. Jekyll and Mr. Hyde (Rouben Mamoulian). "The fact that Mamoulian made *Jekyll and Hyde* and *Love Me Tonight* in the same twelve-month period is amazing to me. One of them is a perfect Lubitsch impersonation, maybe even better, and the other one this really beautiful horror movie. I'm desperate to find his first two movies, *City Streets* and *Applause*."

Dracula (Tod Browning). "It might be a blasphemy, but I have the version with the Philip Glass score. I find it unbelievably insane somehow. It didn't occur to them to put a score in it originally, so the Glass score doesn't replace anything, but provides wall-to-wall music. I like the audacity of a movie that has nonstop music. *The Black Cat*, by Ulmer, has almost wall-to-wall music."

East Side, West Side (Mervyn Le Roy). "Lots of great stars in this one. Van Heflin sure is a mysterious entity. He sort of looks like an animal with a fat ass or something. Anyway, it's another great James Mason movie."

The Fall of the House of Usher (Jean Epstein). "The very first movie that Buñuel ever worked on. He learned everything he knew about filmmaking on this shoot."

The Horror of Dracula (Terence Fisher). "I must have watched Christopher Lee's death sequence in this movie five hundred times at least. Only trying to climb a flagpole can come close to replicating the feeling it gives me."

How Green Was My Valley (John Ford). "I will now proudly declare my love of *How Green Was My Valley*."

Joe 90 (Russ Dyck). "Every bit as delirious as its director. I can't figure out what that movie is about, even after many conversations about it with Russ."

Johnny Guitar (Nicholas Ray). "One of my favourite Westerns of all time."

Kansas City Confidential (Phil Karlson). "I love John Payne's name and his face, which are perfectly matched. There are some really painful *mano-a-mano* fights in there, and I love those. I collect them, in fact."

The Leech Woman (Edward Dein). "This movie seems to be at least sixty percent stock footage of jungle animals."

Leolo (Jean Claude Lauzon). "My favourite Canadian movie by a Secretariat's margin. It's better than anything else ever made in Canada."

The Little Match Girl (Jean Renoir). "I love this movie. When I was getting the famously taciturn Terry Reimer to help me shoot *Archangel*, the first day's rushes came back looking far too clean. So I showed him *Little Match Girl* and said I wanted it more high contrast, like this. I'm not sure if he said anything, but I think he nodded. And the next day's rushes were much better, though still outrageously clean. I never had the nerve until maybe *Hospital Fragment* or *The Heart of the World* to make the images as degraded as they really should be."

Mad Love (Karl Freund). "A bunch of great cameramen worked on this, and it has Peter Lorre and Colin Clive, two of the greatest voices of all time. And I love the *Hands of Orlac* story so much that I want to do my own version some time. I see myself as Orlac sometimes."

The Miracle of Morgan's Creek (Preston Sturges). "One of the cruellest, most frantic masterpieces ever."

Los Olvidados (Luis Buñuel). "One of my fondest Christmas Eve memories was after I'd dropped my daughter off at her mother's place and had nothing left to do and was feeling kind of despairing. Everyone else in my family was off doing other Christmas things and I was feeling all alone in the world. I went off to that great secular curmudgeon's place, the House of Snyder, and he had a print of *Los Olvidados*, a movie in which children are hit with sticks, and dancing Chihuahuas dressed in tutus serve as euphemisms for the sex act, to watch on Christmas Eve."

Le Plaisir (Max Ophüls). "Unbelievable décors. I loved the dance hall set in the first story and wanted it for the inside of Dr. Solti's palace in *Twilight of the Ice Nymphs*. With all the cost compromises it turned into something not related to it at all. It only takes three compromises or so, and you end up with something like a dog house with a whistle on the top. So I keep *Le Plaisir* around as a reminder to resist those compromises as Ophüls must have had to do."

Quay Brothers Collection. "They really are an art direction standard for me, so they're really important. Plus they're pals."

The Quick and the Dead (Sam Raimi). "I love this movie. Go figure."

The Red and the White (Miklós Jancsó). "My favourite Cinemascope moving-camera movie. It's got twenty-minute-long shots with depth-of-field from two inches to two miles."

Road House (Jean Negulesco). "Richard Widmark is one of the all-time great sweaty-faced squealing cowards ever, and he gets shot to death orgasmically by Ida Lupino in this movie."

Rose Hobart (Joseph Cornell). "This is Cornell's tribute to his favourite actress. I like it quite a bit."

La Roue (Abel Gance). "I have as much Gance as there is available on videotape. I love directors who are obviously possessed, and Gance was possessed by the greatest case of hubris ever, plus a big cocaine addiction."

The Seventh Veil (Compton Bennett). "A great melodrama, and maybe the sexiest James Mason role ever. He plays the angriest, sternest, limpingest piano teacher ever. He smashes a little girl's fingers with a cane and things like that."

La Signora di Tutti (Max Ophüls). "I love everything by Ophüls except *Lola Montes*. And I don't like *La Ronde* that much either: the structure is too exhausting. But *La Signora di Tutti* has that great Cronenbergian gas mask that comes down over the title character's face just before she goes under the knife at the beginning of the movie. I made notes in the Dikemaster's Daughter script to include a *Signora di Tutti* gas mask."

A Star Is Born (George Cukor). "I want it on the record that I have *A Star Is Born* on my shelf for James Mason, not Judy Garland. There's a difference. And now, having apparently dispelled any conjecture about my sexuality, it should be noted that I have nothing but adulation for Joan Crawford."

Storm Over Asia (V. I. Pudovkin). "A wild movie, great propaganda, with lots of plutocrats being blown away."

Strike (Sergei Eisenstein). "I sort of got into Eisenstein backwards, starting with the *Ivan the Terrible Part III* fragments and working my way back. But now, having watched *Strike*, I have to admit that he was great from start to finish."

Svengali (Archie Mayo). "A super seminal influence on me."

Sweet Smell of Success (Alexander Mackendrick). "Absolutely fantastic, and my favourite dialogue in movies ever."

Terror in a Texas Town (Joseph H. Lewis). "When my brother died, my uber-zaftig Aunt Lil came into the living room to tell me, and she put me on her lap and cried and told me that my brother had gone to heaven and wasn't coming back. And I noticed that on television, a big fat African American woman, like Hattie McDaniel or someone, was sitting and crying with this little African American boy on her lap. So there was this weird negative image thing happening.

"Anyway, that was a fine myth until thirty years later when I decided to find out at the archives what movie it was. The T.V. listings for the time said it was *Terror in a Texas Town*. I would tell people this and they would say 'You mean that all-midget movie?' But this was a sacred myth for me, so finally I ordered it off the Internet, and when it came two days later I fast-forwarded through the whole movie to find this scene. It wasn't anywhere to be found, and there wasn't even any big fat black woman in it. So here. You take it."

They Won't Believe Me (Irving Pichel). "A Robert Young picture that's the ultimate cowardly man noir, and there are an awful lot of those."

Three Songs About Lenin (Dziga Vertov). "I'll watch anything by Dziga Vertov. That guy can really shoot, as can his brother, Boris Kaufman."

Throne of Blood (Akira Kurosawa). "Worth owning if only for the arrow scene at the end. And, let's face it, Toshiro Mifune's always good."

Trouble in Paradise (Ernst Lubitsch). "The other great Lubitsch triangle movie. Everyone loves it, but I consider it and *Design for Living* interchangeably great."

Tunes A Plenty (Greg Hanec). "This is a local film, and it's really got something. I'm not sure of what it's got, and I don't know if Greg knows what it's got, but it's got something. Just the way [Hanec] almost made *Stranger Than Paradise* with his other feature *Downtime*, he almost made *Spinal Tap* with this one, but without realizing it."

The Unknown (Tod Browning). "*Dracula* is great, but it must have been some sort of assignment, because the usual starting point for a Tod Browning picture involves, at the very least, a guy in drag and a cigar-chomping midget wearing a diaper."

Vampyr (Carl Dreyer). "Might have more textures of ambient degradation on the soundtrack than any other movie."

A Walk in the Sun (Lewis Milestone). "I have that there to remind me that there's a bit of Ian Handford in all of us. It's an all-male movie about men marching all day in the sun. Richard Conte's in it and lots of other great guys, all talking to the rhythm of marching. It's pretty great."

White Zombie (Victor Halperin). "One of my favourites. I think it's pretty obvious that Coppola was paying tribute to it in *Dracula* when he had Gary Oldman's eyes appear in the sky."

The World of Henry Orient (George Roy Hill). "It has a wonderful sequence of two fourteen-year-old girls dressed in plaid skirts running all over town jumping over anything phallic, like fire hydrants or bald men. The camera takes every point of view possible, and it's shot in a really well-crafted early sixties way that's kind of nice."

Zabava (Greg Klymkiw). "Greg directed this, and it starts off as a very nice, charming portrait of the Drones, and there's even a character that's recognizable as me. But by the end I'm hoping it's not me, because they all start talking about gang-bangs and 'pulling train' and things like that. It's a very nice movie at the beginning, but doesn't really have much of a follow-through for me."

Zoo in Budapest (Rowland V. Lee). "A very charming movie that seems Lubitschian to me, and it stars that odd proto-Reagan Gene Raymond guy."

Final Note: "At the tail end of almost all my tapes are snippets of Winnipeg Jets games because I knew from a certain point that their days were numbered."

"I may be straying into a minutiae that even *I'm* not interested in at the moment"

Guy Maddin/2000

Extract transcribed from the audio commentary track of *Tales of the Gimli Hospital*, published by Kino Video, October 17, 2000. Reprinted by permission of the publisher.

I may be straying into a minutiae that even *I'm* not interested in at the moment. Maybe I should talk more about what even made me make the movie in the first place. I guess whenever I heard about my ancestors, they always had impossible to remember names, Alpha Agelsdotter, Snowleg Sniggboggesen, etc., and they always seemed to be going through such terrible hardships. This first batch of Icelandic immigrants had gone through a grasshopper pestilence, volcanic eruptions, drought for a few years, and a number of diseases back in Iceland before they came to North America, picked up smallpox in one of the quarantines in Kingston, Ontario, and then brought smallpox to the New Iceland region of Manitoba and wiped out all the Indians who'd never encountered North Americans before. It was kind of their gift to the First Nations people. A common practice throughout North America, but one the Icelanders were particularly good at.

I found their stories, told with a singularly humorless aspect that most Icelandic stories seem to have on the surface, to be incredibly funny. Maybe I was getting the joke without realizing it and felt good about it. But whatever it was, the atmospheres of these little family anecdotes—which eventually congealed into the book *Gimli Saga*, because many families told these stories and eventually wrote them down in the book—but just sitting around the family and not particularly listening to these dead serious Icelandic stories, just presented such dark and tragic tones, and gave to me the same kind of delight the super empurpled dialogue of Greek tragedies gives to me. I just love *Medea* and how far it's willing to go, and while I don't go that far with the Icelanders here—because after all I am a Canadian and an Icelandic Canadian on top of that, the only thing we're willing to far at is drinking—so just this atmosphere, I had this atmosphere in my head, kind of like someone whacking a tuning fork on a table, it just left me with this pitch that I knew was a tone that didn't exist in any other movie. Whether the movie would be good or bad, it would have its own tone at least. And that emboldened me to make the picture. I knew I could create a picture that had its own tone.

I think my biggest complaint about movies now, just in the year 2000, is that for the longest time they've all had the same rhythm, the same sort of punch line cadence, just the same flavor, a little bit off the rack, and I was pleased—this isn't boasting, it's, believe me, spoken with most extreme diffidence because I'm very sheepish about looking at my own stuff—but I felt I had a tone, and that was reason enough to make this thing.

"Well, maybe now's the moment"

Guy Maddin and George Toles/2000

Extract transcribed from the audio commentary track of *Careful*, published by Kino Video, October 17, 2000. Reprinted by permission of Zeitgeist Video.

George Toles: Well, maybe now's the moment to talk about the color for this world, and then maybe I'll say something about trying to find dialogue to match the color.

Guy Maddin: Sure. Originally when this script was finished, I always pictured this movie in black and white, just like the Riefensthal mountain pictures. But I was pretty much told by my producer and distributor that it had to be in color, that it didn't matter how good the movie was, the Japanese are buying up anything in color. It seemed like the Japanese were just buying film stock—and running it in theaters unprocessed, even—to hear these people. But I was initially depressed by that. But watching this almost anonymous little picture, Paul Whiteman's *The King of Jazz*, just the primitive two strip Technicolor gave me the courage to proceed. And I thought by limiting the palette to pretty much just two colors at a time—even sometimes two strip Technicolor can produce a mysterious third color—and then cautiously retreating into one color at a time, such as the opening sequence, this sort of sepia tobacco color, that I could approximate something that was antique, but something that felt refreshingly different and therefore modern. So it was simple enough. It has an all-Caucasian cast, so the faces would be kind of orange, and orange is a great color complement to a host of other colors. So it was just a matter of picking another color. In this scene it's blue and orange, other scenes green and orange, and purple and orange, whatever.

George Toles: Now the soundtrack has obviously that crackle and hiss—

Guy Maddin: Um hmmm.

George Toles: —sizzling along throughout. But then you've got your sound almost entirely on one plane, which is a little bit forward of the film, and, on this, highly selected sound effects. How did you see that going with the color?

Guy Maddin: Yeah, my taste in sound has kind of evolved separately. I think a lot of people would assume that I would try to create the most crackly degenerated sound possible for the movies, but I wanted to make sure that the words were as clear as the mountain air, and audible, and I know that the acoustics at high altitudes are rather strange anyway so I was happy if the words were completely clear, and I wanted them to have that old theatrical, part-talkie enunciation—clarity—and so it's true they do end up floating somewhere a few feet in front of the lips of the actors sometimes, and they definitely have a different sound perspective than the sound effects and than the ambiance and so they're not all married up. It's like plywood that's been pried apart. And then it just seems to become the way I work with sound now. I don't know why. It's just evolved, like everything else that has happened while I've learned to make movies.

George Toles: One major source for the dialogue style in *Careful* was Herman Melville's incest novel *Pierre*.

Guy Maddin: Yeah, a beautiful novel.

George Toles: Written a year after *Moby Dick*. And what I . . . obviously a movie that looked like this could not have conventional *Masterpiece Theater* period dialogue, and I wanted something which had its own kind of strange coloration to it. What Melville's dialogue has in addition to having parody . . . on one level he is sending up conventions of domestic fiction, but at the same time there is an authentic hysteria in the book that the parody and the sentiment never effaces, and to get some of that mixed in with the other stuff was at least an ongoing hope in the writing, so you would have, yes, laughter and mischief, but never just that.

Guy Maddin: Yeah, I think you could have a very worthwhile film career just aspiring to repeat Melville's unique recipe. You have plenty of room for emotion. Hysteria is always welcome at my door. My filmmaking door, anyway.

George Toles: This scene, by the way, owes something to Harold Lloyd's *Kid Brother*.

Guy Maddin: That's right.

George Toles: That great scene where Harold Lloyd climbs up in a tree higher and higher to see his girl leaving in the distance and waving to her again and again.

Guy Maddin: It's beautiful. I remember you telling me about this long before I saw it and I was determined to do it, but actually it was too much trouble bringing a tree into this studio, so . . .

George Toles: Also in that previous scene just to revive eavesdropping which I've always loved in life and in theater. But it always seems inexpressibly absurd on stage when people are eavesdropping in bushes, but to be able to eavesdrop in the mountains—

Guy Maddin: Where the mountain acoustics are very peculiar. Where you can hear someone's thoughts across a chasm. And around lakes, as well. Down at Gimli where I grew up it was *amazing* how you could hear two people *kissing* about a mile away across the bay on Willow Island. I always liked those acoustics, and having the sounds so clear and yet so scratchy at the same time gave me a perfect chance to play with those acoustics.

Tales of Guy Maddin

Mike White/2002

From *Cashiers du Cinemart*, issue No. 13, interview conducted in 2002. Reprinted by permission of the author.

Guy Maddin lives in the twenty-first century, near the windswept Icelandic shores of Manitoba's Lake Winnipeg. Maddin's films, however, live in the first few decades of the twentieth century, in a mountainous land outside of Prussia.

Maddin's films hark back to the primordial days of cinema. He shot his first feature, *Tales from the Gimli Hospital*, primarily as a silent film. Described by Maddin as "a tone poem in tribute to ambient crackle," *Gimli* is a beautiful tale of rivalry and pestilence.

Maddin's most accomplished works recall fleeting movie moments. Though made in 1990, *Archangel*, Maddin's second feature, falls neatly into place with films made circa 1929 during the trepidatious transition between silent films and "talkies." Like Alfred Hitchcock's *Blackmail*, Maddin's *Archangel* employs its sound subjectively. Characters' voices hover before their lips, aiding in the creation of a world of unreality, perfectly suited to a story populated with amnesiacs.

Archangel tells the stories of Boles (Kyle McCulloch) and Danchak (Sarah Neville), war-torn lovers in the Hun-infested titular town. The characters become increasingly obsessed and forgetful in this moody movie chock full of ironic, dark humor. The inhabitants of *Archangel* have a tenuous grasp on their sanity; likewise, the film teeters between silence and sound, as if the soundtrack might flutter away.

Maddin's subsequent film straddles the crevasse between the monochromatic and harshly hued realm of color cinema. Peppered with tinted black and white stock, Maddin shot the majority of *Careful* in archaic two-strip Technicolor—a process notably used in Chester M. Franklin's 1922 work, *The Toll of the Sea*. Painted with a limited palette,

Careful can be at once muted and garish. Sweaty, anxious faces shot through lenses smeared with petroleum jelly bare red hues that flutter about their faces.

In the mountain village that is the setting for *Careful*, the constant peril of burial under an avalanche makes residents wary to speak above a whisper. In an attempt to deter obstreperous livestock, the villagers' animals have their vocal cords slit. Now, if only those noisy geese would go away! Living under this burden of silence, the local folk have odd aspirations. Grigorss (Maddin regular McCulloch), the hero of *Careful*, wants nothing more than to successfully complete "butler school" and serve under the village patriarch, Count Knotkers (Paul Cox). Meanwhile, his brother Johann (Brent Neale) flunks out and, just when it looks like he might be destined to share space in the attic with his shut-in brother Franz (Vince Rimmer), the love of his mother (Gosia Dobrowolska) "saves" Johann from Franz's haunted fate.

Despite its incest, self-mutilation, and Melvillean dialogue, *Careful* ranks as Maddin's most accessible work that showcases his anachronistic style. Years after *Careful*, Maddin directed *Twilight of the Ice Nymphs*, a film that strayed from his venerable cinema. Shot in 35mm with a cast of familiar faces, *Ice Nymphs* shares Maddin's twisted humor but moves at a sluggish pace, as if bloated by lavish craft services. Despite Maddin's tangible unease about the project (witnessed in Noam Gonick's behind-the-scenes documentary, *Waiting for Twilight*), *Ice Nymphs* should count among Maddin's successes.

Beautifully filmed in a lavish soap factory-cum-movie studio *Ice Nymphs* has a mood somewhere between a fairy tale and myth. Nigel Whitmey stars as Peter, an ex-con returning to his home—an ostrich farm run by his sister, Amelia (Shelly Duvall), and the crazed handyman, Cain Ball (Frank Gorshin). Along the way, he falls for the evanescent Juliana (Pascale Bussières). Peter longs for Juliana while bedding down with the sylvan Zephyr (Alice Krige). If *Twilight of the Ice Nymphs* lacks the outright experimental use of stock or sound, it shares several motifs with Maddin's other work. More than the eccentric dialogue, lush cinematography, and infirmed characters, *Ice Nymphs* feels as though it comes from another era.

Twilight of the Ice Nymphs came about five years after *Careful*. In the meantime, Maddin shot several shorts and worked on an unrealized project, *The Dikemaster's Daughter*. The aborted film, coupled with a shoot Maddin considered too "big budget," soured the director for a while. It wouldn't be until the end of the twentieth century that Maddin would find his filmic footing again.

Maddin was one of several Canadian filmmakers invited to participate in the twenty-fifth anniversary of the Toronto International Film Festival by creating a "prelude" piece to celebrate the festival and, moreover, cinema itself. In Maddin's case, it wasn't so much "film" that he reveled in but "kino." With *Heart of the World*, Maddin rejects all that he found distasteful about his larger budget work. Here, the plucky director returned to cinematic basics—shooting on Super 8mm Tri-X stock. The film is without spoken dialogue, relying on a handful of title cards, a driving score, and fantastic editing. Maddin found inspiration for his short in the fervent era of early Russian cinema. His five-minute piece would make Eisenstein and Kuleshov proud, with its intense editing and daring cinematography. *Heart of the World* reintroduced Maddin to the delight of filmmaking, and stood out as the most loving display of cinema in decades.

Judging by Maddin's latest feature-length work, *Dracula: Pages from a Virgin's Diary*, the director is back on track and once again playing in the realm of silent, black and white cinema. With its manic editing style and ballet sequences, Dracula resembles Maddin's *Tales from the Gimli Hospital* in terms of its technology, but displays a maturity far removed from the director's initial cinematic efforts.

Cashiers du Cinemart: Your love of film—at least from the "primitive days" of filmmaking—is obvious. How much have you studied the early days of cinema?
Guy Maddin: My fellow Drones and I found an orphaned 16mm projector—an old Pageant swaddled in newspaper and smelling as if it had soiled itself with burnt mildew or bulb dust. There were cans of film on the floor beside the little unloved one. Among these was Erich Von Stroheim's *Foolish Wives*. We watched this some thousand times at least, until we screamed out in agonized ennui at the over-memorized routines of Maude George, Cesare Gravina, Dale Fuller, and even "retarded, deaf, and dumb" Malvina Polo as they retraced their steps ad infinitum like so many ants in a silent movie ant farm.

Long after any flavor had been sucked out of this movie, the inscrutable chirographies of these long-dead actors entrenched themselves in our brains as lucid language of imperatives. Deeply inscribed behind our sleepy pans was Stroheim's occult Constitution—his Moral Code! It was with his erectile gait we soon strode about the apartment, our faces rippling with Prussian sneers. Constantly pressing monocles to our eyes, we inspected each other's habiliments, cuirasses, and plumages in an endless mutual pass and muster. Between sips and snoozes, we served deliriously as both master and adjutant in an army without ranks, without much wakefulness, without even the wherewithal to exit the apartment.

I managed a daring escape from the apartment with my life. I never really saw, or needed to see, any other movies before picking up a camera myself. I've since seen other titles, but never more than once.

CdC: How have you managed to see these prototypical films? I know that German Mountain Movies aren't the *du jour* of the local multiplex . . .

GM: I've never seen a "mountain picture" except the one I made myself. I hate research. I need my sleep. When Leni Riefenstahl sent me a fan letter, I didn't even know who she was. I wrote back because she sounded hot to trot, a bit of a floozy. I thought, if I'm ever going to get laid, maybe this'll be the one to do it. We arranged a meeting in her hometown, in one of those German meat taverns, where legendary Bavarian aphrodisiacs like ox breast and deer soup are served. Since I'd never been away from home before, I sent Drone Emu in my stead. One week later, he came back from Riefenstahl shell-shocked and mute. He took what happened to him to his grave.

CdC: What of other modes of cinema? What are other avenues that you have explored, or that you enjoy? Can you turn off your brain and let the latest Joel Schumacher film wash over you?

GM: I like almost anything from Bollywood. I'm afraid I can't abide Schumacher, but I do love Adam Sandler, especially *Little Nicky*.

CdC: You've said that you've had a story lined up to explain the minstrel character in *Gimli*. Can you share this?

GM: Spike Lee said it all, and many times over, with *Bamboozled*, but this middle-class white Icelander is proud to boast he said it a little earlier, albeit differently.

I use an obsolete movie vocabulary. I love this vocabulary, but that doesn't mean I want to live in the era from which it comes, the days before [Frederick] Banting and [Charles] Best [discovers of insulin] and other medical advances, the days of entrenched segregation and legislated sexism, no matter how great the music, film, and painting from the twenties. I felt it unfair to celebrate the vocabulary of this era without acknowledging other, more shameful movie conventions, the expletives of the language then in common parlance—for one, the blackface.

You'd have to be a complete fucking idiot not to find the use of blackface a heinous insensitivity. At the same time, however (and even Spike found this), the minstrel is an instant way into the attitudes of an era, attitudes that have donned different disguises in order to survive to this day. Anytime one can be made to feel the past so readily, so slap-bracingly, one is perversely exhilarated and excited, hopefully along with being angered or moved. The sight of a burnt-cork minstrel in modern times is strange and sobering, outrageous and funny in an immensely wrong way. It belonged in my movie. Since Buñuel had already sliced open a woman's eyeball, I had to settle for this second-best strategy for achieving all of the above-mentioned effects.

CdC: I experience a sense of malaise when watching *Twilight of the Ice Nymphs*. However, I can't determine if this stems wholly from the film, or if seeing your unhappiness with the project in *Waiting for Twilight* influenced me. What are your feelings about the film now, and what were the critical reactions to this project?

GM: There are things I'm very proud of in *Twilight of the Ice Nymphs*, but I was not happy with much of it (neither were most critics), and it's all my fault.

For a couple years, I blamed my producer for falling short of my hopes, since he's a fatuous and meddlesome moron—like having Ted Baxter of the *Mary Tyler Moore Show* produce your movie. I blamed my director of photography for keeping me away from the camera, for conspiring to shoot in 35mm just for the sake of his résumé, and for working too slowly. I blamed my miserable marriage for keeping me unfocused.

Ultimately, I must accept all blame for the malaise that made it to screen. I was indecisive about what my next movie should be like—whether I should continue in the same primitive vein as I had been, or perhaps make a movie to modernize somewhat. The people who were assigned to the project against my will—I couldn't even get my eighteen-year-old daughter on as a production assistant trainee—all hated my movies, if they'd seen them at all. They all pushed for modernization, something I should have resisted with all my soul.

I've always made movies that are filmic equivalents to the music from basement bands. I've always averred that it's a tragedy when a good basement band learns to play its instruments. I was surrounded by philistines who knew how to play the instruments. Lawrence Welk's

Orchestra knew how to play their instruments in much the same way. I should have had the strength to blow these people away. Then I would have made a break for it, shot the picture even more primitively than *Flaming Creatures*. Had I done this, I wouldn't have done such a grave disservice to the script written for me by George Toles. I'll never make that mistake again!

It took two years to repair my friendship with George after mangling his scenario, hurting his feelings, and self-delusionally including him among the blameworthy. Now, George and I are back writing together again and it feels brilliant! I'm very optimistic. But all interlopers beware: it's death to the philistines! Don't tell me you love my vision and then insert your own stuff up my ass. Just tell me you love my vision, please.

CdC: How does it feel to be considered a "national treasure of Canadian cinema"? Is there a real sense of Canada having a "national cinema?"

GM: I'd like to firmly establish the notion that I'm a national treasure. Perhaps I'd earn more than 15K a year, somehow. You don't really want me to talk about Canadian national cinema, do you?

CdC: Yes, please, go ahead!

GM: Okay, I'll try, but I run out of gas on this one every time. Any discussion of "our national cinema"—and keep in mind, we're not exactly a politically repressed and perfervid revolutionist band of outlaws fighting for any particular cause up here—always makes me feel like I'm filling out one of those big fat grant applications. Half of the films made here are diluted approximations of the American product, with weak little myth-making impulses where you guys have rope-thick nerve. Characters in Yank pictures are always "bigger than life," in good films and bad, in naturalistic films and in fantasies. Somehow, Canadian characters seem "smaller than life." We're even scared that naturalism would be implausible. Thank God that De Sica was born in Italy; as a Canadian he'd consider a bike theft farfetched. The other films made here are reactions against American trends, but somehow, by unknowingly garbing ourselves in American film conventions, as we do, we are as rubes standing before a carnival mirror, laughing and pointing at the ugly bumpkins reflecting back to us. We indict ourselves with much slobber flying. Humiliating.

CdC: It seems that only in the last few years has there been recognition of Canadian cinema. Without fail, the works of Atom Egoyan and

David Cronenberg are lauded in conversations involving your country's cinematic prowess. How does this make you feel?
GM: I'm proud to know David and Atom a little bit. They're gracious and hilarious. I get a little jealous of Atom sometimes because he's slightly younger than I am, or so he says.
CdC: I've been reading the book of Alejandro Jodorowsky's *El Topo*. Jodorowsky cited von Stroheim and Keaton as "filmmakers who make poetry." Meanwhile, you've stated that before making your first short film, *The Dead Father*, you had seen "only a handful of von Stroheim movies and some Keatons." At face value, I can't think of two more dissimilar filmmakers than yourself and Mr. Jodorowsky. What do you think of his work?
GM: I love Jodorowsky! And to further the coincidence, my French distributors say Jodorowsky came into their Paris office one day and bought all my movies on video. A huge thrill and honor. So did Yves St. Laurent. (In other brushes with celebrity, I sent my first movie to Irving Berlin, hoping to coax the 101-year-old out of retirement to score my next picture, but the old grouch kicked the bucket before—or even while—seeing the tape.)
CdC: Titles like *Sissy-Boy Slap-Party* and *The Cock Crew* sound as if some of your shorts might have some homoerotic overtones. True?
GM: No more than any [J. S.] Watson and [Melville] Webber gem. *The Cock Crew* is actually an adaptation of Herman Melville's *I and My Chimney*, with a little extra sperm from *Moby Dick* thrown in. I've tried for as much homo-mischief as Melville pulled off—no more, no less.
CdC: Do you have any desire to try to make *The Dikemaster's Daughter* in the future, or has that project's time passed?
GM: I shot a short called *Sea Beggars*, which takes my favorite scenes of that ill-starred feature. I've no use for that sad dalliance with all things Dutch any longer.
CdC: What have you been up to lately?
GM: All I've been doing the last nine weeks is editing the ballet film, *Dracula: Pages From a Virgin's Diary*. It's *Dracula* as a ballet. Don't worry, I don't think it's a very good idea either, but it paid me a good salary, and I got to work with nonstop music and fluid camera along the way, then cut it all up with little halting hiccup-cuts, jump-cuts, and good ol' fashioned bad continuity. It may not be scary as a gothic tale, but the finished product seems to have scared my producer and my broadcaster.

They hate the cutting style I've been using, and I'd like to say things are headed for a showdown, but since they have final cut approval, I might just have to Smithee the whole damn thing.

The arbiters of taste here in Winnipeg say it will revolutionize dance film. If so, that may be one revolution no one cares about.

CdC: What are you hoping to work on next?

GM: I want to remake famous lost films, but in an extremely short form. Almost every director from that generation born 1895–1910 has at least one film on his filmography that is lost forever. I want to reconstruct my own glosses on as many of them as possible. I'm also planning a hockey-hairdressing film noir called *Cowards Bend the Knee*.

CdC: A hockey-hairdressing film noir?

GM: It'll combine my favorite aspects of the Greek tragedy *Electra* with some stuff from the French penny-dreadful *The Hands of Orlac*. To give the story authentic human psychology, I've made it as autobiographical as possible, setting all of the action in my two childhood homes: The Winnipeg Arena and our family-run beauty salon. I know there's life in the old genre yet, the hockey-hairdressing noir.

"Now here we have..."

Guy Maddin and George Toles/2002

Transcribed from the audio commentary track of *Twilight of the Ice Nymphs*, published by Zeitgeist Video, March 26, 2002. Reprinted by permission of the publisher.

George Toles: Now here we have a—
Guy Maddin: Well it's a shot I've always wanted to do. Through an ostrich and down a fourteen-by-two-foot-long table, ending with Frank Gorshin hacking up some phlegm.
George Toles: Do you want to say how it is that the Icelandic sheep farm of our first draft of the script evolved into an ostrich world in which . . . well, let's say the practical demands of farming have blown away like so much pixie dust.
Guy Maddin: Well, it was awfully nice of you to crossdress as an Icelander for me as a screenwriter, but I've had enough of sheep. I'd read my Halldor Laxness, and I'd been wearing wool diapers as an infant. I've . . . so . . . and as I said earlier I'd been reading a lot of decadence and I just thought that these curly, phallic, stamen-like ostrich necks could adorn the margins of the story the way, I don't know, the way Aubrey Beardsley might squiggle something on the margins of a play . . .
George Toles: Did you initially wish with the decadence to efface completely—I mean did you want it to be remotely Nordic decadence or did you want to move the whole thing closer to the Mediterranean or to some impossible geography that we needn't trouble to identify?
Guy Maddin: Well, your script is so fiercely Nordic in many ways that no matter what I did, no matter how many tropical breezes I pumped into the studio, there's a peculiar hybrid of Mediterranean and Nordic—
George Toles: North and south.
Guy Maddin: —yeah, seemed to result in the studio. And Frank Gorshin, whom I love, projects really neither Greek nor Icelandic but . . . He's from Pittsburgh and you can hear it right there, and I love it.

George Toles: My father adored Frank Gorshin.

Guy Maddin: He was right to do so.

George Toles: He was one of the few people on *Sullivan* that consistently made my father laugh uproariously, and so I studied everything that Gorshin did . . . like a religious zealot trying to find the key to my father's effusions—and rather rare effusions—of hilarity, and I certainly couldn't approximate Gorshin's take on Burt Lancaster or Kirk Douglas, but what I did try to emulate was the rubber-faced chameleon-like demeanor of Gorshin whose face and . . . his gift for making his body rigid and then contorted and swinging about and a pivot . . . I mean I've been turning myself slowly into Frank Gorshin ever since.

Guy Maddin: Yeah, well for me my introduction to him was just Riddler. But it wasn't just an introduction, it was an epiphany. I spent the next three years drawing pictures of myself as a companion arch villain madman in my costume to match . . . A perfect sort of complement to his lime green Riddler's leotard was a white straight jacket with a violet colored bowler and I think I had exclamation marks all over the bowler or something.

George Toles: Jim Carrey went rubber face to rubber face with Gorshin playing the Riddler himself and it's, I'm afraid—

Guy Maddin: I'm sorry, he finished a distant, distant, distant second.

George Toles: —wasn't even on the playing field.

Guy Maddin: I think he finished a distant third behind John Astin, actually.

George Toles: But it suddenly occurs to me that the facial contortions of Gorshin are a kind of lofty precursor to Carrey's own genius mobility of countenance, and yet entering the master's domain was a mistake for Jim and he's lived to regret it.

Guy Maddin: Yeah, he took one step onto the trap door and I haven't really seen him do anything interesting since. You know, my biggest regret, coming out of this movie, is that I haven't really phoned, well, no, I just plain and simple haven't phoned Frank Gorshin since, and I love him. I hope he hears me somewhere on this dialog track.

. . .

George Toles: Is it time to address the, well, the matter of the split acting identity of Peter?

Guy Maddin: Well, certainly. Peter Glahn, the protagonist, is played by two people. It's almost a Buñuelian trick except that—

George Toles: —*That Obscure Object of Desire*.
Guy Maddin: —yeah, except this has I guess a different genesis. Nigel [Whitmey], here, performed the visual part of the performance, and Ross McMillan, a naked extra, who appears later on in the movie—
George Toles: Who's the only other actor visible in the film besides the six principals—
Guy Maddin: —yeah, and an infant that appears briefly—
George Toles: —who are legislated by executive fiat as to the size of our cast. But that's really an Alliance discussion.
Guy Maddin: So this naked extra who appears later actually supplies the vocal half of the performance and it's kind of an odd elevation from nude extra to male lead voice. But I thought it worked really well. There was twenty days to shoot this picture and twenty days to replace all the voices—all the actors' voices are replaced—but in Ross's case he had to put his voice on the lips of another person. Everyone else did their own. I really liked the result, and it's almost a pointless exercise, one might think, but Ross knows you really well, and he really knows the language really well, and he really makes a host of each and every syllable. And it was a very bizarre exercise reconstructing the performance syllable by syllable over seven days.
George Toles: I think Nigel was, through no fault of his own, somewhat baffled by those turn-on-a-dime mood shifts and mind shifts that are, for good or ill, the basis of Peter's character.
Guy Maddin: My way of shooting this thing set him up for a big fall. It was horribly unfair. I shoot in a crappy old warehouse with no acoustics. I have fans blowing constantly just to keep feathers and spores and sparkles falling through the air. And so I can't even hear the actors' performances until months later when I'm editing, and so I have no real way of tracking how people are interacting vocally and that's never really been a big problem in the dialog-light movies. And all of a sudden it became a surprising . . . it was a problem, I felt. And it was beside the point that I felt it might be a problem. As a matter of fact I was constantly defending him from attackers at [Atlantis] Alliance, and my producer, and everyone else who seemed against him, and so Nigel and I struggled on and he came back for the ADR, the Automated Dialogue Replacement, but Ross came in and Alliance chose Ross's voice over Nigel's. And it's for the better. And I love this schizoid . . . the fact that I can hear Ross—a very familiar friend of mine—I can hear his voice coming out of a man, a man who hates me, the face of a man who hates me, but you know

Ross worked hard on it, and it was intoxicating . . . the ADR, for anyone who's ever been lucky enough to do it, is very strange. You put a headset on and you turn off all the lights and you look at the lips of a performer and listen, not just to the vocal performance of the new performer but you can hear his tongue poising like a seal ready to leap off a rock, just getting ready to slide off the molars and go into the next sibilant or next ululation or whatever. It's very private and personal and it's just you and this other performer and I know I shouldn't say it but . . . no I won't say it now, but I'll move on, but . . . It was very exhilarating and strange to see one performance just completely transformed by another person.

Purple Majesty: James Quandt Talks with Guy Maddin

James Quandt/2003

From *ArtForum*, June, 2003. Reprinted by permission of the author.

"Cult" and "coterie" cling like barnacles to the reputation of Winnipeg director Guy Maddin, a situation that may change with the release later this year of his new film, *The Saddest Music in the World*, starring Isabella Rossellini and scripted by novelist Kazuo Ishiguro. Maddin's work—five previous features, eighteen short films, and an installation piece commissioned by Toronto's Power Plant, where it debuted in March—is eccentric, even hermetic in its pursuit of the filmic primeval. "I work under the banner of primitivity," Maddin has proclaimed, and for the past two decades he has invoked the codes and forms of silent cinema and early talkies, of the film noirs and color-coded melodramas of the '40s and '50s, in his search for the cinematic sublime. Such Maddin classics as *Tales from the Gimli Hospital* (1988), *Archangel* (1990), and *Careful* (1992) aim to look exhumed, their tales of amnesia, incest, death, and transfiguration decked out in low-rent expressionism and dime-store surrealism. Whether shot in high-contrast black and white or aggressively artificial color (as in the exquisitely tinctured *Twilight of the Ice Nymphs* [1997]), the films rely on such superannuated devices as the iris, the lap dissolve, and superimposition, and on the cheap, dreamy blur provided by Vaseline, store-bought fog, and fake snow. The radical anachronism of this style is wedded to empurpled dialogue, crackly, muffled sound tracks, and a playhouse aesthetic in costume and set design, in which everything looks handmade, outsize, and illogical, keyed to the (soap) operatic passions and masochistic emotions of Maddin's bushy-browed characters. Non sequiturs and convolutions proliferate in both narrative and style, until one is left adrift in an obscure, obsessive spectacle conjured up from disinterred art forms and private compulsions. (Though Maddin is frequently compared to David Lynch and the Quay Brothers, his funny, puzzling, and often overstretched first films have surprising affinities with the early work of German director Werner Schroeter.)

Maddin insists that no matter how outlandish his films are, they are all in some way autobiographical. Born in 1956 in Winnipeg, he escaped the laconic, Lutheran culture of the prairie Icelanders by watching films in the local cinemas, on late-night television, and, later, at home after he discovered a trove of 16 mm silent films. This mock-Canuck *Cinema Paradiso* account of his childhood underscores the semi-apocryphal nature of Maddin's biography, whose formative events—his father's Willy Loman life and early death, his brother's suicide on the grave of his girlfriend, his own youth as a slacker surrounded by equally slothful male friends called "drones"—sometimes sound "heightened," to use a favorite Maddin locution. An artist who invents the traditions that inspire him, is influenced by films he hasn't seen, and makes versions of films that don't exist and whose stock-in-trade is imagined memories and fake nostalgia, Maddin often rebuffs analysis, leaving the true believer in the sorry role of chump or gull. So it is with *Cowards Bend the Knee* (2003), his first foray into installation art. Structured as a ten-chapter film projection viewed through sequential peepholes in a wall, it recounts the life of one Guy Maddin. The director claims, with disarming sincerity, that this lurid work about a botched abortion, a ferocious Electra complex, and transplanted murderous hands contains the "poetic truth" of his life story.

The following interview took place in Toronto as Maddin was beginning to edit the forty-four hours of footage he had shot for *The Saddest Music in the World* into a "penetrable" feature to be unveiled this fall on the festival circuit. Despite its stars (Rossellini, Mark McKinney, Maria de Medeiros), its "big" budget ($2.5 million), and its literary script, *Music* sounds, on paper, like another mad Maddin fantasia. The characters include Lady Port-Huntley, an amputee bar owner whose glass legs are filled with beer; an amnesiac nymphomaniac; and the motley bands (including a klezmer/flamenco/Afro orchestra) competing in a display of mass masochism to play—what else?—the saddest music in the world. Enjoying a brief moment of Maddin mania, with a director's spotlight at the Rotterdam Film Festival in January; the critically acclaimed installation at the Power Plant this spring; retrospectives of his films in Vienna,

Toronto, and (next fall) Washington, DC; and the release of his superb ballet film, *Dracula: Pages from a Virgin's Diary*, at New York's Film Forum last month, the director nevertheless maintains his persona of immoderate mildness. Self-deprecating, boyishly nervous, Maddin punctuated his thoughts on cowardice, artistic influence, and the revival of melodrama with the occasional fusty Fauntleroy phrase, enough to remind us that, *chez* Maddin, artifice is all.

James Quandt: Isabella Rossellini says that your films remind her of her father's, which is surprising since Roberto Rossellini was the father of Italian neorealism. But his films, though it's rarely remarked on, are full of artifice and melodrama—making them all the more moving. You've often said that "ultrarealism"—you cite Harmony Korine as an example—is a kind of falsity, or contrivance, and that such modes as fairy tales are often more emotionally resonant. What are your notions of melodrama and realism and how each gets at truth?
Guy Maddin: It's peculiar that I'm a big fan of fairy tales and melodrama, yet love the neorealists too. Melodrama, neorealism, and, of course, surrealism all get at something true by heightening, the way a dream can heighten the truth by exaggerating it into another form altogether, and making it some sort of immediate fear or terror or desire. The bedtime stories told to us as children can never be completely fathomed, but they can be felt—much the way sophisticated art for adults operates, so I make virtually no distinction.
JQ: You reject the designation of "camp" for your films and prefer "melodrama." Both terms are slippery because they are so promiscuously used, like "noir." Do you find them derogatory?
GM: "Melodrama," definitely. "Camp" feels like it's derogatory, but at least it's fun. Somehow it implies shallowness. People have often assigned the terms "camp" or "postmodern" to my films. It's a point of pride to elude classification, so I'm happy to occupy all those territories.
JQ: Directors like Todd Haynes and Pedro Almodóvar have moved away from campy, derisively ironic melodrama toward a form that searches for authentic emotion, even sincerity. You have always wanted your films, quite desperately, to have an emotional effect, something other than mannerism or mockery. In fact, you've talked about wanting to make a film that is emotionally flaying, or "filleting." Traditionally, your kind of irony would be seen as a force opposite or inimical to sincerity.

GM: People talk about irony and melodrama as if they're mutually exclusive, but I'm not so sure they are. When melodrama isn't working, I crave irony. If the sweetness isn't working, I need something savory, something very salty or something horrible, caustic to undermine it. The ironic temperament is tattooed onto all of our sensibilities. People laugh at Sirk movies but get sucked into them if they have any heart at all. No matter how delighted you are by the look, the excess, the sheer madness of a film like *Imitation of Life*, how could you not be absolutely wiped out by the final scene? The beautiful thing about Sirk is what he calls his "false-bottom endings." Universal Studios demanded a happy ending, but he's an old Euripidean. He sets them up so if you consider what will happen to the characters a few days after "The End," you realize they're all doomed. I can't believe that I used to feel superior to his films. The first few times I saw *Written on the Wind*, I was delighted but never emotionally affected. And then I had a sneak attack by Robert Stack. I could just feel the dread he had in being Kyle Hadley for an entire lifetime. I was destroyed by the movie. You never know when a wrecking ball will come swinging out of the Technicolor rosebushes in one of these melodramas.

JQ: You recently exhorted audiences to see as much as they can of the cinemas of Joan Crawford and Carl Theodor Dreyer. Of course, you're trying to be provocative, but do you, in all seriousness, aspire to the gravity and grandeur of Dreyer's art? As in his *Ordet*, there are a lot of resurrections from the dead in your cinema.

GM: I love *Ordet* and *Day of Wrath* and *Vampyr*. Maybe I have the wrong take on the first two, but I find them funny. I grew up in the Lutheran "fishbelt" of Winnipeg, and I recognize my Lutheran comedies. Just watching those old men shuffling around in *Ordet* and that son who thinks he's Jesus and the pure melodrama of the plot in *Day of Wrath*—the son stealing his father's bride away, and people denouncing witches—that stuff is right up there with Joan Crawford. She gets to suffer for six decades, there's a kind of anguish there, and Joan kept rising from the dead. I'll take your word for the resurrections in my films.

JQ: There are lots.

GM: If there are, they would be a quick shorthand for the desire to see someone again who has been removed from me, or from a character, through death or rejection. It works in *Hamlet* . . . and in Mexican soap operas. It works in—

JQ: *Twilight of the Ice Nymphs*!
GM: Well, nothing works in *Ice Nymphs*. But it certainly works in Dreyer's plutonium-weighted dramas. I love the rhythms of *Ordet*—they're hilarious, just the nerve it took for Dreyer to pace the movie so methodically. Watching an old man shuffle across the room to open a door just to find another door, it's really *Three's Company* slowed down.
JQ: He made comedies, actually, early in his career. He's like Ozu—this sense of him as an austere master is just partly right.
GM: I once watched a Buster Keaton movie shown at eighteen frames per second [silent speed], and the gags took forever to unfold, like *Ordet*. Maybe if we watched them at nine frames per second, they'd be funny again.
JQ: Art has been an important reference and inspiration for your work—Caspar David Friedrich especially. In 1995 you made *The Eye Like a Strange Balloon Mounts Towards Infinity*, a lovely short film based on a painting by Odilon Redon. And now you're in a major museum yourself. What was the genesis of *Cowards Bend the Knee*, a major new development in your career?
GM: It's been the most fun I've had. Philip Monk, the curator at the Power Plant, approached me about a year and a half ago with the idea, and I told him that I hadn't even seen enough installations to dare one myself. I likened it to a guy who's never read a novel sitting down to write one. He suggested I construct a set. Once in my childhood, I spent a lot of time spying on people, and I thought now I'd let people spy in on me through a series of little films viewed through peepholes. I try to make all of my work psychologically or poetically plausible, autobiographical in some way. I condensed a melodramatic plot down to five minutes in *Heart of the World* [2000], so thought maybe this sprawling autobiographical script could be condensed to a series of short films. I went on a shooting spree, and the megalomaniac in me went for something closer to feature length. I really regret it. It's next to impossible to view the whole installation. You'd have to be ludicrously devoted, with stalker-like devotion, to get through all ten chapters.
JQ: Curators and critics anguish over how to present installation work that is durational or narrative so that viewers actually attend to it. Ironically, *Cowards* is your most linear and structured story, so, perversely, it has to be seen sequentially. In Rotterdam, somebody was always at holes one or three or eight, and if I didn't elbow Dutch people aside,

I couldn't see it in order. It's a very provocative and evocative title, as "bending the knee" has associations with supplication, contrition, praying, begging, even blowjobs.

GM: I wanted them to make the holes large, cock-size, so they would at least be eye friendly.

JQ: Somewhere between an iris shot and a glory hole. The title and the way the installation forces one to crouch a little to see into the peepholes implicates the audience as cowards. You're a coward, I'm a coward . . . but cowardice is a tricky idea.

GM: It just feels like the male state of mind somehow. In the battles of the heart, men are cowards. In the battle of the sexes, women seem to have the bigger army and the chemical weapons, and the only way a man can swim upstream, almost like a lowly little sperm trying to get at the egg—maybe I'm getting into *Cremaster* territory here!—men will always take the slipperiest way. "Be a man" means John Wayne, but the men I know are more like Daffy Duck or George Costanza. It feels cathartic to just say, "I'm a coward" and to let you peep at me. It's an illicit, lurid, horrible, shameful confession, but I'll make it. It feels good to tell the truth, and people with really tough eyeballs can check it out. Much to my surprise, the thing came out in one piece, in five effortless days of shooting, just burning through film on a Super-8 camera, as a wildly elliptical but cohesive melodrama full of feverish hyperbole.

JQ: Do you feel any affinity with Joseph Cornell? I often think of your films as little nostalgia boxes, in which you put your private mementos, your trinkets and obsessions, dreams and desires all lovingly arranged.

GM: My first encounter with Cornell was his movie *Rose Hobart*, with the actress he fetishized. He took the much derided jungle adventure melodrama *East of Borneo*, which I love, and he tore out scenes like a boy tears out pictures of his favorite actress and puts them on his bedroom wall. There's a joyous sloppiness to the way he assembles it that is intoxicating. I like the way the records of the Brazilian sambas that are played with the images are so random. It reminded me of the way Buñuel DJ-ed his own screenings of *Un Chien Andalou* and roughly scored *L'Age d'or* with a bit of Beethoven here, some tangos there. That's the banner I wanted to work under. I knew I would never be a neat and tidy craftsman. It's a thrill to be a primitivist.

JQ: Your love of the primitive seems to have no bounds—you collect 78s, for instance—and words like "musty" and "fusty" and "curio" are not pejorative to you. Ken Jacobs said what seems to be a paradox:

"Advanced filmmaking leads to Muybridge." You resurrect a lot of tropes of early cinema.

GM: I'm excited by the word "trope." When I hear it, my pupils dilate. The most exciting movements in art in the last century and a half have been reactions against technical sophistication and have gone "backward" to find honesty and truth, the essences of things.

JQ: Amnesia and suppressed memory are constant themes in your films, from *Tales from the Gimli Hospital* to your latest, *The Saddest Music in the World*, which features a nymphomaniac with amnesia.

GM: That's right! The ultimate amnesiac would forget any obligation to fidelity, and that's the kind of amnesiac I've been at times.

JQ: "Forgetfulness was the very tenor of his existence," you say about the groom who has had amnesia since his wedding in *Archangel*. This doesn't seem to be merely a fond trope—there's that word again!—from old melodramas but a very central theme in your work. And amnesia has been turning up a lot lately in literature and in films—*Memento* and Kaurismaki's *Man Without a Past*. Is this pattern just coincidental, or does it say something about the times?

GM: Amnesia is a timeless storytelling device. Forgetfulness is a kind of anesthetic for the painful life we all live. We're forced constantly to think about the shameful things we've done, the painful things that have happened to us. We owe most of the feelings we have, as sensate beings, to shoddy memories. The sheer erratic nature of memory keeps life a Luna Park.

JQ: You "swear to the veracity of your recollections" of your life, yet you also say, "I'll confess that it's self-mythologizing when I'm filming." There's a tension between what seems intentionally or compulsively apocryphal, a kind of manufactured biography, versus real events, sincerity, depth of feeling. Many biographical facts have turned up transmogrified in your films—several deaths and suicides, a number of rending events in your life. You also call *Cowards Bend the Knee* autobiographical, which is hard to countenance. What is camouflage in your work, and what is actual or sincere?

GM: The audacious fact is that I haven't camouflaged much of anything. I just try and put things into forms that will be fun, and if anything, it feels just too good to blurt out the truth. Also, I haven't done that much in my life.

JQ: *Cowards* makes it seem like you have. As I watched it, it struck me that you're the only filmmaker who could make a connection, on every level—semiotic, poetic, etc.—between hockey and hairdressing, between a hockey net and a hair net. Those became two poles in your life as you were growing up—the world of women, signified by your Aunt Lil's hairdressing salon, and the world of men, the hockey rink and the locker room. Your films often seem to be, like Nick Ray's, about what it means to be a man. There's this strange simultaneity of the rarefied and poetic and delicate, and the guyish stuff—the jealousy, competitiveness, the blustering . . . and the violence. You say *Dracula* is about male jealousy and men's trouble dealing with female desire. *Cowards* ends almost condemning men for their fear of, inability to deal with, women, the world of women.

GM: I was condemning them too much, and I don't like making absolute statements, so I had to give the men a museum that celebrated them: the Museum of Men, or wax men. In my dreams about my dead father, he hadn't died but had really gone to live with another family. He couldn't admit that he didn't like us. I always forget his death and his funeral in my dreams, and so oneiric amnesia allows me to get that narcotic hit of visiting a beloved—my father, who turns out to be the biggest coward in the world. I realize he probably wasn't happy, he probably was dying to get away, yearning to escape.

JQ: *Dracula* is a project removed from you in twenty different ways. Yet it's 100 percent Maddin.

GM: Strangely enough, I had never read the Bram Stoker novel. I could barely get through it when I was hired to shoot it. As a child, I loved monster movies except vampire movies. I forced myself to watch the Tod Browning version but finally got into it through the Philip Glass–scored video rerelease. It's so dreamy and slow. It's slower than *Ordet*. With Glass's incessant, nutty arpeggios urging on something that refused to move, I found it kind of nightmarish. I thought that was the real ballet, and wondered, "Why am I doing this? The damn ballet version of *Dracula* has already been done." Then I realized that none of the other movies approached what made the novel so durable: Dracula, the being, is made possible by male jealousy. This is the way I see all my movies, all my stories, because I've gone through a horrible period of jealousy myself. I'm a jealousy war vet.

JQ: You recently said that "a really good score can save a movie's ass." *Tales from the Gimli Hospital* opens with the nurse saying to the children, "All right now, let's let your mother rest and listen to her music." *Heart of the World* in some ways functions as a music video for the Sviridov composition. There's the pastiche of two Mahler symphonies in *Dracula*, the mock Prokofiev in *Twilight of the Ice Nymphs*.

GM: I love it when narratives lose logical sense and take on a musical sense, when plots and pictures work like music. Not tonal or atonal, but they take me someplace as instantly as music can. I use music to get myself out of trouble, to get out of lazy planning or poorly shot or badly acted sequences. I'm always applying giant musical Band-Aids, hoping they'll stanch the flow of life that's ebbing out. My latest film is a giant orgy of self-pity, where every nation of the world sends delegations of musicians to vie for the title of the "saddest music in the world." In Kazuo Ishiguro's script, it's a political allegory. Like panhandlers who do some sort of limbo of pathos, the countries see who has the saddest song to sing and is therefore the neediest and most worthy of international charity. It's a story about how Third World countries can survive only by losing all their dignity, or keep their dignity by panhandling in a very clever way. I didn't want to make this a political satire, so we inserted a family melodrama in the foreground, in which various family members—all musicians—are also manipulating each other through self-pity, fake pathos.

JQ: To situate you or your films, critics always invoke three or four directors or movements—you know, "He's Cocteau and Welles and Eisenstein and Buñuel, and German Expressionism and Heimatfilm and Surrealism . . ."

GM: All I've been doing is gathering up things, carrion basically, from a big scrap heap of old dead masters; it sure seems like these people weren't all that well known when I first started watching them. I've used these "vocabulary units" from the canon-writers and directors—and used their language to tell my stories.

JQ: Citation and homage are part of your arsenal, but I can never put my finger on where your allusions come from. They often seem elusive, indirect, dredged up from some half-remembered dream. "Is this Dreyer's *Master of the House*?" "Which Murnau film is this from?"

GM: Often, the references are to movies I haven't even seen or that were never even made.

JQ: Manufactured memory, then. But some references are explicit, like *Night of the Hunter* in *Gimli*; some are insiderish, private, like the figure of Liliom in *Cowards*, which refers to your own Aunt Lil but surely also to the films of that name by Fritz Lang and Frank Borzage—which stars Rose Hobart! You say you haven't seen some of the films you allude to.

Your first film, *The Dead Father* [1986], sometimes reminds me of *Ordet*, but you hadn't seen any Dreyer films before you made it.

GM: No, I hadn't, but I read about the films. For *Eye Like a Strange Balloon*, I read about Abel Gance's *La Roue* and thought I'd never be able to see it, so I decided to make my own version. A lot of these are partially imagined or dreamt versions for me, too. Some of them I regurgitated ineptly, so maybe that's why they are hard to recognize. It pleases me that people can't put their finger on it; that's actually the most pleasurable compliment I can get.

JQ: In Lang's *Liliom*, the central character goes to heaven, where he's shown films, newsreels of his life, that reveal his transgressions, against women in particular. What newsreel of your life would they show you in heaven—would it be *Cowards Bend the Knee*?

GM: Pretty close, yeah. Although my life story would be something filmed in heaven by Andy Warhol, very long, sort of static. It would be called *Nap*.

"Hi, I'm Guy. I made this thing"

Guy Maddin/2003

> Extract transcribed from the audio commentary track of *Cowards Bend the Knee*, published by Zeitgeist Video, September 20, 2003. Reprinted by permission of the publisher.

Hi, I'm Guy. I made this thing, *Cowards Bend the Knee*. It was first commissioned as an installation at the Power Plant Art Gallery in Toronto, to be viewed through ten separate peepholes. I had so much respect for art galleries, I really feared being viewed as a wanker, so I think I had to introduce the project with that image there. The movie is hugely autobiographical. I chose to make an autobiography out of cowardice. I had so much respect for the art gallery that I just felt the only thing I knew anything about was my own life and so drawing on childhood memories of my life in a hockey rink and a beauty salon—my father was treasurer and general manager of the Canadian national hockey team and the Winnipeg Maroons, my mother and Aunt Lil were hairdressers in the family-owned business—I set out tell my own story set in these two great Winnipeg venues, the Winnipeg arena and Lil's beauty shop. I was always struck by early NHL photographs by how noir-looking they were . . . I guess it's because early sports photography was always done in those darkened arenas with the flashbulb and only the athletes in the immediate foreground were illuminated and everyone else seemed to disappear in thickest night, and so you got the idea that hockey was played more in a back alley, so it felt really lurid and frightening and no one wore helmets, except helmets of Brylcreem, and it seemed like players could disappear into the murk and come back out with the puck in some surprising place and almost mug another player and that a lot of frightening secrecy took place in the playmaking on the ice.

So this was just a chance to film hockey the way I always felt it must have looked in my prehistory. I decided to set the film in my prehistory—I was born in 1956—but just kind of vaguely set it in some kind of silent movie past just because that's where it felt like my life really began, where all the interesting melodramas, the myths that made me what I am, took place. So I just took all these frighteningly honest recollections, incidents, melodramatic historical facts from my own life and decided to project them onto a movie screen and let them reflect my own story back to me.

'Course I tried to cram so many things into the one-hour running time of this movie that I had to end up sort of stomping on them to make them all fit, and the reflective surface broke and a lot of the facts of my life end up being kind of reflected back to me in little distorting shards and so the facts come back to me in sort of the oddest places.

There is a character there, Darcy Fehr, playing Guy Maddin, but I strangely found that my own autobiography was popping up in most of the other characters as well, so that every one of these characters is me, in a weird way. Louis Negin is Dr. Fusi. [I] cast Louis Negin on the basis of a very strong audition film that I made of his hands and of his face and I was struck by how closely he resembled Cesare Gravina, an old Erich von Stroheim character actor, from, famously cut out of *Greed*, and in *Foolish Wives* and in Paul Leni's *The Man Who Laughs*. I love that Gravina and Louis Negin does seem like the reincarnation of him.

Early childhood memories of hanging out with a lot of nude men at the Winnipeg Arena. That's an actual Allan Cup championship ring won by my father's team in 1964. I like the fact that it doesn't really fit Guy. He's not worthy to wear it. Vic Cowie plays my father here. I needed someone sort of imposing to play my father, and I really wanted to—fetishize is kind of a lame word to use to describe what I wanted to do with hands in this movie. I noticed when I made a ballet version of *Dracula* a year earlier how expressive ballet dancers' hands were and how I ended up using their hands by the end of the shoot as much as their faces in expressive close-ups, and so I thought it might be fun to tell a story using hands as much as faces for close-ups. And by coincidence, organically enough I made a story in which hands feature as prominently as any other element.

"Squeeze of the Hand," a chapter in *Moby Dick*, my favorite chapter, I recommend all of you read it. This is a chance to shift over to my childhood home, the beauty salon. There was actually a rival beauty salon down the street called The Black Silhouette. I liked that title more, it's a little more noirish. My family's beauty salon was just called Lil's. My mom and my aunt kept really long hours, often up at 5:30 to perform the coiffure perfection on professionals before they would work and then after work—this is back in the day of the weekly coif, preserved every night in a hairnet at bedtime, so there were great regular customers all the time coming and going very early in the morning before I got up and leaving very late at night after I went to bed. It's very mysterious what went on in that beauty salon. And our house, designed by my mother, was built on top of and behind the beauty salon, and crisscrossed with a series of hair chutes and garbage chutes and laundry chutes and secret passages that afforded me many a great view of the goings on there, but I still was never able to figure it out. I guess my first erotic memory is just a row of swollen nylon-clad ankles lined up beneath the row of roaring hair dryers.

But we did have a back room used for storage where visitors would come and go, and there was always a fleet of taxicabs out front no matter what time of day, and my Dad's hockey playing friends would come over quite a bit to kibitz at the sinks, sometimes washing each other's hair, just for fun. But back here Amy Stewart playing Veronica, sort of the ultimate childhood brunette for comic book reading me, comes back for a little medical procedure. That's Tara Birtwhistle, who had a lead role in my *Dracula*. She was a last minute replacement for Alice Krige, whom I had used in *Twilight of the Ice Nymphs*. Alice is a dear friend of mine, but she got really sick at the last second and had to bail out, so I asked Tara if she'd consider coming in. She had to cancel a week's work at the Royal Winnipeg Ballet and come in and put on the same cheap wig I had Isabella Rossellini wear a couple of weeks later in *Saddest Music in the World*. Tara ended up being an interesting replacement, a completely different read on what Alice would have given, but an unbelievably athletic death scene, which really only a ballerina could have done, so it was a fantastic trade off and I've always felt that Tara's one of the greatest silent movie actors of all time.

Guy Maddin Discusses His Film Career

Terry Gross/2004

From Fresh Air, April 26, 2004. Interview provided by WHYY, Inc., producer of *Fresh Air with Terry Gross*. All rights reserved. Reprinted by permission.

Terry Gross: Guy Maddin, welcome back to *Fresh Air*. Your movie, *The Saddest Music in the World*, is adapted from a screenplay that was written by Kazuo Ishiguro, who wrote *Remains of the Day*.
Mr. Guy Maddin: Right.
Gross: But his screenplay was set in the '80s, and yours is set in the 1930s, during the Depression. I think you probably reworked a lot of the original concept. Talk about your idea for what the contest would be like to find the saddest music in the world.
Mr. Maddin: Well, the original premise of such a contest was Ish's, and he saw it as a political satire mostly about the way it's kind of sad that countries that are already suffering from the worst deprivations imaginable still have to pretend to be even worse off than they really are just to get some sort of international sympathy and charity, and that everyone is forced into this undignified limbo contest of exaggerating their misery just to get some charity. And for me the contest was a great backdrop for the way families and people in love manipulate each other in much the same way that countries do. And it was a great chance for me to have an orgy of self-pity, not just among nations but among family members. You know the way families really mess with each other's minds. And so I just found sort of a microcosm within Ish's political satire. And my obsessions are always with family melodrama anyway, so it was just a matter of putting that peanut butter on Ish's chocolate and coming up with something that pleased us both.
Gross: Let's talk about the music a little bit. There actually is a contest in the movie for the saddest music in the world, and representatives

from countries around the world show up to perform their music and vie for the cash reward. How did you go about finding performers from around the world to use in this contest? 'Cause you have real performers from different countries.

Mr. Maddin: Yeah. Most of them live in my hometown of Winnipeg.

Gross: Oh, really?

Mr. Maddin: Yeah.

Gross: Oh, I imagined you going around the world actually . . .

Mr. Maddin: That's right, on a big talent search.

Gross: . . . putting classifieds in newspapers around the world.

Mr. Maddin: That's right, going to Moscow and . . .

Gross: Exactly.

Mr. Maddin: . . . Stockholm.

Gross: Scotland.

Mr. Maddin: Yeah. We just put an ad in the paper and actually dealt through the Winnipeg Folk Arts Council and just arranged for a massive audition. We just told various, you know, El Salvadorian musicians, Portuguese fado musicians, Ukrainian bandurists to show up in costume with their instruments in full plumage and to play the two saddest songs they had in their repertoire. And we just invited them all to come up to this very tiny, crowded ballroom we rented in a hotel. They all had to ride up in an elevator, a very tiny elevator, so a big mariachi band would crowd out of the elevator while the Heather Belles, the all-female highland bagpipe troupe marched in. And it was great just to see the clash of colors, plaids, sombreros. It was really exciting, and I realized I kind of had half my musical problems solved right there at the audition. It was just a matter of picking my favorites from this and just getting a nice balance of colors and costumes and musics from these people.

Gross: How did you explain yourself to them?

Mr. Maddin: I kind of didn't, and that was kind of fun, just looking at the sheer puzzlement on their faces. And at one point in the auditions, I always encouraged the last group of musicians to stay on while the next one came on, and I would have them play at the same time and actually have them try to cross-pollinate or actually get down lower. I was thinking in terms of limbo, and I would tell the Klezmer clarinetist to get down below the Ukrainian clarinetist and try to get down lower, lower in pitch and lower in physicality and literally compete and cross swords with clarinets. And it was really kind of fun to watch these people literally competing for the tears of the judges and me and my producers musically. And it was all just sort of playing itself out the way it did in the movie.

Gross: Yeah, it's kind of like a battle of the bands except that they're all playing incredibly sad music.

Mr. Maddin: Yeah. And it really was just like, I guess, just watching the self-pitying aunts at a tea party just going at it and trying to top each other's stories of woe. I grew up in a family where people did that all the time. We're Icelandic, and all stories about our family are about tragedy and misery and, you know, plagues, blight, volcanic eruptions, etc.

Gross: Let me play the song I'd probably vote for if I were a judge in this contest for the saddest music in the world, and I'll just play an excerpt of this. This is a Mexican song, sung from the point of view of a mother who's singing to her dead baby. And as we hear the song, we'll also hear the announcers who are announcing this contest as it happens. And, of course, they're totally undercutting the tragedy with their absolutely clueless explanations of what's going on. So why don't we hear the scene?

[Soundbite of *The Saddest Music in the World*; soundbite of song.]

Gross: A short scene from Guy Maddin's new film, *The Saddest Music in the World*. Guy, tell me . . .

Mr. Maddin: I actually have a songwriting credit on that song, by the way.

Gross: Oh, did you co-write it?

Mr. Maddin: I cannot read music, but I wrote the lyrics. I can't speak Spanish, either, but I had the singer translate it and I just have to trust the translation.

Gross: What went through your mind as you were writing this?

Mr. Maddin: Well, I just . . .

Gross: I mean, how did you come up with this idea of the woman singing to her dead child?

Mr. Maddin: Well, there's nothing sadder than that. But, you know, in spite of the recent epidemic of dead child movies that have been put out there, I find it extremely difficult to even approach the magnitude, the enormity of such a feeling. So the only way to present it for me was to undercut it instantly somehow and just to let off the clear message that I wasn't going to try to reach anybody's heart at that point. It just had to be goofy.

Gross: I'm thinking back to the last interview that you did on *Fresh Air* after your ballet version of *Dracula*, and somehow we were talking about grief, which of course relates to this new movie, and you had mentioned that your brother killed himself when he was nineteen, that he shot himself on the grave of his girlfriend.

Mr. Maddin: Yeah. When I was seven or just turning seven, I remember thinking it was quite thoughtless of him to do that just a week before my birthday. Yeah, it was, you know, obviously a horrible tragedy, and it's the worst thing that can happen to parents. I was young enough that it was turned into a romance for me, the idea that he got to go to heaven with his girlfriend and that they were somehow being richly married there, and that our two families, the family of the dead girlfriend and my family sort of considered each other in-laws as a way of making sense of this gesture of their sadnesses. It just seemed very romantic to me, the idea of, you know, very *Wuthering Heights*, you know, the idea of just giving your whole life for the love of somebody. And maybe that's what made me more receptive to romantic literature later. I don't know. But it seems like the little garden from which I sprung was well watered with tears. This isn't self-pity talking; it's something I just observed as a way of growing up. Like I said, I couldn't have had a happier childhood. I loved it.

Gross: How did your brother's girlfriend die?

Mr. Maddin: In a car accident. You know, it was horrible, and it just ruined him, you know. He hung in there for about six months and then couldn't take it anymore.

Gross: There's a car accident in this movie, too.

Mr. Maddin: Yeah, there is, although the words "car accident" don't mean anything to me. They probably are horrible words to hear for the girl's family. But I don't know, all the trappings of that incident were kind of just—they were just as artificial as a TV show to me at that age. So I don't cringe or tweak when I hear those words.

Gross: It didn't scare you to death that your brother in one gesture was able to take his life away?

Mr. Maddin: Well, you know, I don't how to make sense of what I thought of it. I know I was given his bedroom the very night that he did it, and he had a way better bedroom than I did. So, you know, I was pretty happy about that. I shared it with my other brother, who couldn't stand the sound of my night breathing. You know, it sort of haunted him a lot. And I immediately thought I was him and, you know, immediately started thinking what it would be like to die or to kill myself and, you know, in those ways that every child daydreams about just wanting to go away when things don't go right, to remove yourself. But, you know, I never really seriously considered it. It was just kind of a play daydream that I like to replay all the time.

Gross: I'm thinking back to something else you said in that first interview that we did. You said that when people who were important to you died, you felt you didn't grieve at the time and that you even had to fake tears at their funeral. And I was thinking, you know, this just seems so connected to me, to this new movie, *The Saddest Music in the World*, because, you know, one of the characters just is incapable of grieving and he kind of walks through life as if it were like a bleak comedy. And another character goes through life, because her grief is so deep, she falls into amnesia. Her only way of surviving is just totally to forget.

Mr. Maddin: I guess you're very astute, Terry, because I think you have picked up on some kind of autobiographical trait that I've put in the movie, maybe without even thinking about it. I know when I was in my mid-teens, my father developed a very serious heart condition and I just lived in terror of him just dropping dead of a heart attack. And the words "heart attack" literally launched me—whenever I happened to hear them on TV or in a conversation—would launch me into a procedure of elaborate superstitions, you know, crossing my fingers, knocking on wood, backing out of a room left foot first, and all sorts of elaborate, strange, exhausting procedures. And I think when my father finally did have a heart attack and die, or when he did die of some heart-related thing, that a fuse went in me and I couldn't grieve. It was everything I had feared and worse because it really happened. And I just felt nothing. And I felt a bit ashamed of myself for not feeling anything, but I'm sure it's common that some people just can't feel anything. I guess it's just simply being in shock, although it didn't even feel like being in shock. I remember actually kind of enjoying all the company and sympathy I was getting around funeral time. It's pretty gloomy stuff we're talking about, but then I did grieve on the installment plan. For years, I was revisited by my father in regular dreams, just probably a pathological number of dreams. And so these characters, this woman who virtually is visited with amnesia when her child dies, is kind of a version of that, I guess. It's just a matter of her being faced with something that's unbearable and amnesia's the only way to go. Amnesia and nymphomania, as it turns out.

Gross: That's right, she's got that, too.

Mr. Maddin: Yeah, that's two Band-Aids on top of a trauma.

Gross: Let me quote two things about sadness that are said in the movie. One is, "What good is memory? Why make yourself sad?" And the other is, "Sadness is just happiness turned on its ass. It's all show biz."

Mr. Maddin: Yeah, I'm just trying to make sense of what sadness is. I know I don't like being sad very much, and the weirdest things make me sad. I don't know.

Gross: Like what?

Mr. Maddin: Sometimes a movie that's mediocre for some reason. I like a really bad movie or a really good movie. But a movie that just somehow—there's a certain combination of notes that mediocrity combines to form and that just about has me suicidal. For some reason, the second *Matrix* movie had me on suicide alert. I had to make some hotline phone calls after walking out of that theater. I don't know.

Gross: Why? Because mediocrity wastes your time or because there's something emotional in a mediocre film? Like, what is it?

Mr. Maddin: Yeah, well, I started daydreaming a bit about my brother, something I almost never do, and I know he was a bit of a science fiction enthusiast and kind of a technical freak. You know, he built a stereo with his bare hands when he was fifteen years old, and built a radio station and was arrested for broadcasting, you know, from a pirate station when he was a young teen. And so I just started thinking of—I was sort of daydreaming that I was watching this movie with him for some reason. This is something I've never done before. And then the movie was so overwhelmingly filled with effects that he would never have been able to comprehend at his young age. But then it was so incomprehensibly boring at the same time that I remember just sort of thinking that maybe my brother would decide that he should have lived all along just because these movies are so cool and so technically slick and the excitement of science would have made it worthwhile to keep on living. And then I realized I was losing him as the movie got worse and worse and that by the end of the movie, he was back in his grave and I was looking for one for myself. I don't know.

Gross: Oh, gosh. This is what happens when your mind wanders when a movie's really dull, I think.

Mr. Maddin: Yeah. I probably just should have gone to see, you know, *Charlie's Angels: Full Throttle* again.

Gross: Was that better?

Mr. Maddin: That was way better. I love that movie.

Gross: There are images of hockey in several of your films, and I know your father was the treasurer and manager of Canada's national hockey team.

Mr. Maddin: Right.

Gross: You described yourself in our first interview as spending most of your childhood in front of the television with your dog.

Mr. Maddin: Yeah.

Gross: Did you play hockey, too?

Mr. Maddin: No, I didn't, and believe me, that was the source of unbelievable shame. Growing up in Winnipeg, Canada; father featured frequently in the city's newspaper, you know, talking about Canada's national hockey team, and not being able to skate. I don't know. I just spent too much time in front of the TV. Even my dog was stupid, not even paper-trained or anything. We were both very underachieving organisms. And I finally couldn't stand the shame anymore, and I bought a pair of skates when I was about eighteen, and just went out after dark and taught myself how to skate and then just fell in love with it. Became obsessed with it; dropped out of the university and just spent all my time playing hockey with twelve-year-olds until I was good enough to join a team, and I still have that kind of learned-late skating style. I skate too straight up and down, and you know, people know I was a latecomer to the game. But believe me, every stride I take on the ice feels like I'm undoing the shame of my childhood, and I'm not quite done yet. I'm still playing; I'm forty-eight years old now, and I still play and I'm not kidding. Every stride I take feels like I'm repairing damage.

Gross: Too bad your dog didn't live long enough to undo his reputation.

Mr. Maddin: Yeah. No, my dog lived a pure life—underachieving to the end: didn't even get out of bed to die. Died on my feet while I was sleeping.

Gross: Well, Guy Maddin, thank you so much for talking with us.

Mr. Maddin: Oh, thanks so much, Terry.

The Reconfiguration of Film History: Guy Maddin

Jonathan Marlow/2004

From *Green Cine Daily*, April 28, 2004, and November 15, 2004, and early December, 2004. Reprinted by permission of the author.

Reviewing Guy Maddin's latest film, *The Saddest Music in the World*, for the current issue of the *Village Voice*, J. Hoberman succinctly nails what's most unique about one of the most enigmatic living filmmakers: "Like everything in Maddin's oeuvre . . . [it] is a contribution to the imaginary history of our times." Maddin's *Music* recently screened at SFIFF, prompting a long and leisurely conversation (by telephone) with filmmaker Jonathan Marlow about his work.

"A really strange recipe of feelings."

Marlow: When I was in Vancouver in October, I bought the diary *From the Atelier Tovar* and I was a little curious. We actually talked about this at Sundance briefly—what prompted you to get around to publishing them?
Maddin: A perverse caprice. I happened to have them on me in Toronto one day. I don't live in Toronto but I was staying there for a few months, this past summer to edit, and I go there every now and then.
Marlow: You edited *Saddest Music* there?
Maddin: Yes, *The Saddest Music in the World*. So I guess I was having coffee or something with a friend of mine during one of my business trips, and I had my diary and a friend of my friend joined us. It turned out to be Jason McBride of Coach House Books and he was talking about diaries for some reason—because I had them on me I guess— and he said, "Would you ever consider having your diaries published?"

And I thought, "Maybe someday, when I rewrite them." Because I just thought, "Maybe as a memoir," you know? Ah, but he said, "Would you mind if I took a look at them?" And I said, "No, here." I found myself giving my diaries to a total stranger. Maybe not a perverse caprice but a moronic caprice. Then he just sort of charmed me or persuaded me into publishing. He said, "Would you allow me to publish them?" And I said, "Eh, whatever."

Marlow: Is it only published in Canada or is there a distributor in the U.S.?

Maddin: I don't know how the distribution works anymore. So many things are available on the Internet anyway. When I was in New York recently, a bunch of people came up to me with copies to autograph, so they're getting a hold of them somehow. I've sold about a thousand copies so far. I don't know if that's good or bad or what.

Marlow: Was the jacket design yours or was it something that they came up with?

Maddin: I like the jacket design on that.

Marlow: It's beautiful, yes.

Maddin: Some guy named Darren Wershler-Henry. He's one of the employees at Coach House Books. He did a good job, I thought.

Marlow: It looks like something that would . . . Well, obviously there's one part that is from a film of yours, but the actual design seems to evoke . . .

Maddin: Yeah, they're very thoughtful people there, and I'd like to do something else someday and actually take some time to write it. You know, I was so harried when that diary was put together, which is just as well anyway because I would have been tempted to do so many revisions that it would have lost all "diary-ness." I still haven't read it, anyway. I haven't even read my diaries. I intended to read them many years from now, and I have this odd thing where I have a book out that I myself haven't even read.

Marlow: There are people out there like myself that know more about your past than you remember.

Maddin: Than I would at least know; I've probably forgotten many things I wrote. I definitely don't know what aspects of me you know because it was edited and the diaries are very long. Those are just a selection. From what I've been able to understand, it sounds like it's mostly . . . Half of my diaries are little fictional miniatures and I think those are

not selected, so it's mostly the diary-ish things that are in there. A lot of the self-loathing and the self-pity.
Marlow: Yes, that's what surprised me.
Maddin: Name-dropping, you know.
Marlow: The amount of self-loathing that permeates the book is somewhat overwhelming.
Maddin: When you're writing a diary, you don't really feel the need to balance anything, so it's not like I hate myself all the time. A diary isn't a perfect reflection of what you're up to. The days in which my life's really humming along and I'm busy and happy, I don't have time to write in my diary. It's those days with lengthy stretches of "down time" that you have all the time in the world to write in a diary. Those days that you don't really feel so good about how your life's unfurling. The shitty days tend to get the lion's share of the print, you know. There's some kind of weird natural selection that goes on, that weeds out the strong days and keeps the weak.
Marlow: That definitely puts things in perspective.
Maddin: Yeah, but having said that, I am a loathsome person.
Marlow: Your films tend to mirror the history of cinema. In fact, in Caelum Vatnsdal's book (*Kino Delirium*), you say that you're bent on rewriting Hollywood history. As such, the early films seem like this quasi-silent period, and then your first color film is almost a mirror of the two-strip Technicolor period. Now, with *Saddest Music*, you're almost in this period of the early-1930s musical. Except, mixed in with this chronology, you have *The Heart of the World*, *Dracula*, and *Cowards Bend the Knee*, which are almost even "earlier" than your earliest films because they are almost pure silent films.
Maddin: I've gotten off the straight-and-narrow path, shooting through the decades of the twentieth century. I'm sort of tackling all sorts of branching lines, loops, and blind alleys. I'm traveling a pretty ramified path up through the reconfiguration of film history. It's whatever capriciously seizes hold of my interest for a while. Each project has its own slightly different demands, although I'm sure they all look the same to a casual observer. They all look like old movies. They do have minor distinctions.
Marlow: I think they're pretty significant distinctions. Take *The Dead Father*, for instance. You mention it was influenced by *Sanatorium Under the Sign of the Hourglass*. I don't know if there is any special thing that

continues to re-create itself around your relationship with your father, but there's obviously this root that forms around all of your films. There is also some kind of core inspiration and, in this case, it was [Bruno] Schultz's writing. How did you come about putting *The Dead Father* together?

Maddin: I thought, from the very first, that it was always the subject of the first film I was going to do. In a way, my reasons for making a film and how I made it all sort of intersected at one point and that was with the dead father. I knew I would never be able to make a very sophisticated looking movie, like more young aspiring filmmakers try to make. They try to make an exact replica of their favorite movie or something like that, like those kids that reshot storyboard panel for panel *Raiders of the Lost Ark* starting at age ten and finishing at age seventeen or whatever. I knew that I just didn't have the technical expertise to make anything that would have any sort of continuity or sort of "Sean Penn style." I would never be an actor's director at that stage of my career anyway, probably never will be.

Having seen Luis Buñuel's early films enough times (*Un chien andalou* and *L'Age d'or*), I was very impressed with the effect Buñuel and Dali could get while being film novices . . . primitives, actually. I knew that was the route I had to take. The kind of accidents you have when you're a klutzy novice filmmaker lend themselves to surrealism. *L'Age d'or*, their second film, is more narrative than their first, or more recognizably narrative—it's a love story with some surreal trimmings. I knew that I could probably have a narrative that was as continuous as that and as discontinuous as that and maybe, I would hope, as effective as that. It isn't, because *L'Age d'or* is a great movie, and *The Dead Father* was sort of an interesting learning experience. I knew that I wanted to make something that wasn't just a piece of wank, so I wanted to make something autobiographical. I also had this burning desire to just put down on celluloid what Bruno Schultz managed to get on paper, these dreams that people have about return visits of dead loved ones that leave you with such a strong feeling afterwards. A really strange recipe of feelings. I just thought that I would try to put these autobiographical reveries down in some kind of artificial structure, some sort of narrative order, in the freewheeling style of Bruno Schultz's writing.

Marlow: Were you familiar at the time with Lynch's *The Grandmother*? Had you seen that at all?

Maddin: No, I hadn't, but *Eraserhead* really hit me hard. I was really impressed. It was a big influence. When I discovered that Lynch's first major short film was the same length as *The Dead Father* and was about his grandmother, it just really seemed like he'd felt the same need. He's exactly ten years older than I am, and I know he's felt the same need to go autobiographical all the time. As soon as I saw *Eraserhead*, I knew he, like I, had experienced unplanned pregnancy and taken all those feelings of delirium and disorientation that comes when all the terrain you're standing on is suddenly pulled up from under you. You find yourself standing in a completely new domestic situation. Especially in the middle of the night when you just can't believe what's really happened to you. On those trips to the bathroom where you go, "I'm in the bathroom in my wife's apartment, the one I share with her, and I have a child," you kind of dream these odd moments and realize where you really are in the world.

Marlow: Surrealism is a natural tendency out of that.

Maddin: Yes, it is. There are many different ways of getting at the truth. There's melodrama, there's surrealism, there's naturalism. When it's done well, surrealism is as good as anything at getting at those irrational moments, those certain fears. It's a unique species of feelings that David Lynch fits into *Eraserhead*. It always impressed me and emboldened me to just go after a story in a nonlinear way. I felt it was important to be true to the feelings I had and to get them up on the screen. Now, I failed. Nowhere do I see in *The Dead Father* the feelings that I get from my dreams. But it was an interesting experiment. I found some things worked better than I thought they would. Other things just never worked, even if I went back and reedited it. About halfway through shooting, I discovered a visual style that I would stay with for quite a while. So it was really valuable.

"A perfect dream of a movie."

Marlow: I don't want to dwell too long on your first film, but John Paizs was something of an inspiration as well? I'm quite a fan of *Crime Wave*, although I may be only one of a few dozen folks in this country that's actually seen it.

Maddin: I like that film a lot, too. John and I were friends. I introduced myself to him—much the way you introduced yourself to me—after seeing one of his films. He made a series of pretty great half-hour films; he must have made six or seven thirty-minute films. It's an unique length.

I think I'd seen his third one one day—he brought it to a class and screened it—and I came up to him afterwards and talked to him. We hit it off pretty well. You know, we never became best friends, but we came close enough that we hung out together for the next three years or so. It never even occurred to me that films of such accomplishment could be made by people my age, in my mid-twenties. When I met him, I think I was twenty-four and he was twenty-three. I don't know if you've seen his other films, but his half-hour films are already as accomplished as *Crime Wave*. His style's there. They were a real inspiration to me, and I knew right then that I wanted to make one someday. It took me a few years to get up off my ass and go at it myself.

Marlow: And you have a part in one of them, *The Internationals*?

Maddin: Yeah, I do. I'm a terrible actor, though. I actually didn't even realize I wanted to be an actor. John just casts friends in parts, he didn't bother [to cast things the usual way]. I don't think 'til *Crime Wave* did he even bother casting people he'd never met before. We all hung out and watched movies together at a friend's place. Almost every night of the week he made this movie, or he was in preproduction on it, and he cast all of my friends except me. I couldn't believe that I actually found myself saying, "Well, can't I have a part?" I honestly had never wanted to be an actor and can't imagine why anyone would want to be one, but I found myself saying this. I think it was just because I was the only one who wasn't [cast], and he said the only part he had left was a woman, a woman's part. I said, "I'll do it, I'll do it!" I can't believe it. I guess you're just never too far away from becoming a shameless actor. I did it, but holy smokes, I never got comfortable performing and that had nothing to do with the drag. I just can't get comfortable in front of a movie camera, especially with the slate and all those things that get said before "Action." Maybe if they just suddenly said "Action," I could do it.

Marlow: You seem relatively comfortable in *Waiting for Twilight*, but then you're just appearing as yourself, I guess.

Maddin: Yes, but I also knew that I would never watch it. I promised the director [Noam Gonick] I would never watch the movie, so he could feel free to cut it any way he wanted to and I could be free to do whatever I wanted.

Marlow: It seems to be a reasonable agreement.

Maddin: Yes.

Marlow: With your first feature, *Tales from the Gimli Hospital*, with that one effort, you became Winnipeg's most famous director. Is that too bold of me to say?

Maddin: Actually, it depends on what you mean by "famous." There's a number of Winnipeg filmmakers that up until very recently were more well known than I was locally. You know, they work on Movies of the Week all the time and they get a lot more regular work than I. One of them, Norma Bailey, is from Gimli, where I spend summers. This resort town, an hour's drive [from Winnipeg]. I wasn't even the most famous director from Gimli! And then Neil Young is from Winnipeg. He's made a Super-8 feature, *Greendale*. I think he would have to qualify as the most famous.
Marlow: Yeah, except that he didn't make it under his own name.
Maddin: No, that's true. It's "Shakey-something" [Bernard Shakey], and I guess he's not famous for filmmaking.
Marlow: No, not exactly.
Maddin: But he'd be the most famous filmmaker from Winnipeg.
Marlow: Yeah, now . . .
Maddin: Unless Monty Hall made a film, somewhere . . .
Marlow: Did he?
Maddin: I don't know.
Marlow: He might have. [He didn't]. It seems in *Gimli* that you were able to strike on another Maddin hallmark, one that doesn't appear in *The Dead Father*, exemplified in this case by the "Angels of Mercy." You have this knack for finding the most beautiful women to appear in your films. I don't know how it's possible, but they're always there. You have this thing for faces . . .
Maddin: Yes, and they have to be anachronistic faces. They have to seem somehow that they belong to another time or place. I was a little beyond my years already. I'd already adopted that forty-something habit of hanging out in cafes alone with a notebook. That sort of "foreign legion of the middle-aged men" who are just sort of always scouring and scouting the world's surface for faces. Male or female or whatever, and if you get a few with acting ability, it's sort of a bonus. They look good. Some of them. I filled up most of the cast after that movie with thirteen-year-old girls, actually. I have this theory that girls could look a lot older on film than they really do if they wear makeup. I noticed that during Halloween. It's from the six-year-olds that look like badly used thirty-year-olds. Because, what do you dress up as if you're a little girl on Halloween? A hooker. So I see a lot of the coal-eyed treatment. Paid a heavy price for it, though. Showbiz parents hanging around all the time, who don't really love their children but are doing something sick [to their kids]. Whatever it was that I was doing wrong, they were

doing far worse, so I retired a few of the thirteen-year-olds and replaced them with twenty-year-olds and things like that because it just wasn't worth the trouble. Parents that are willing to step on their children to get closer to the director. It was really strange. A really strange scene.

Marlow: This is your first collaboration with Kyle McCulloch. He appeared in the first three pictures.

Maddin: John Paizs discovered him somewhere. He was a good little Mormon boy at the age of eighteen when Paizs put him in a movie. Next thing you know, Kyle was smoking and drinking—things a good little Mormon boy should do. He disappeared for about a year and a half. He was a Neil Cassidy kind of guy in real life, despite being alone. Kind of a charismatic to the ladies, kind of a drifter, and he just hopped on a boxcar one day and disappeared. All sorts of rumors drifted back to Winnipeg. That he had died or that he had won the lottery—I remember those two were the two most common. And then finally he just came back to Winnipeg. He had neither died nor won the lottery. He'd just gone boxcar-hopping for a year and a half. He came back just in time, 'cause I'd had him in mind while I was writing this thing.

I didn't know many actors, I only knew the few that John Paizs had used. John decided he hated Kyle McCulloch by that point, and he didn't want to use him anymore. I was happy to use him. Kyle and I became very close filmmaking buddies. We hung out mostly while working on films together and then only occasionally during other things because he . . . I can't stand not having a roof over my head, and he doesn't mind just sleeping on a pile of cardboard. It's not so true now. He's married and he lives in a beautiful home in Los Angeles with his wife. He's got this job as a writer for *South Park*. But when he was younger, he was one of those guys that could just sort of go play pinball all afternoon and then fall asleep on the sidewalk. I always needed to be home for dinner at 5 PM even though there was no one home to make it for me. I had to be home or my imaginary parents would get mad at me or something. Even when I was an adult. He was sort of like the fox in *Pinocchio*. He wasn't into method acting or anything. He takes his acting seriously, but I could just tell him to do something. I could just show it to him, and he would imitate me perfectly and then improve on it. He's really funny; he'd do improv and stuff. He is "Mr. Expressionism," you know. He's where a person's inner landscape is reflected in the outer landscape, and he augments it with all sorts of great sort of miming. He sort of had that set of false modesty gestures that I use all the time down pat.

Marlow: It isn't likely that you'll ever work together again?

Maddin: I'd love to work with him. I don't know if it's likely, you know, 'cause he's busy on his writing job. A year and a half ago, I called him up to offer him a part in this movie *Cowards Bend the Knee*, playing me. I thought of him first. He's maybe seven years younger than I am. We're both about the same size, and he's always been sort of a reflection of me because he does a good impersonation. But he was busy working on *South Park*, and there were scheduling difficulties so I asked a new slimmer, younger me to come on and take my place.

Marlow: Then *Archangel* followed *Gimli*. It was given the National Society of Film Critics award for Best Experimental Film. Here you have this "part-talkie," a beast which really only existed between 1927 and 1930, but you had to make one and there it is. Intertitles, occasional dialogue, voiceover—everything all in one big picture. How was your experience on that film?

Maddin: I loved making that movie. I really thought right up until the day I had it finished that I'd made a masterpiece. I watched it for the first time during a process of the sound mix. It used to be called the interlock, where you'd put up all these magnetic soundtracks all at once really for the first time. Normally, when you're editing on a Steinbeck, you can only hear two tracks at once. I think I only had three or four tracks on the movie, but I finally heard them all at once. I really felt like I'd made a dream, a perfect dream of a movie.

It wasn't. I had no objectivity on it. I didn't even realize until I watched it with an audience and then . . . it was very crushing. I didn't have a test audience on the film in those days. I didn't trust them. I didn't realize that I'd made a film that was incomprehensible to everybody else. It wasn't so much "dreamlike" as "sleep-inducing." But I feel that the completely self-deluding experience I had when I first watched *Archangel* might be one of the best film viewing experiences ever. I was very proud of myself when I watched it with Greg Klymkiw, who was my producer at the time, and we were just so thrilled at how beautifully it turned out. We both fooled ourselves. We just drove around all night going, "Wow, that is so incredible." You know, we got our comeuppance.

Marlow: I think that it has a first in the history of cinema, though— the intestinal strangulation scene. I was quite surprised by that.

Maddin: I was proud of that. It felt like a first. If I stole it from anyone, it was definitely a subconscious plagiarism.

Marlow: It's played seriously, which I think helps considerably. It's a very strange sequence, though.
Maddin: [laughs] Thank you.
Marlow: I think this whole technique was pretty much fully formed by the time you get to *Careful*, where you're making your first color film. I watched it again last night, and I felt it to be a Freudian fever-dream. Until very recently, it was my favorite of your films.
Maddin: I feel Freud has been discredited. No one takes him seriously anymore. I thought it would be kind of fun to just embrace the good old days, when there was that great mania for Freud in the 1940s and 1950s in Hollywood. There were so many films with shrinks; sort of the Greek chorus. I thought it would be fun. I didn't know much about Freud. I read the first chapter of his *Interpretation of Dreams*. It was really just fun to play around with these obvious symbols. I was forced to do it in color by the distributor, but I was really glad I was forced because it would have taken me a long time to get around to it otherwise. I was so respectful of the power of color, its mystical power. I started to try to harness it and control it as much as possible. I remember, I thought, "How could they force me to shoot color? Don't they realize how difficult color is?" Think of *Don't Look Now* where that red raincoat is worn only by a homicidal dwarf and a drowned girl. If you don't control every color in the frame, you might accidentally shoot a fire hydrant, and the fire hydrant will take on all the same importance as the homicidal dwarf and a drowned girl. I didn't want to have fire hydrants all over the place, so I determined I would have to control the color of absolutely everything in the movie and make it only two colors at a time.
Marlow: That's why you shot it exclusively indoors?
Maddin: Yeah, because if I shot outdoors I would have to pull an Antonioni and paint the golf course or whatever it was.
Marlow: Did you think, when you were making a mountain film, that it had to be black-and-white and then . . .
Maddin: I felt like it had to be black-and-white because mountains seem like black-and-white things—although I guess *Heidi* would look good in color. I had never seen a Leni Riefenstahl picture prior to writing *Careful*, but I saw *Tiefland* shortly before shooting. *Tiefland* was in black-and-white and I thought, "Yes, mountains, black-and-white's the way to go," but I'm really glad I was forced to go color. I like the color in about three quarters of the scenes.

Marlow: I suspect that you were familiar with Robert Walser's *Jakob von Gunten*?
Maddin: Very familiar. I read it. I had read it, but I didn't have a library card. I couldn't take it out of the library, so I read it in the library once. I read it way too quickly because you can't read Walser quickly. I like the butler stuff. It was actually George Toles, my writing partner, who suggested we stick a butler academy up in the mountains. I just wanted to make a mountain picture and I had some other plots in mind but George had read another Walser in the *Masquerade* collection. There's some butler hijinks in that story. I got all the Walser attitude that I needed from that short story.

At the time, I didn't realize that the Brothers Quay were working on their own adaptation. I'm a huge fan of the Brothers Quay, and they'd already beaten me to doing a Bruno Schultz adaptation when they did *Street of Crocodiles*. When I found that they were doing *Institute Benjamenta*, it just sort of confirmed that these were people I had to meet someday. I've since become really good friends with them. I really admire them, and I visit them whenever I go to England . . .

"Perhaps I was a little bit of an arrogant mother."

Marlow: How is the Quay Brothers' latest feature [*The Mechanical Infanta*, aka *The Piano Tuner of Earthquakes*] coming along? Have you heard much about it?
Maddin: I think it's still sort of in delivery throes right now. No one has quite given them the go-ahead to start. I think it's in that state where everyone is waiting around hoping that they'll get the word.
Marlow: You finally met Steven and Timothy [Quay] at the Olympia Film Festival, the same time that we were introduced. There's a reference in the *Atelier Tovar* to "dinner with tons of wine before the *Twilight* screening," which was a dinner that we all had together. You also mention showing up at Scarecrow Video, a company that I worked for at the time [Marlow operated a movie theatre on the second floor of the store in the mid-1990s].
Maddin: I liked that video store. It was great.
Marlow: It's still quite a place. Can you talk a bit about casting Paul Cox as Count Knotkers? Because, as I understand it, Martin Scorsese was at one point going to do it and then Bobby Hull . . .

Maddin: That's right, yes. I received a lot of encouragement about Scorsese from his vice-president [of operations] at the time, Melanie Friesen. She's a Manitoban, actually, my home province, and she now works for the Vancouver International Film Festival. She used to phone me up every now and then to request a tape or a print from me because Marty was interested, and I talked to her. Naturally, being self-centered like all filmmakers, I tried to turn this to my advantage somehow. I wanted to get Marty in this part, you know, and I tried. She finally just said, "No, he's too busy." [Scorsese was editing *Cape Fear* at the time.] By then, I became determined to get a celebrity, so I thought along the lines of celebrity athletes for some reason. O. J. Simpson hadn't killed anyone at that point yet. I was thinking of Jim Brown, the former football player who had, I think, thrown a woman out of a window or something. No one talks about his unbelievably homicidal tendencies, but he struck me as a great sports hero turned rotten. I knew Bobby Hull was charged a few times for slapping his wife around and things like that, so I thought, "This is great, he's Canada's—and especially Winnipeg's—huge hockey legend. Plus he'll have this echo, a sort of after-career echo that's really rotten and that will be my own private joke." I think he smelled a rat or he was too busy bashing someone, but he was interested in theory for only a couple of weeks. And then, I just got it into my head that I needed a hockey player, so my producer [Greg Klymkiw], whose dad [Julian Klymkiw] used to play in the NHL in the 1950s, knew Maurice Richard [of the Montreal Canadians] and so I wanted to get Maurice. He did a lot of Grecian Formula hair ads in Canada in the 1960s and 1970s, but apparently he was getting too old, even in the early 1990s, to be considered. I don't remember all the other people we thought of.

Finally, Greg had become friends with Paul Cox at a film festival. Paul is a great drinker and he just likes hanging out with other filmmakers. He's sort of a grassroots kind of guy, which Greg really liked. Paul made *Golden Braid* with Gosia Dobrowolska and eventually married her. When we cast Gosia as Zenaida in *Careful*, Greg just thought it might be handy to ask Paul, her husband, as well. Paul and Kyle McCulloch had this strange rivalry over Gosia. They had been working together for a few weeks before Paul even arrived in town, and Paul sniffed something was up. I choreographed their fight after Leni Riefenstahl's *Tiefland* knife scene. I'd watched it the night before and basically lifted the storyboard panel-for-panel from that because I didn't know how to do a knife fight. It sort of encouraged me; incompetence rendered it unrecognizable, but it was a nice starting point. There are a lot of shots in that scene, two hundred or maybe 150. I don't know if they all made it into the movie, but I shot a lot of setups. Paul and Kyle were using these fake knives, but even those were kind of sharp and they were genuinely stabbing each other. Just stabbing away all day long. They truly hated each other. They were pretending not to, but you could tell that there was some sort of sexual rivalry going on there. Anyway, the marriage is over and the rivalry's over. Everything's over.

Marlow: Seeing the film again last night, I was surprised at the duration of that sequence. It's very difficult to block action scenes and make them seem believable. The rest of the film is so loose—to shift into a compelling fight sequence right at the end is a bit of a surprise.

Maddin: You know, I was very proud of that because I edited it myself. I edited the whole movie myself. I'm pretty proud of the movie, but I wish it were about fifteen minutes shorter. I think I allowed my girlfriend at the time to talk me into putting her in the movie and . . .

Marlow: What part did she play?

Maddin: She's that girl chained to a rock. An unnecessary detour in the movie. I had to create a lot of stuff around the rock to make it a justifiable piece. If I went back and cut it out, I could just fix that movie up, but you're not allowed to cut out things from our lives, so . . .

Marlow: Well, it seems that everyone else is doing it these days. Imagine, a Director's Cut of *Careful*—other folks put missing scenes back in, but you'd be taking existing footage out.

Maddin: I'm very sad to report that the guy who narrates the introductions to both *Careful* and *Archangel*, Victor Cowie, just died yesterday.

Marlow: Oh, no.

Maddin: Yeah, I was very close to him. He was very sweet. He had a small part in *The Saddest Music in the World* and it fit. I had given him a tape [of the movie] a couple of weeks ago because he was dying of cancer. His wife phoned me today to tell me two things: That he'd died and that he liked the movie. She was so sweet. He was a perfect gentleman and always made a point of followup calls. It would be so unlike him to die without passing on word that he thought he had done okay. It really is a touching gesture from this woman who had just lost her husband. She was sort of acting as a "gentleman of proxy" or something like that.

Marlow: This is the actor that portrayed the father?

Maddin: [Herr Trotta], the father of the girl.

Marlow: He's so fantastic in *Careful*.
Maddin: They go down in the little avalanche in the end. I really loved Victor Cowie.
Marlow: That's such a shame. The score in the film is your first non-cobbled together composition, I guess. John McCulloch, he is related to . . .
Maddin: Kyle's brother.
Marlow: That's what I figured. Even though it's his score, there are a handful of quotes from other pieces. For instance, there are a few bars from Stravinsky's *The Rite of Spring* in one sequence. Did you influence him in that way or is that something he simply wanted to do for the film?
Maddin: You know, I'm not even aware of that quote, because I don't even know *The Rite of Spring* that well, but I know that we spoke in those terms quite often about [Bernard] Herrmann or [Erich Wolfgang] Korngold and things like that.
Marlow: . . . like a classic Hollywood score.
Maddin: Yes, I just sort of wanted it to feel like certain things. He lives in Vancouver and I live in Winnipeg, so there was a time difference. We would sort of collaborate on the score over the phone. He'd play me little things, and I'd say, "Oh, that sounds good." When it was all orchestrated, there were little things in there, and sometimes I would ask him to put in paraphrases of things. I can't remember specifically right now what they were, but I liked it when things sounded Herrmannesque, even if Herrmann belonged to a entirely different era than the one the movie seems to evoke. I don't really care because I didn't really want to just make an imitation of any specific time period anyway.
Marlow: I remember when I saw the film in a theater, shortly after it was released, and all of the added surface noise, like old run-out grooves of records, I just thought was fantastic.
Maddin: It really broke John McCulloch's heart because he was begging me to let the sound be full Dolby Stereo Surround, 'cause he'd really written a nice score, I thought. It was my belief that all other movies had full Dolby Surround scores, and I just didn't want to sound like other movies. He'd written a great score I thought, and it sounded great in mono. I later took his advice but one film too late.
Marlow: It would seem inappropriate for that film to have it in stereo . . .

Maddin: I thought so, but I know it broke his heart, 'cause he really did beg me. He's a very insistent person, very persuasive, and it's the only time I ever really dug in my heels with him. When one of my producers, Greg [Klymkiw]'s partner, Tracy [Traeger], just assumed we were doing Dolby Surround so that the avalanches could really kick ass, I was thinking, "You fool, did *King Kong* need Dolby? What are you even talking about, you preposterous nincompoop?" So I was literally, completely insulted when someone mentioned the word Dolby around me. Perhaps I was a little bit of an arrogant mother.

Marlow: There is another oddity that I noticed in *Careful*. Sarah Neville appeared in *Archangel* and *Careful*, and then she seemingly disappeared, but Katya Gardner, whose first role was in *Careful* as Klara's sister Sigleinde, has gone on to do a lot of television and other feature films as well. How did you find Katya for the film?

Maddin: Katya was my very first casting agent find. I really was having trouble finding that part. I was thinking of using Angela Heck, who was the blond girl in *Gimli Hospital*, but Angela was going through some sort of "earth mother" phase, and she was intentionally making herself look tired. She looks great now. I think she was sick, frankly. I don't know what it was . . . I realize now, she told me a few years ago, that she got so mad when I didn't cast her. That's right, she told me she had cancer. That's what it was. She didn't look so hot and, without realizing that she was sick, I just thought that she was . . . I remember now, it's all coming back. I'm piecing these two halves together now. I thought that there was something about this "back to the land" look that she was adopting that made her look like she was literally lying with her toadstool collection at night or something. It didn't look healthy and sort of disappointed me, so I did know whom to cast. Katya was suggested to me by a local casting agent. She's in Winnipeg and she came and I talked to her and she sort of reminded me of Angela a little bit. She's sort of Winnipeg's Charlize Theron. She was always sort of seriously disappearing from the set to testify in court at the murder trial of her stepfather or something like that. Someone came to the door and killed him. Sarah Neville works in Toronto as well and both Katya and Sarah live in Toronto. I see Sarah in Ivory Snow commercials and she does some theater and things.

Marlow: So, *Careful* seems to mark an end of an era, filled with all these little cinematic treasures and a number of shorts that I'm still dying to see . . .

"It's the only film that turned out exactly the way I had hoped."

Marlow: Closing that decade is what I believe to be one of the finest short films ever made, *Odilon Redon or The Eye Like a Strange Balloon Mounts Toward Infinity*. I think a lot of the folks that were heaping words of praise upon the wonderful *Heart of the World* apparently had never seen *Odilon Redon* because your incredible abilities were readily visible there.

Maddin: It doesn't get seen that much, I don't think.

Marlow: I guess not. That's unfortunate because it's fantastic. Something that you mentioned in *Kino Delirium* was an attempt with *Odilon Redon* to remake Abel Gance's *La Roue* without ever actually seeing it. What other films would you like to remake that are lost or that you've only read about? Would you want to tackle [Tod] Browning's *London After Midnight* or [F.W] Murnau's *Four Devils*? Would that ever interest you?

Maddin: Precisely those titles. I made a little list of lost films that I thought would be fun to make into four-minute productions. Those two were there. I've since seen a reconstruction of *London After Midnight* on that Lon Chaney DVD that's just come out. It doesn't interest me that much anymore [ed. besides, Browning himself remade this film as *Mark of the Vampire*]. *Four Devils* I would love to make, although shooting trapeze artists would be very tough. I would like to slowly make them, something to do between big projects to fill in the gaps. Almost every major director has at least one lost film. It was really fun and liberating to make *La Roue* without having seen it. I've since seen it; I own it on videotape now. It's kind of fun to watch a two-and-a-half-hour version. And I'm a huge fan of Gance.

Marlow: As am I. Now we're up to *Twilight of the Ice Nymphs*—"very lush and full of ostriches!" Like Paul Cox in *Careful*, Frank Gorshin wasn't your first choice. The film wasn't really your first choice, either. You were going to make *The Dikemaster's Daughter*. Will you ever get back to that project or is it one that will stay on the shelf?

Maddin: I was lucky that one fell through. I wasn't ready to make that one. The script wasn't quite ready there. We were into preproduction, and we had some people cast already but it just . . . it was going to be a big mess. That's one of the reasons it folded. When financing was cut in half by the government, we did have the choice of continuing or not. We could have restructured and gone nonunion and made it for less money than we'd made the previous film, *Careful*. I was already starting to have doubts about this project anyway. When everyone was so devastated by getting 50 percent of what we thought we were getting from Telefilm Canada to make the film, I just used that as an excuse to bail on it, in a way. It wasn't just that. It was a terrific slap in the face, I felt; a terrific display of a lack of confidence in me and aptly so [laughs]. I think the funders read the script and felt the same kind of concerns that I did. It was a good first draft, but it wasn't ready to go. They didn't say that, though. They just said, "No!" Then they gave me a figure. I think we wanted to make it for $1.8 million and we were going to be forced to make it for $900K [Canadian]. In 2004 dollars, that would be like making the movie for $2 million; that wouldn't be so bad. I just thought, "Nah, I better get out of this picture that I don't really want to make." It needed to be rewritten. I wasn't ready to shoot a musical, either. I was barely ready to shoot the musical that *Saddest Music in the World* is when I shot it. A lot of work goes into those things. I hadn't done any of it, and we were just a few weeks from shooting. It was going to be like that Nick Nolte musical [*I'll Do Anything*] that was shot a few years ago where they finally just cut out all of the musical numbers and released it as a drama. That would have been its fate for sure.

I remember feeling, just as I was finishing *Careful*, that for almost ten years, since I picked up a camera for the first time, I had already been messing around with making these old-looking movies. I really felt like I'd done it once too often, even. I just needed to spend a few years drifting around until I found some enthusiasm for the pictures again. Unfortunately, I made a movie right in the middle of this period where I had no enthusiasm for making pictures . . .

Marlow: . . . and that's *Ice Nymphs*?

Maddin: Yeah. I feel that good directors have got to be able to get through that anyway and just work; to put failure behind them and just keep moving. I shouldn't have lulled around so much, but I just didn't feel a burning need to make a picture. I didn't know what kind of visual language to use, which is why there is sort of a different visual language going on in *Twilight of the Ice Nymphs*. Sort of a determined Ouija-style by unknown forces at work on the set. Different people determining different things. Some very loyal pals helping me out that were doing imitations of me in the décors. Every now and then I would work up the energy to supervise really nice "Guy backdrops." I like those in the movie. It was a learning experience, but I shouldn't have let the film's sort of cursed existence get me down so much. I should have just reminded myself that even Hitchcock laid a rotten egg now and then.

Marlow: Quite a few of them, even. If you had a checklist of film techniques that you were crossing off as you make these features, you covered Orson Welles's classic trick of redubbing someone (although you didn't do the voice yourself).

Maddin: Exactly. I'm not in love with my voice. But I do love Ross MacMillan's voice, so he could be my "vocal Orson" any time. There's only so much an actor in Ross's position can do. He understands the music of George [Toles's] writing and he could put the "George" back in the George lines. Nigel [Whitmey, star of *Twilight*] had no sense of irony or playfulness. He was a bit of an imposter. He was from RADA [Royal Academy of Dramatic Arts], this distinguished academy in London but, I don't know, it just seemed like he was from Calgary to me. Strangely enough, when we were finishing *Saddest Music in the World*, and we had some preview screenings, there were some suggestions that we replace Ross MacMillan's voice [Ross portrays Roderick, the "sad Serbian"]. [laughs] I couldn't believe it. His voice was almost replaced. It would have been the strangest irony that I hired him to replace someone's voice in one movie and then hired him again only to have his voice replaced. Whatever.

Marlow: This was the producers of the film that wanted you to do it?

Maddin: I'd better not say who it was.

Marlow: Let's forget it then.

Maddin: It was some people up there that luckily didn't have any sort of veto power or anything. It was some bigwigs . . .

Marlow: You took this period after *Ice Nymphs* to finish off some shorts that you had shot earlier but hadn't finished . . .

Maddin: A lot of them are sort of stillborn, and it may be a while before they see the light of day. I've shown them to friends. I have about four shorts that were financed by my aunt Lil who died and then left her entire estate to her nephew. Not me, a different nephew. Now he claims ownership of them. One of them is *Sissy-Boy Slap-Party*, so I've reshot it just recently. That will be released as a remake. He can have the first one and I have the second one. The second one's better anyway.

Marlow: We screened *Hospital Fragment* at the Grand Illusion in Seattle. It seemed to be an outtake from *Gimli*. I don't believe that it really was; perhaps it was only inspired by . . .

Maddin: I shot it many years later. Mike Gottli, the fat guy from *Gimli*, had been in a horrible car accident. He hit a moose with his Austin Mini and went into a coma for about a year. When he came out of it, he needed speech therapy. He can't talk, actually. He lost about five years worth of memories, including making the movies with me [Gottli also stars in *Archangel*]. He needed to walk with a walker. His health has since failed even worse, and he's doing really badly. He's had a stroke. He's only thirty-five years old, and he's in horrible shape. Before he had his stroke, I thought it might be nice to have him come and do a little scene, just for something to do. So, on the day that JFK Jr. went down in an airplane, I just called up Angela Heck and Brent Neale [from *Careful*] and I got them all together in my bedroom and we just shot this thing. It was done in 1999, a full twelve years later than *Gimli Hospital*.

Marlow: I wasn't sure if the footage was shot earlier and then assembled in 1999. I suppose, if I compared them side-by-side, it would be rather obvious. Wasn't *Maldoror: Tigers* shot earlier and finished, I think, in 1999?

Maddin: It was shot when Kyle was heavier, I know that.

Marlow: From the lone still that I've seen, it was clearly photographed after *Careful* but I can't tell when.

Maddin: It was shot around 1997.

Marlow: Now we're into the big guns. You had this fallow period and now you can't be stopped.

Maddin: [laughs]

Marlow: *The Heart of the World*, of course—the shot heard 'round the world. Nearly everyone's seen it. It's on disc, fortunately, so folks that have only heard about it now have the chance to see it as well. In only six minutes, you're able to pack more story than nearly every feature film released in 2000.

Maddin: [laughs] Yeah, it felt pretty good. It's the only film that I've ever made that turned out exactly the way I had hoped.

Marlow: Plus, I'd wished that when people were talking about *The Passion of the Christ* and rattling off all of the great cinematic Christs that they would mention Caelum [Vatnsdal] but they didn't! I don't know why . . .

Maddin: He's a pretty good one. I was pretty lucky there. I've always been lucky in my career. Lucky to get way more mileage out of my talent than I deserve. I felt like everything that could go wrong went wrong on *Twilight of the Ice Nymphs*. The spell I like to work in was gone. All of the sudden, I felt lucky again. Caelum lives just a few blocks away from me. I phoned him up and said, "Do you mind if I just come over and look at you?" So I rode over on my bicycle, and I was there within ninety seconds. He opened his door, and I just said, "Heal me!" He's got these long, skinny, boney fingers, and he became a German Expressionist Christ there on the spot. I cast him. I just felt so lucky. He'd never really done much acting, but I thought he was perfect for it. I had an audition even, where I had these people showing up, and they'd memorized chunks of the Bible, giving me Christ monologues. None of them were as good as the nonactor Caelum.

Marlow: He has that great Ivan the Terrible beard.

Maddin: Yeah, and since I wanted to make a Soviet agitprop thing, I thought he looked quite sinister. Christianity really is the sinister opiate of the masses.

Marlow: That free style that you use on *Heart of the World* seems to surface again in *Dracula: Pages from a Virgin's Diary*. This all-over Super-8 shooting style, assembled in a way that really doesn't resemble anyone else's film.

Maddin: I just started getting more and more confident with my "primitivity." Just deciding that the more I intentionally, aggressively, got primitive, the more it embraced mistakes and made them into strengths. I really started to hit my stride right around *Dracula* that way. I just felt good, and it's been kind of a strategy I've been using lately.

Marlow: The same style goes into *The Hands of Orlac*, which I thought was really clever . . .

Maddin: I loved the premise of *The Hands of Orlac*, and it never seems to get told properly. I'm not saying that I've done it properly either but, like in *Mad Love*, it always becomes bogus about two thirds of the way through. That's a wonderful movie. I love Peter Lorre, it looks great, but the script sort of fell apart. I thought I'd try my hand it. It's been shot six times at least. I had all of these other stories sort of simmering in my head, and *The Hands of Orlac* as well. I was really worried that, by fusing too many metaphors together, I'd just make a big dog's breakfast. I feel that it worked out okay.

Marlow: Well, more than okay. Obviously, conceived as an installation, I think that the single-channel film is really exceptional.

Maddin: I sort of let down the Power Plant [Contemporary Art] Gallery [in Toronto] that commissioned it because I made a film not an installation. I feel badly about it. They've been kind enough to let me show it as a film from now on.

Marlow: IFC Films picked up *Saddest Music* and Zeitgeist is distributing *Cowards*?
Maddin: Yeah.
Marlow: I'm pleased that people will have a chance to see it.
Maddin: It is going to open at the Film Forum in New York in August with a Quay brothers film [*The Phantom Museum*] and probably with *Sissy-Boy Slap-Party*.

"I still remember my head hurting, so I guess that I was excited."

Marlow: How did this idea of coming to the Pacific Film Archive come about? Did Edith [Kramer] approach you?
Maddin: Edith made a phone call to me. I was quite excited to talk to Edith—I hadn't talked to her in a few years.
Marlow: Since 1993, right?
Maddin: Yeah, but she's one of those people whose opinion really matters to me. Whenever I made a movie, I used to send a tape of it for her to watch and then wait for her response. Sometimes you could tell if she was busy and hadn't had a chance to see it properly. She'd say, "Congratulations," and then she would cite something that she liked about it, usually something that happened in the first few minutes. I was beginning to get frightened that I had fallen off of her radar altogether. To get a call way back whenever it was, last February maybe, about coming here when I was already getting sick of traveling. I had sort of sworn off all trips but I accepted this offer in a second.

The chance to do a retrospective plus the carte blanche [to show the sidebar, "Director's Choice"] was a tasty piece of bait. It was fun to pick other movies. It was great talking with Edith, and then she quickly delegated it out to Steve Seid. He's really an amazing programmer. He really knows his stuff. A lot of people say that he's maybe the best programmer in the country and things like that. It was really nice to work with him. He's really funny. He's kind of a merciless kidder as well. There's not even a molecule of obsequiousness in him or anything. I feel like he's a friend already, somehow, although we probably won't ever speak to each other ever again! At least not for a couple of years.
Marlow: You've definitely had a flurry of productivity over these last few years.
Maddin: Maybe I can be back here eventually or soon or something.
Marlow: When *Saddest Music* screened at the recent San Francisco

International Film Festival, the staff were apologetic that you weren't present to introduce it.

Maddin: I'd had it. I'd had it with travel. I think it was happening during the school year and I was teaching, for one thing. I had just traveled so much, and I'd talked about the movie so much that I didn't think I was capable. Now it's getting a French release, so I'm going to have to go there. French film press. Staggeringly huge. I'll have to do a lot of interviews. I'm just going to have to gird myself for another blitzkrieg. Maybe I should think up a new mythology for the movie or something.

Marlow: Perhaps you can try some of those ideas out now?

Maddin: Yeah, I'm dry I think.

Marlow: Is that the hardest part? After you've worked so hard on the film, to have to go around and explain it to these people who probably don't have a clue.

Maddin: Sometimes it was kind of fun. When I made *Archangel*, a movie which, while I was making it, I was very hubristic, I thought that I was making something wonderful. Then, when it came out, I realized with a very painful blow to the skull administered by the public that the movie was incomprehensible. I had a lot of fun talking about it and trying to make it more accessible to people, trying to literally hide in these interviews explanations and enlightenments and ways into the movie and things like that. That was kind of a fun challenge. I never got tired of that because I liked the movie enough. It was just this little movie of mine walking around on leg braces. I gave it all the special attention it needed.

Marlow: Were you giving conflicting explanations for the film?

Maddin: I was giving any explanation.

Marlow: You were trying to provide any detail that could provide a gateway into the story?

Maddin: Yeah, whereas with *Saddest Music in the World* it's somehow a movie that can stand more on its own. I quickly found myself running out of things to say. Maybe this came with age but I felt less mischievous; I found myself less interested in lying. Not very playful. The biggest challenge was *Twilight of the Ice Nymphs*, where I had to talk about how, since it was a movie set in the forest, I was going for a "deciduous" acting style. Trying anything to help people into what few sylvan charms were in there. But *Saddest Music in the World* seemed to stand well enough on its own. I really preferred reading or hearing what writers had to say about it rather than hearing me myself saying it. I wanted to give myself the pleasure of reading some takes on it or hearing about it, you know? But then you're standing there with a microphone or a blank piece of paper and you've got to say or write something. I found myself using up all the material that I have. When you're a director and you are talking about your movie, you're pretending to be a viewer and talking about the viewing experience.

Marlow: How did you and George [Toles] approach the story? Were there any special challenges in taking the story and adapting it into a film?

Maddin: One of my favorite stages of filmmaking is the writing of the screenplay—my other favorite part is the sound edit. The treatment was really fun. The screenplay was kicking around since 1985, I think, and it was something that Ish [Kazuo Ishiguro] had written before he was a famous novelist. We were told, not by Ish but by our producer, that we could do whatever we wanted to make it "live" as long as we kept the basic premise and the title and Ishiguro's name on there as a pedigree. One of the first things we did . . . George and I have almost never collaborated in person. We just talk on the phone. Our friendship was formed over the phone. He's a person that has a phone-shaped dent in the side of his head from 1968. You can put a phone in there and you can just hang it up.

Marlow: He does his best thinking through this device?

Maddin: Yes, and he's really strangely articulate. He speaks in these long, complicated sentences but with correct punctuation—dashes, colons, semicolons, exclamation points, periods, pauses . . . and then, just when you think the whole thing is going to topple over in some dramatically incorrect mountain of participles, he just finishes it up in a couple of words and the whole thing stands there, shimmering. He's a real Nabokovian that way. He's fun just to listen to, so we've always just collaborated by editing out all other things except for the sounds of our voices over the phone. The more excited we get—I don't know about George but, judging by the dent in his head, he is probably the same as me—I start pressing the phone further into my ear and by the end of the conversation I usually can't straighten my arm up, my tendons are close to snapping, my head hurts—but we peeled away all the things in Ish's script that didn't thrill us and added some personal obsessions of our own. We came up with a structure that we felt could support all of the through lines in a clear, audience-friendly way without sabotaging any of our concerns.

We were quite excited after just one ten- or fifteen-minute conversation. Then it was a matter of having one more conversation like that. Even though it was a short conversation, I still remember my head hurting, so I guess that I was excited. Then, my job is always to write it out in purpled prose to get right away to the tone of the movie. At least that's what I like to do. I'm sure that people in the industry don't want to read that and I've probably done myself no favors by writing in that way. Trying to write in the style of the last decade of the nineteenth century or something like that; trying to get some flavor of decadence into the project, something frightening to the producers but something that gets my mouth watering for the project. I wrote a twenty-nine-page treatment just based on our conversations.

"They're just silent movie actors that don't know it."

Marlow: Were there certain things that you found in the original script that seemed to suggest the typical obsessions that would appear in your films or did you feel that it was open enough to add those items in here or there? It doesn't seem greatly different from *Careful* or *Tales from the Gimli Hospital*. It's definitely a "Guy Maddin/George Toles" concept.

Maddin: There were some things that we've been working towards. There was a project that we didn't make, this Thomas Edison biopic [*Edison and Neemo*]—it's being shot but not by me; George sold the script to an animator and it's being made into a cartoon [by Perfect Circle Productions in Vancouver, B.C.]—but I had sort of sworn that I would have a proactive protagonist in my films from now on. With Thomas Edison, you had the ultimate American proactive protagonist—a guy that just sort of grabbed and stole and took a lot of credit and things like that.

Right away, we switched around Ishiguro's script into something that was more of what we had become recently. The competition in Ishiguro's script didn't even involve Americans. They were in there but only in a tertiary role. We just thought, "No, it has to be about America and this proactive character." Since we're Canadian, there has to be a Canadian character, and they might as well be brothers. There had to be an old world way. Then, we quickly developed this way of speaking over each other's lines and finishing each other's sentences. We talked about how America always repressed its sadness in music and pop culture and how Europe always seemed to embrace sadness and present it to the world without any guise, especially its music. Think of all those Tin

Pan Alley songs of the Great Depression that came out of America, like "We're in the Money" or "Happy Days Are Here Again" and a million others. Only a couple of Tin Pan Alley hits of the 1930s acknowledged the Depression—"Brother, Can You Spare a Dime?" is the most famous one, I guess. The rest are highly polished songs concentrating on romance.

Marlow: In Hollywood, they rarely wanted to address the Depression in any cinematic dramatic way, except for a handful—Wellman's *Wild Boys of the Road*, for instance.

Maddin: Yeah, there's a few. The Warner Bros. stuff was kind of gritty, and there's something tawdry about everything Busby Berkeley does but, for the most part . . .

Marlow: They knew that audiences were seeking some kind of escape.

Maddin: Audiences didn't want to see a movie about shacks because they were living in them.

Marlow: We're kind of in that period again. Making shallow entertainment that denies our situation.

Maddin: The new opiate of the masses. Anyway, we thought it would be fun to make a movie that would be full of music. This was something that I had been working towards for a long time anyway and something that I was able to do with my ballet, *Dracula*—a melodrama that's wall-to-wall music.

Marlow: Was it always the case that you were going to exclusively use Mahler for *Dracula*?

Maddin: I came to the ballet after it had already been staged [by Mark Godden] three years earlier, and it had been choreographed to Mahler. I was stuck with the Mahler. I didn't love it at first, but I learned to like most of it a lot.

Marlow: I think that it's used effectively and, at times, it sounds like it's played off of an old 78 RPM turntable, which suits the imagery. That sets a whole other story in the development of this style of shooting in many different formats and using multiple cameras, moving all over the stage.

Maddin: I had to cover that one almost like a hockey game.

Marlow: In a sense, you're treating ballet as a sporting event.

Maddin: The ballet dancers struck me more as athletes than as artists. I think that they think of themselves more as athletes. They don't go into a method actors trance in between stints on stage. As a matter of fact, I went to a number of ballets and watched from the wings. As I got to know the ballet dancers, they would come running off of the stage and they'd go, "Hey, Guy. What did you do on the weekend?" And I'd go, "You know, I got too drunk," or whatever. I'd go, "How about you?" "Oh, I went fishing . . . just a minute." And they'd run out and have a love scene and then come back, literally like talking to a hockey player between line changes or something like that. They are so athletic and they perform as a team. They do act with their faces, but it's that uninhibited magnified melodrama, like in silent movies. They're just silent movie actors that don't know it. It was neat working with them and I've used them since. One of the female leads [Tara Birtwhistle] from *Dracula* I used in *Cowards Bend the Knee* but in a cheap wig.

Marlow: Which part did she play?

Maddin: She's the mother of Meta who gets strangled. She's unrecognizable in that cheap wig.

Marlow: I didn't make the connection at all. I also didn't realize until recently that your mother [Herdis Maddin] appears in the film.

Maddin: [Laughs] Where her ballet training came in handy was when she was being strangled. She could really make it seem like she's going through a lot of pain and she's being tossed around when in fact she's leading. The actor is supposed to be strangling her with a hair net when in fact he's just following her around while she's leading with her throat. Dragging herself but making it appear that she's being dragged underneath the hairdryer and having her head rammed underneath while putting her hand on the helmet of the hairdryer as if to try to resist it when, in fact, she's pushing it down. She sort of does everything in reverse. She knows how to die since she's died a million deaths on stage—stab wounds, stakes through the heart, poisonings, broken hearts, and all sorts of other things that a ballerina has to die from. That one really paid off.

Marlow: This would be similar to when a number of early silent filmmakers used opera performers to bring that level of experience to the screen. Have you ever thought about directing an opera?

Maddin: I've had a few offers recently.

Marlow: I think that your talents would suit the stage rather well. Watching *West of Zanzibar* the other day [one of Maddin's selections for "Director's Choice"], I thought that it was a perfect story, this tale of misplaced revenge, for an opera.

Maddin: Maybe you're right. Maybe it should just be sung. Maybe I'll send you a case of champagne for that idea if I ever do it! The first opera that I was offered was Jánacek's *From the House of the Dead*, but I got fired. It would have been nice, but it didn't work out. I'm still not sure why. Perhaps because over coffee with the maestro I told him that I actually enjoyed Gounod's *Faust*. About three people started spitting up their coffee at that point, and one of them announced that it was the most loathsome opera ever written. The next thing you know, none of my calls were being returned.

Marlow: Just for a simple comment?

Maddin: The other theories are more litigious sounding so I'll just stick with that one.

Marlow: Many opera companies rely heavily on directors with a significant theater background, but these directors seem better suited for a smaller stage. They generally spend much of the performance moving the singers and supernumeraries around in circles. Of course, they're often dealing in those types of productions with singers who simply are not great actors.

Maddin: Right, and they often can't get them to sing and act at the same time either.

Marlow: Were there special difficulties in starting with a movie entitled *The Saddest Music in the World* with writing or finding music that would be perceived by audiences to be the saddest music? One person's "saddest" is definitely not another's.

Maddin: I just sort of believe that there is no way for there to be a "saddest music in the world." It's different for everybody. George was really pushing a while for "Happy Birthday." I was up for it because I told him that in my personal experience, "Happy Birthday" is the saddest, not because it marks another year passed, another year older. Actually, it's been sad for me since I was about five years old. I could always sense that around birthday time I was going to be getting a lot of presents that would be kind of useless and disappoint me. I always had to feign happiness. I could always tell that my loved ones—my parents, my aunt, my grandmother—could tell that maybe I was faking and then they were trying to conceal their disappointments. Then there were all of these mutual reassurances that everyone loved the presents and, even if we didn't, we still loved each other anyway. It just became an annual occasion for a lot of deception, discomfort, and pressure to please.

As the years went on, these memories accumulated into a highly concentrated unpleasant feeling. The music for me is awful. Plus, I have a girlfriend who demands an orgy of celebrations every year for her birthday. Whenever her birthday rolls around, I feel like I'm in the pennant race but without any pitchers. Every year, it's awful. I start out the spring with the buds on the trees, feeling like the New York Yankees, and I end by feeling like the Montreal Expos. To me, it's just the saddest music in the world, but I knew that it wouldn't necessarily be so for everyone. For my girlfriend, for instance, it's the happiest music in the world. In the first draft of the script, we decided on climaxing the movie, after the contest, having Mark McKinney/Chester Kent's mother come to the piano and everyone would be laid to waste again by the devastating effect of the song. But it's too abstract and it couldn't be accomplished through a montage. Besides, the rights to that song are notoriously expensive!

"It was my favorite experience."

Maddin: Right away, I discarded that notion [of using "Happy Birthday" as the saddest music]. Remembering how musicals worked, old Hollywood musicals set up a piece of music in one context and then replayed it throughout the movie in different contexts and then, hopefully, that sets the viewer up for the ultimate proper context that is the exact flipside of the original idea. It starts off being a happy piece of music and then it gains some demonic associations when it's played finally. That was something that I thought that I'd try to do. It was just a matter of picking a piece of music that was versatile enough.
Marlow: Then whereabouts would you approach . . . how could I say this nicely? How did you select a composer that is mostly associated with writing the happiest pop music in the world, Christopher Dedrick of The Free Design, to write the score for your film?
Maddin: You know of The Free Design? "Kites Are Fun"! He was up for it, and I think that he did a pretty good job.
Marlow: He does a great job.
Maddin: Yeah, he's really proud of his work and he should be. He's won some Canadian movie awards for it. I wasn't that familiar with "Kites Are Fun" at the time. I don't know how I missed that because I was a real pop music buff in the late '60s when "Kites Are Fun" was a hit.
Marlow: You weren't the only one that missed it. The song, along with much of their work, is largely forgotten now, despite its relative popularity at the time.

Maddin: He's a real sort of charmed, levelheaded figure. He seems to have a harmonic way of playing through life, but he's really professional and hardworking. I wasn't quaking in my boots with the realization that I might have to swing this guy around. He was willing to turn the dial darker. It was just a matter of saying, "More Wagner, more Herrmann." I had this Jerome Kern song that seemed to be the most versatile song ever. The lyrics to it seemed to apply to almost any situation that the human heart can get itself into, "The Song Is You" [words by Oscar Hammerstein]. So I decided to make that the firepole that ran the length of the movie. Chris [Dedrick] could sort of slide up and down that thing to get to various "darknesses" or lighter than air.
Marlow: Such as the "flapper-esque" version.
Maddin: Yeah, there's a foxtrot, a dirge. All along, I knew that wanted to take one song and keep it as a motif. I thought that it was worth it to pay for the rights to this Jerome Kern classic. It's a song that, at one point, he was best known for, but it seems to have been forgotten by so many people. So, it felt good to partially exhume it and recycle it. Then it was just a matter of finding incidental music, and I was really worried about that. I just held auditions in Winnipeg and, it turns out, among its many immigrants are tons of musical groups. We held auditions and we also told them to bring their own costumes and their own instruments and play two of the saddest songs their ethnicity could muster. They were allowed five minutes each and we just picked people that had their own costumes to save some money.
Marlow: IFC stepped up to the film after it was finished, right?
Maddin: After seeing it at the Toronto Film Festival.
Marlow: How did you finance the film initially?
Maddin: I have no idea. I know that I didn't have to pitch the movie once, which felt good. I guess my producers did the pitching this time. In the past, I've had to pitch my movies a little bit. It's kind of strange to make a movie now without even pitching it.
Marlow: That's where you're at now!
Maddin: Pitching it afterwards.
Marlow: With MGM releasing it on video, it will probably be seen by more people than any of your other films.
Maddin: I hope that they release it in the proper aspect ratio [the Canadian release, evidently, was full-frame; the U.S. release is 1.85:1].
Marlow: Did you create a commentary track for the film?

Maddin: I did some commentary in Canada, Mark McKinney and me. Maybe they're buying the commentary. [They didn't—the U.S. release contains two featurettes and three short films instead].

Marlow: Was Mark always your first choice for the film? Did you write it with him in mind?

Maddin: No, we didn't write it with him in mind, but we didn't have anyone else in mind either. I guess he was my first choice. He was the only choice. We thought of some other people, briefly, but I have no regrets. I think that it was really the way to go.

Marlow: There is a real chemistry between Mark and Isabella [Rossellini].

Maddin: Isabella was in our minds all along. I'd given brief thought to my friend Alice Krige, with whom I'd worked on *Twilight of the Ice Nymphs*. I'd cast her and even bought her a plane ticket for *Cowards Bend the Knee*, but she got quite sick so I replaced her with that ballerina at the last second. Then we shot *Saddest Music in the World* instantly after—you know, I shot those movies back-to-back. I shot *Cowards* during the preproduction of *Saddest Music in the World*.

Marlow: I told you this before but I'll mention it again—*Cowards* is my favorite of your films. It used to be *Careful*.

Maddin: I think that it might be my favorite, too. It was my favorite experience.

Marlow: To exorcise those demons, in a way?

Maddin: It felt really good. Plus it was so easy to make. I had a friend [Shawna Connor] that needed a job, and so I paid her some money to be the production designer. I found a studio, an abandoned snowplow garage in Winnipeg, so I gave her some money to build some sets. I basically just gave her the script, and I just let her do it herself. I only showed up on set maybe twice before shooting, to make sure that things were going along nicely. She took so much pride in her work; she had so many volunteers working for her. I had really nothing to do with it. I just made sure that it looked good to me. So I just showed up on the first day of shooting with a bunch of actors.

Marlow: She was your Cedric Gibbons, in a way.

Maddin: Yep, I just let her go and she does great work! I gave her a salary, too, and she spent her whole salary on materials as well. She was living in complete poverty, sleeping in her car. The costume designer, Meg McMillan, was the same thing. She also did the costumes for *The Saddest Music in the World*. She was sleeping in her car with her two Scottie dogs.

People were pouring their own salaries into the movies. I owe them a lot of gratitude.

So, I just showed up with these actors. I guess that I had cast the actors myself. That was slightly time consuming, but they were all hand-picked from people that I knew. Meg put them in costumes, and I put them in the sets that Shawna built. Then I pointed a Super-8 camera at them and started filming them. I sort of snuck five days away from *Saddest Music in the World* into this snowplow garage.

Marlow: It was only a five-day shoot?

Maddin: Yeah. Five pretty short days, too, because I had to check in at the other place first thing in the morning and then report back in at lunchtime.

Marlow: Sounds like an Edgar Ulmer schedule.

Maddin: Yeah. We'd shoot from ten in the morning until four in the afternoon everyday with a ninety-minute lunch break while I would drive across town to the other studio. It was fun shooting a secret movie in a parallel universe. The only thing that would have made it better was if I was shooting at the same time on both sets, but that would've been impossible. I actually tried that once. It doesn't work. A producer for a rock video hired me once to be the director of the video, but he secretly really wanted to direct it himself. So he scheduled it, rather craftily, at the same time while I was scheduled to shoot another short movie of mine. For a while, I was literally riding my bike back and forth between the two locations. This was back in 1994 when I was making the *Odilon Redon* short. The video was for a group called Grand Theft Canoe. I ended up finally giving up after about three bike rides and just letting him take over. It was clear that he was going to do it anyway.

Marlow: This chaotic shooting schedule seems to suit you. *Odilon Redon* is an amazing film as well.

Maddin: I like the imposition of outside restrictions somehow. You wouldn't think you'd want that, but I kind of like it. I like working with producers that make it clear to me what they want. The producer of *Dracula* really made it clear that she [Vonnie von Helmolt] wanted it in HD-TV color.

Marlow: Although it is neither of those things—HD or color.

Maddin: When I fought with her over it being in black-and-white and on film, Super-8 film even, I finally had to make a strong case. You sort of find out which of your arguments are good and which ones you don't even believe yourself. As long as you're dealing with a reasonable person who isn't just using their veto power, it's pretty productive actually. It was like that with the producer of *Saddest Music in the World*, Niv Fichman, with whom I argued constantly. He had this sort of rule, which is very sweet—once an argument is settled, it's never brought up again in the form of sour grapes or whatever. And consensus—once the two of you have decided on a path, you back each other on it. Quickly, amnesia sets in and you don't remember which side of the argument you were on, whether you lost or won.

Marlow: Because you had agreement.

Maddin: Yeah. It was pretty good, actually. There was never any, "Ah, shit! I knew I should've shot it in color." Or something like that. "Why did I let you talk me into it?" There was none of that, ever. I beat myself up over some second guesses, though.

Marlow: Why did she want to shoot *Dracula* in HD?

Maddin: Well, it was her project right from the start. She approached me as a gun for hire. She just knew that she wanted it for TV and she loved the production that she'd seen on stage. She wanted it to be on cutting-edge technology, thinking that it would improve its export chances for Europe and American television.

Marlow: Was she wrong?

Maddin: I don't know. I think, for me, she was. It wasn't a good fit for me because I like to murk things up. I don't really like watching ballet films. A lot of times, you're not seeing enough because the camera is too far away from the human face. Then, when they do go in for a closeup, you're seeing too much. You're seeing bad stage makeup or a person whose face isn't mysterious enough. I thought that HD would be the worst possible approach.

Marlow: It seems that your technique, which you were perfecting on *Dracula*, accurately represents the way that the human eye perceives things. Shifting the focus, picking up different details.

Maddin: Yeah, there is a time to reveal something and a time not to. In writing, in painting, in photography, in drama and storytelling. It's not like I'm the only person doing stuff like that. You see it in commercials all the time, in advertising where the smartest people are, the most manipulative at least. That's where I get daily inspiration. I buy the big, thick fashion magazines and flip through them. I sort of wish that I could be a fashion writer, as a matter of fact. There is a particular flavor to the kind of spun candy that appears in those pages.

Marlow: Did you ever want to be a sports writer at all?

Maddin: That would be fun, too! A dream that I held, quite seriously, was to be a hockey color commentator. I knew that I couldn't be a broadcast play-by-play man because I just don't have the voice for it. I don't even have the voice for his companion in the booth, either. That was a dream that I had for a long time, and I'm meaning, recently. In my late thirties, I was still sort of planning on it.

Marlow: The whole film thing is a sideline.

Maddin: They get paid like $30,000 a year, but it was what I wanted to do.

Marlow: Dreams have nothing to do with money.

Maddin: Of course, that's about $20,000 more a year than I get paid now!

Mr. Beaks Gets to the Root of Brilliance with Guy Maddin—An Absolute Genius!

Jeremy Smith/2004

From *Ain't It Cool News*, April 30, 2004. Reprinted by permission of the author.

We're only nearing the end of April, and I've already seen three films—*Eternal Sunshine of the Spotless Mind*, *Kill Bill Vol. 2*, and *The Saddest Music in the World*—that are not only locks for my year end top ten, but damn near sure things for my top five. Hopefully, you've already seen the first two I listed (a hearty "Fie" in your direction, if not), and now, if you live in New York or Los Angeles, you're going to finally get a chance to see the latest work of peculiar genius from Guy Maddin, *The Saddest Music in the World*.

The film tells the strange tale of the glass-legged Brewery Baroness Lady Port-Huntly (Isabella Rossellini), who has commissioned a contest to bring the world's saddest music to Depression-era Winnipeg. Competing for the $25,000 prize are two estranged brothers (Mark McKinney and Ross McMillan) and their decrepit father (David Fox), along with representatives from almost every nation on the planet. It's a wacky idea that gets typically surreal treatment from Maddin, who is at his most accessible here if only because he's working from a somewhat conventional narrative. It's a film of singularly rough beauty, seeming, like Maddin's best work, as if it just arrived in a time machine from the 1920s. If you've never imbibed the director's consciousness-warping cinema, *The Saddest Music in the World* is definitely the drug to start with.

Below is the transcript from my fascinating one-on-one interview with Maddin conducted at the Avalon Hotel several weeks ago. Enjoy!

Smith: First, one hockey fan to another, I've got to ask who you favor for the Stanley Cup.

Maddin: A certain part of me wants the Ottawa Senators to win just because it would destroy the NHL's television ratings in America, and because it would break so many hearts in Canada. But my son-in-law is a huge Toronto Maple Leafs fan, so I feel out of solidarity I have to pull for them.
Smith: It's tough. I grew up near Detroit, so I now root for what's become the New York Yankees of hockey.
Maddin: I love the Red Wings. I've always loved them: Alex Delvecchio, Ted Lindsay, Gordie Howe. Not that I was alive in their heyday, but just the legend of them. I loved when Igor Larionov played for them, and I'm sad that he's now benched most of the time as a forty-two-year-old who's not getting any respect even though he's one of the greatest players of all time. He deserves to be in the Hall of Fame.
Smith: He does. It's amazing that these guys, at their advanced age, keep getting out there to play such a brutal sport.
Maddin: I really wish he hadn't left Detroit. I wish Scotty Bowman could've stayed there.
Smith: I think we all do.
Maddin: Dave Lewis is doing a fine job, but I just wish it could've stayed that way for a while longer.
Smith: Yeah. It had kind of a magical glow about it.
Maddin: I guess I'm not married to any one team, but certain teams give me a lot of pleasure and Detroit is one of them, that's for sure.
Smith: I was reading an essay that said you once contracted a rather serious cold that left you with a permanent neurological disorder.
Maddin: That's true.
Smith: Which gives you the sensation of feeling like you're touched by ghosts all of the time?
Maddin: It's true. It's suffered by many people at varying degrees. It's called myoclonus. I have myoclonic seizures, and it does feel like what you just described. They can be controlled by medication, which I'm on for the rest of my life. So, I don't feel the ghosts all the time now, steering me around. Believe me, though, for a while they just terrified me. First of all, because I was scared of ghosts. Second of all, because I thought it was a disease with initials. [Laughs.] Or a disease named after a baseball player. The doctors thought it was, too. Finally, it turned out to be an easily controlled thing. I wet the bed every now and then, but other than that.
Smith: Do you credit that otherworldly feeling with informing the distanced, dreamlike aesthetic of your work?

Maddin: Of all the ailments to get, that's certainly an odd coincidence that I would get one that would seem to match-up, or dovetail, with my filmmaking attitudes so perfectly. It is kind of odd. But I got this while making my second feature, *Archangel*. I had already started making films, but . . . I wanted that movie to be full of haunted feeling. It was about a bunch of . . . dead World War I soldiers without memory, without life any longer, being filmed as dimly remembered characters. And, then, to be sort of haunted myself by something neurological seemed very chilling. I almost felt like I gave myself the disease.

There were some other things, too. In my following picture, my lead actor's character had a hole driven into his heart by a stake, and then he was diagnosed with having a hole in his heart after the film wrapped. He had to have surgery to have it closed. And one of the amnesiacs in *Archangel* actually hit a moose with his car, and ended up with amnesia. He now has no recollection of making two movies with me.

Smith: To have that following you around, I don't know if that's strangely empowering or absolutely frightening.

Maddin: I've warned Isabella to watch out for her legs, and not to fall asleep near any train tracks.

Smith: Given your condition, and these other bizarre calamities, yours would seem a wholly honest formalist aesthetic.

Maddin: I'm glad you used the word "honest." I try to be as honest as possible all the time. It may seem odd that a movie with as many apparently bizarre things in it could be described as honest, but I like to put things in for a reason. They have to have a certain psychological source—a neurotic source, or even a paranoid source. Some sort of source or emotion that I've experienced, at least. I don't feel that I'm any different than the average person; I'm just trying to put the human condition up there in all of its multi-varied forms. The result is, I hope, honest.

Smith: I don't think you can help but be honest when you're throwing so many absurd things at the audience. I mean, it doesn't feel like absurd for absurd's sake, as we often see. It does have, and I know you get compared to David Lynch all of the time, but your films do have that kind of genuine oddness.

Maddin: In his best films, he's honest, too. *Eraserhead* is an amazing confession of what it feels like to be a father in an unplanned pregnancy, which I was, as well. When I saw it, I saw my autobiography, and it hit me like a wrecking ball. This was a guy who everyone else was touting as an absurdist or surrealist or whatever, and I just saw him as making one of the most honest, most cathartic and *not pretty* pictures of the self. It was really interesting and exciting.

Smith: Would you credit that film as one that got you into filmmaking?

Maddin: That would be one of them. That one and *L'Age d'or* by Buñuel, his second film and second collaboration with Dali. Both he and Dali claimed it was a series of unrelated gags that were funny for now explicable reason. But the fact is: whether they're unrelated or not, the overall shape of the narrative resembled that of a love story, of an unrequited love story, or a mad love story; something that, if we're lucky, we've all been through, with all its pain and insanity. Actually describing love is the mandate of the surrealist. That one was pretty inspiring to me because . . . actually, in both cases—with *Eraserhead* and *L'Age d'or*—they were movies that were primitive in many respects. They were low budget, they used nonactors or nonstars, they used atmospheres and ideas, and were unbelievably honest, frank, and, therefore, exciting to me. They made moviemaking seem possible to me. I knew that I was not the kind of person who would ever be a technically proficient filmmaker. Well, I wasn't interested in it, anyway. What excited me was finding exciting effects in low-tech, and the ideas and story. Believe me, I love great performances in films, and I even enjoy special effects pictures: I loved *Charlie's Angels: Full Throttle* and *Terminator 3* as much as anybody. I did. But nothing replaces the excitement of a primitively fashioned, surprising idea to me. And that's also doable to me, as opposed to those other pictures. So, both of those movies, *Eraserhead* and *L'Age d'or*, probably simultaneously kicked me, one in each buttock, into the director's chair.

Smith: It is an intentional artifice. When you discovered that after your first film, working backwards, were you consciously trying to emulate a certain style as an organic outgrowth from those mistakes?

Maddin: Sometimes it was. I had two concerns which kind of ran concurrently, and if they dovetailed, fine. If they didn't, that was fine, too. I wanted to design little stories that were, I hoped, original ways of showing people themselves. But I also wanted to just indulge myself in the surprisingly tasty textures of audio scratches and acting devices and cutting techniques of a forgotten film vocabulary. And for some reason, that film vocabulary seemed just as sexy and new as the women in those 1920s films. They seem sort of eternally new every time I look at them, and more beautiful each time, almost. I almost feel as if the excitement I feel is necrophilia of some sort. If that's what necrophilia is, then so be it.

Smith: At least no loved ones are getting defiled in the process.

Maddin: No one's getting hurt. Like in most cases of necrophilia, there are no victims.

Smith: Is it a lot of work to achieve your weathered style? To make it look so primitive?

Maddin: It's simpler. Although, every now and then, you have to watch that it's not straying. There's sort of a natural buoyancy in your film crew; people that . . . just know too much. They've learned to play their instruments. They're no longer a basement band, and if you're not careful, you'll accidentally allow them to bring the primitivity up to a level of mediocrity, where it's neither primitive nor sophisticated. I like keeping things raw. It was tricky with *The Saddest Music in the World*. I wanted the primitivity to be just so. I wanted it to be an almost subtle form of primitive. I didn't want to be a punk rock band; I wanted to be a good songwriting basement band. So, we really worked on the script, and made sure it was as sophisticated as possible. We worked on the music score, and everything. But the images I wanted to create the impression that they were sort of fast and loose. So, we shot with many different cameras and many different film stocks. My thinking was that I needed a working analogy to embolden me to say, "This is going to be primitive." Just by having three different cameras—three different formats of cameras—going, with each one giving a slightly different look, different film stocks and sometimes push processing, which increases grain and sometimes not. It would be like putting yourself into a childlike trance where you're creating with crayons and fingerpaints and collage and . . . whatever you feel like using at the moment. So, quite often I would say, "Give me the camera." They'd say, "Which camera?" I'd say, "Just surprise me." It kind of had that daycare kind of primitive feeling. I wanted to have at least one aspect of childhood at work in my head at all time, and that early mythmaking time, when children haven't quite figured out how the world works.

Smith: Where they create these vast inner-worlds . . .

Maddin: Yeah. And then they form their own spontaneous and erroneous connections. Just sort of fill the film with those little errors that keep harkening back to that kind of childhood invention.

Smith: But there must be some kind of tremendous skill to be able to catch those accidents, get them up on the screen, and not look like a rank amateur.

Maddin: Yeah. I'm getting a little bit better at it. I've learned to move the camera a bit more recklessly, and just trust that happy accidents will happen along with the unfortunate ones. Just to trust inevitability enough. And if they don't happen, then there's some other reckless plan that will come to the rescue.

Smith: Are you, then, left with a mountain of film at the end of the shoot?

Maddin: On this one we had a pretty high shooting ratio. I think it was ten- or twelve-to-one.

Smith: Not quite Michael Bay levels, but—

Maddin: No. But every now and then I shoot something, and it's just one-to-one. Not surprisingly, that's even more primitive. On this one, though, I got the cooperation of my DOP, a really sweet guy, Luc Montpellier. I just said, "I hope you don't mind other people shooting every now and then. For one thing, I really need to look through the camera myself, and pull the trigger. And I'd like to cover some scenes like a drunken crew would cover the Super Bowl, people just swarming around with Super 8 cameras and 16mm cameras, and just film things from as many angles as possible." Work quickly. Sometimes, I get really discouraged on a set by how slow and meticulous everything gets. It takes all of the life out of the shoot, and fills me with ulcers. I'm just ulcerated at the end of one of those things. But it becomes a point of pride for me to get as many shots as possible. Plus, you get different eyes and different aesthetics working that way. It's still lit by the DOP in consultation with me, but with the various shots there's different framing. It's endlessly surprising when you're watching rushes.

Smith: You've worked with a lot of different cinematographers, and shot quite a bit yourself. Does it take much work getting your DP's to respond to your style?

Maddin: It's kind of weird. I want them to understand what I like right away, but I'm also this weird utopian; I want everyone to feel they're contributing, and that they can satisfy themselves with their own contributions. But it's hard finding the right combination. I think Luc was the best because he made it a point to watch all of my movies. And we watched other movies together, and talked about what I liked. So, he sort of understood how far he could go with me, and he made a million suggestions that I would never have thought of, but they were within the boundaries. Plus, he has a great temperament. I'm one of those people who don't like confrontation that much. Quite often, just to avoid it, I'll just give into the collaborator, and that's when the picture becomes less me. That's why I found the perfect partner here. He's got the ideal temperament for me; he's so gracious and nonconfrontational. I don't know how he liked it, because I become a horrible minefield on the set. I go off so easily, but he never set me off once. He really delivered the goods.

Smith: You said you watched a lot of different films. You also said earlier that you were inspired by Lon Chaney. Were you watching any of his films?

Maddin: A lot of his films aren't particularly shot that well. I watched those almost just for script inspiration. There *is* only one Lon Chaney; you can't direct people to act like that. He's irreplaceable. It'd be like trying to say, "Do it like Buster Keaton would." Some of Chaney's films are shot rather unimaginatively, but they're just so inspiring anyway. They seem so timeless and exciting. They're more like inspiring banners to wave over the production just by watching them before or during. Other movies that I like to watch, just for the look of them, are Max Reinhardt's *A Midsummer Night's Dream*, anything ever shot by Vigo or his cinematographer, Boris Kaufman, and then just John Alton film noirs and things like that.

Smith: Henri Alekan?

Maddin: Yeah, yeah! These things just have instant atmosphere. They just seem to define the countries or eras they came from. They don't belong to the eras; they *are* the eras.

Smith: You mention defining a country, it's said that your films are quintessentially Canadian.

Maddin: Well, I think Canadians are such lousy self-mythologizers, that I made it a little project of mine to mythologize my own country, maybe get some other people to do the same thing. And maybe, by the end of my generation, there will be a nice little mythos there. Nothing would thrill me more.

Smith: That would be a thrill shared by discerning filmgoers everywhere. Shine on, sir!

The Saddest Music in the World starts today in New York and Los Angeles. It is a must-see.
Faithfully submitted,
Mr. Beaks

"I wanted to use as much Bram Stoker text as possible"

Guy Maddin/ 2004

Extract transcribed from the audio commentary track of *Dracula: Pages from a Virgin's Diary*, published by Zeitgeist Video, May 18, 2004. Reprinted by permission of the publisher.

I wanted to use as much Bram Stoker text as possible for the intertitles. Every now and then I had to tweak some of my own verbiage in there, but strangely enough in spite of this being a danced version of *Dracula*, I aspired to make this the most faithful adaptation of the novel filmed yet [. . .] I was pretty intimidated by the prospect of shooting a ballet. So I read the book pretty carefully. . . . Stoker has a lighthouse in the novel. I think he and Freud were looking over each other's shoulders, while writing around that time, the 1890s [. . .] I felt really lucky making this picture, because of the number of chances I had to integrate filmic things every few seconds, not that filmic things and balletic things are inimical to each other [. . .] There are all these little filmic things—double exposures, some cross-cutting—that just can't be done on the live stage. But there are tremendous opportunities to add little pirouetting props—I use the word "pirouetting" because it is one of the few ballet terms I can still remember from the production. "Boré" is the other word that comes to mind right now. [. . .] There's the first diary in the movie. Diaries seem to pop up quite a bit. I came up with this alternate title for the movie, *Pages from a Virgin's Diary*, because the original broadcasters, the CBC, didn't like the idea of it just being called *Dracula*. I don't know if it was for legal reasons or what. But it was a chance for me to use the word "virgin" in the title, which is always a thrill. And the diary, of course—which is kind of a ticking time bomb for all men. Men get what they deserve when the read their girlfriends' diaries. *I* keep a diary and I leave it lying around for anyone to read, figuring they'll get what they deserve, but no one ever read it, so I published it. Nobody even bought it. [. . .] I've often wondered who the virgin in the film's title is. You always think of women when you hear that, but it's the men who seem to be displaying virginal naiveté, and intense virgin pressured jealousies. [. . .] This whole project was an assignment I didn't want to take, actually. But I'm really glad I did. It's a nice way to spend an autumn afternoon, shooting vampirettes with breast implants. Implanted into their costumes. That was Paul David's idea, not mine.

The Pleasures of Melancholy: An Interview with Guy Maddin

Marie Losier and Richard Porton/2004

From *Cineaste*, Vol. 26, No. 3 (June 2004), 18–25. Reprinted by permission of the publisher.

A zany confection that combines Expressionist Weltschmerz, musical-comedy uplift, and melodramatic twists that might make Douglas Sirk blush, *The Saddest Music in the World* is instantly identifiable as an archetypal Guy Maddin film. Like his previous innovative work, Maddin's latest (and, according to some commentators, most "accessible") film both blends seemingly archaic genres and styles in a self-consciously "retro" fashion and manages to personify an iconoclastic sensibility that transcends his joyous pilfering of the cinematic past. His cinematic scavenging is not in any way aligned to some dreary postmodernist notion of pastiche but in fact reflects genuine, undiluted enthusiasm for the glories, absurdities, and submerged pleasures of film history.

From Maddin's first experimental short—*The Dead Father*—to *The Saddest Music*, his infatuation with movies has also fueled a deeply autobiographical compulsion to mythologize his own life. *The Saddest Music* may have been inspired by every thirties musical with a gung-ho impresario and a wide-eyed ingénue, but the fact that he sets this extravaganza in a fanciful version of Depression-era Winnipeg (his home town) instead of Broadway or Hollywood reflects both a profoundly Canadian sense of self-deprecation and a whimsical desire to transform frigid Manitoba into a locus of glamour and mystery.

Since Maddin has little truck with surface naturalism, he chose to create a gauzy thirties Winnipeg on a set constructed within the city's largest building, the Dominion Bridge factory. Jam-packed with convoluted plots, subplots, and ancillary narrative tributaries, this is one movie that almost defies lucid synopsizing. The cynosure is of course the protracted contest to reward the country either blessed or cursed with the world's most melancholy music. A hyperkinetic Canadian expatriate and Broadway honcho Chester Kent (played by Mark McKinney and named after the Jimmy Cagney character in Lloyd Bacon's *Footlight Parade*), returns home to claim the prize for the U.S.A., a country not noted for its ability to mourn. Kent shows up with his amnesiac, not to mention nymphomaniac, girlfriend, Narcissa, (Maria de Medeiros) and encounters an old flame—the imperious beer magnate and double amputee, Lady Port-Huntly (Isabella Rossellini). Complications abound in an invigoratingly over-the-top fashion when Chester's brother Roderick, who has reinvented himself as a gloomy Serbian cellist, turns up as a contestant, and we learn that he was once in love with clueless Narcissa. As the wacky proceedings reach their crescendo, Mexican mariachi bands engage in doleful battle with Scottish bagpipers, and Lady Port-Huntly achieves temporary bliss with glass, beer-filled legs designed by Chester and Roderick's alcoholic father Fyodor. Fyodor's soulful rendition of "Red Maple Leaves" on an upturned piano cheerfully sends up nationalist fervor; in Maddin's world turned upside down love of country always loses out to l'amour fou.

Of course, a mere plot synopsis cannot do justice to Maddin's intransigently idiosyncratic style. As Mark Peranson observes, "(I)n Maddin's films, viewers are met by the constant changing of perspective, close-ups and long shots, the alternations of iris shots, occasional bursts into color, rapid fire micro-montages, all seemingly approached four sheets to the wind, with a shooting and editing approach more based on intuition than storytelling." This sort of stylistic vertigo is actually somewhat more pronounced in Maddin's earlier films. Yet *The Saddest Music* unquestionably reassembles many of the director's most cherished motifs. Narcissa's amnesia evokes the delirious, memory-impaired soldiers staggering off to battle in *Archangel* during the last days of World War I. Tributes to old movies that are both earnest and ironic (but never facetious) are also apparent in almost all of Maddin's shorts and features: To cite one of many examples, the name of *Archangel*'s protagonist (John Boles, the bland leading man of thirties Hollywood)—and that movie's loving tribute to war movies such as Hawks's *The Road to Glory* and "amnesia films" like Mervyn Le Roy's *Random Harvest*—evoke an overheated melodramatic ambience that exemplifies Maddin's desire to create a "cathartic" cinema. Men vying for the love of the same woman surface in, among other films, *Tales of the Gimli Hospital*, *Careful*, and *The Heart of the World*. Father figures, whether benevolent, malevolent, or tyrannical, loom large in *The Dead Father*, *Careful*, *Odilon Redon*, and *Cowards Bend the Knee*. Equally steeped in classic literature and pop culture, (both respectable and schlocky) Maddin wears his erudition lightly. As the following interview makes evident, he is as smitten with The Ramones as with Nabokov, as tickled by Mexican genre cinema as by Carl Theodor Dreyer. A lifelong hockey fan, Maddin's late father was the manager of the Winnipeg Maroons (winner of the Allan Cup for amateur hockey in 1963.) It also should be noted that this proudly individualistic director's career was nurtured by one of Canada's most resourceful film collectives, The Winnipeg Film Group.

Cineaste interviewed Maddin over French toast while he was in New York in March for a preview screening of *The Saddest Music in the World*, the opening night attraction of the Museum of Modern Art's "Canadian Front" series. We then called him at his home in Winnipeg for a brief followup session. A charming conversationalist, Maddin's interview patter seamlessly combines autobiographical directness with the flair of a seasoned performer.
—Richard Porton

Cineaste: Although *The Saddest Music in the World* is your first musical, I gather that you've wanted to work in this genre for some time. Wasn't your abandoned project, *The Dikemaster's Daughter*, conceived as a musical?
Guy Maddin: Frankly, I don't think I was ready to make a musical. So, when by chance that film fell apart, it was probably a stroke of good luck. I probably would have ended up dropping all the musical numbers. That actually happened with James Brooks's *I'll Do Anything*. It was actually shot as a musical and then all the songs were stripped from the movie before its release.

But I've always liked the idea of a musical. I've never felt that movies are obliged to represent reality. I do believe that, if they want to be good, they are obliged to represent reality transformed.

This is true in many of the arts—not only musicals, but also mime, dance, painting, as well as silent films—anything that isn't a literal document. They can transform reality in mysterious ways and take short cuts to emotion that more literal-minded documents have to work a lot harder to achieve. So my movies have always been as stylized as musicals without being musicals. And I remember trying to promote—if I've ever really promoted anything—my movie *Careful* as an opera without singing. It has the plot of an opera, the sets of an opera, the stylization of an opera; it just didn't have any singing.

Cineaste: The musical number that recurs throughout *The Saddest Music*—Jerome Kern's "The Song Is You"—seems to sum up some of these short cuts to emotion.

Maddin: That song reduces the emotional experience of love to its basics. More than any other audio experience, music is most connected in people's memories to romance. Every crush, every affair, every relationship you've ever had is welded to a song, or a number of songs, forever. No matter what happens to the relationship, that song will make it come alive for you—your chest, your fevered head. I still can't endure listening to two 1976 Peter Frampton releases—"I'm in You," and "Show Me the Way"—without having some morbid flashback. I'm immediately taken back to a urinal that I'm straddling, with both legs and a dripping heart, in a bar in Winnipeg. Those songs sum up the agonies of 1976 twenty-eight years later. And I suspect, any time some one wants to kill me, those songs could be a double-blasted pair of Frampton deathblows. "The Song Is You" is a kind of uber-song; an anthem that signifies everything that music can do to the heart.

Cineaste: Of course, you've always specialized in melodrama—a very "operatic" genre.

Maddin: Right, it's stylized—or as I was trying to explain last night at the MoMa screening, it's life uninhibited as opposed to life exaggerated. It's a legitimate genre, and done well it's beautiful. By the same dictum that everything tastes more or less like chicken, every movie is more or less melodrama. Some aren't very much melodrama. [Laughs.] But, when melodrama is well done, it gets you into one of those great, cathartic crying jags. I'd some day like to make a movie that works as a weepie.

Cineaste: Like a Douglas Sirk film, for example?

Maddin: Yeah, I just finished watching *Imitation of Life* again on video. The first time I watched it I was just delighted by it as a confection and thought it was rather funny, as well as a little bit moving. Now, it just wipes me out.

Cineaste: From what we've read, there's not much of Kazuo Ishiguro's original script left in *The Saddest Music*. Is there a residue of his original conception?

Maddin: Yes, his spirit is there, or some residue, or a smudge. [Laughs.] Whatever the word is; you have to choose the word carefully. But I can tell you what's still there. His title—which I liked and the premise—to determine which country has the saddest music in the world. Political satire has never been my favorite muscle to flex; it often dates quite quickly. But his observations were pretty timeless, especially the sad fact that Third World nations, who are basically in need of alms from the "have" countries, are forced to be in competition with other needy nations. They have to act worse off than they actually are—it's sort of like competitive street begging. It's a horrible, undignified routine they're forced into to exaggerate their own privations when they're already well worthy of sympathy and empathy. This was his chief concern, as well as the fact that there's usually a winner. For example, in the eighties, Ethiopia, with its world-famous drought, managed to get sexy for a few seasons when pop stars were singing all kinds of songs on its behalf. At the same time, many other needy nations could only look on in envy. But, like any other fashion, people get tired eventually. Hemlines drop, the Bolivians have an earthquake, and everyone clambers over to throw their charity dollars at that.

Cineaste: We read—perhaps it was in your diaries—that you consider *The Saddest Music* your "anatomy of melancholy" movie. This seems to key into Burton's implicit assumption that melancholy can be a great source of pleasure.

Maddin: Yeah, you only have to listen to some of your favorite sad songs to realize that they're putting you in a good mood. Dreyer's *Ordet* delights me, as does listening to the boys' choir sing in *Day of Wrath* as the old witch is tied up to the ladder. And listening to Paul Robeson sing "Gloomy Sunday," that famous "suicide song"; that's thrilling to me! I guess it's just cathartic, and catharsis always feels great. I almost wished I pushed it a bit more in the movie. One brother, played by Mark McKinney, is always repressing his sadness with a George M. Cohan effervescence while the other gives in to sadness. I almost wished I had the McKinney character just breaking out and blubbering. Or when Roderick is admiring the glass legs for the first time, he could have cried at their sublime beauty, or cry whenever he fights. There's just no end to it; *The Anatomy of Melancholy* is thousands of pages thick!

Cineaste: You've talked about *Footlight Parade* being an influence on the film. And there are similar impresarios in many other musicals—e.g. the Warner Baxter character in *42nd St.*

Maddin: Yeah, it was dangerous to invoke those names to Mark McKinney. Then you run the risk that he'd imitate those characters, which ends up somewhere on the dial close to sketch comedy. My strategy concerning pastiche has always been to avoid it as much as possible, knowing that it's going to be detected somehow anyway. But I like to make things as straight as possible and make a movie that seems completely unaware of any movie that has come before it. You can then let viewers decide for themselves whether this is pastiche or parody.

Cineaste: And you want to avoid the label of "camp."

Maddin: I've never minded camp that much and I can watch—I don't know if they qualify as camp—"Santo" Mexican wrestling movies for hours on end. But it seems that it's a term that's not usually thrown around as a compliment. It's sometimes hard to avoid that tag, though. I still get it of course. That means someone watched a bit of the films anyway, so I'm pleased [laughs].

Cineaste: Do you and George Toles often write with particular actors in mind?

Maddin: Yes, George Toles wrote the lines in *The Saddest Music* with Isabella [Rossellini] in mind—and this was long before we even approached her. It doesn't mean that she still didn't have trouble getting her tongue around some of them. She sort of feels her way into a role and doesn't necessarily repeat the lines the same way twice. She just likes to get the meaning and say whatever comes to mind. She then leaves it up to her co-actors to respond accordingly; it's more like a theater or Altman-like experience. I also have a few favorite Winnipeg actors, who speak the way the lines are written. The lines are very stylized. My friend George writes most of the dialog in our collaborations, and he actually speaks in this weird, mannered way. He has a strange command of the English language. He speaks like a book written many years ago. Since the dialog is very mannered, it brings actors with many degrees of talent into the film speaking with the same degree of stylization. While making melodramatic movies, it's very handy to have melodramatically stylized dialog.

I had an out of town friend come to Winnipeg—the cinematographer Ed Lachman who shot *Far From Heaven, Erin Brockovich, The Virgin Suicides*, etc. He's in Winnipeg now shooting, and I took him out last Friday night to meet some of my friends. He was slack-jawed with disbelief when he saw that these friends of mine speak like characters out of *Footlight Parade*. They wear spats and get into arguments that would pass the

Hays Code, swearing at each other but not using the usual profanities that I like to use. They're completely anachronistic and it's completely unaffected. They're fully functioning members of society—doctors, lawyers, and magistrates. They're just living in another decade—verbally anyway.

Cineaste: How do you and Toles divide the labor while working on scripts?

Maddin: It varies from script to script and one, *Twilight of the Ice Nymphs*, he wrote in its entirety on his own. We start discussing a basic idea and come up with a treatment (almost always on the phone, for some reason.) When we first became friends twenty-four years ago, we must have spent five or six hours on the phone every day. We were like teenage girls, each of us lying on beds on either end of the phone with cotton balls between our toes talking about movies. Now when we begin talking about treatments, we start bandying things back and forth. After I receive his script and transcribe it onto the word processor, I might add the odd scene or make an embellishment. I feel a bit guilty getting the screenplay credits that I have been getting. I fought, but a bit lamely, to have my name removed from the screenplay credit for *The Saddest Music*. He was fine with my credit. But I don't mind saying, on the record, that he deserved full screenplay credit—with a story by Toles, Maddin, and Ishiguro. And even Nev Fichman, one of my producers, contributed some important story ideas.

Cineaste: Since the dialog in your films is so stylized, I assume there's little room for improvisation.

Maddin: When I first started out, I didn't really work that much with actors and kept them in the dark. I assembled everything through montage. In *The Saddest Music in the World*, it suddenly became different. I had a group of actors, many with theater backgrounds, who were used to playing off each other. They were good listeners as well as good actors. Since they listened to each other's performances and responded to them, each take was drastically different. I let them do just about whatever they wanted to. I figured if I didn't like it I could just cut it out during the editing. I usually forbid improvisation, because it would ruin George's mannered dialog and it would sound inappropriately modern. But everything Isabella [Rossellini] says is so musical and mannered anyway that she got a special dispensation. She could say whatever she wanted. Most of the actors I've hired couldn't improvise more than a few words in the Tolesian manner.

Cineaste: Your fondness for the transition from silent films to sound, and the intermittent Technicolor scenes from the period, seems to come out in *The Saddest Music*. Of course, you had to move the story up to the Depression era.

Maddin: I had to tweak it up to 1933 to find an analogy to what Ishiguro had in his original story. He set it in London during the mid-eighties, just on the eve of Perestroika. This brought down the Iron Curtain and opened up the huge exploitable market in Eastern Europe. The sponsor of the contest was a London-based distiller, who used the contest just to get a lot of free advertising for his business. I found an analogy in the eve of the dissolution of Prohibition, the fact that Winnipeg was near the American border, and the use of radio. But it was close enough to the early sound period. It was still in the pre-Technicolor days. Color scenes were occasionally snuck in for musical numbers—e.g. *Wedding of the Painted Doll*, the Ziegfeld film from 1929, *Glorifying the American Girl*. Howard Hughes's *Hell's Angels* has a costume ball in Technicolor. It was just an excuse to put in a little bit of color. I do like the part-talkie for what it represents—when the camera couldn't have been as mobile as people would have liked. They had the option to have people talk or not talk. In fact, they were adding these talkie scenes after they wrapped production—sometimes three or four months afterwards. In theory, it sounds great. If a scene doesn't need dialog, why do you have to hear people saying, "I love you, I love you too, I love you back and forth"?—the same way a scene only includes those sounds effects that are important or the novelist will only include the descriptions that are important. Anything else would be extraneous.

It thrills me that you needn't be so literal-minded in a part-talkie. You can go into mime when that's appropriate, or into dialog when that's absolutely essential. Of course, in 1929 it added up to mostly a gimmicky act of desperation. Adding talk actually saved the prospects of some pictures. I've chosen to look at it as a great opportunity rather than a horrible, crippling hybrid. Hitchcock's *Blackmail* from this period thrills me. For years, I didn't want to watch early Hitchcock since Hitchcock is all about sophistication to me and I thought primitive Hitchcock would disappoint me. But I love how the sound goes in and out and there's some mime. It's a great period of invention. The world's brightest filmmakers were making up a vocabulary as they worked. It's not like children learning a language from their parents; these were children learning a language that they had created themselves. They learned quickly, and it's really exciting for me to observe what went on in that time. The amount of growth in that period from 1929–1932 is phenomenal. Mamoulian's *Love Me Tonight*, the most sophisticated musical ever, came out just three years after talkies were introduced. It's the equivalent of that great period when Picasso and Matisse were just getting going—so much fecundity and excitement. I try to put myself in that same curious childhood state of mind while making the movies. And I try to make my movies recklessly, as if I'm a child with a full box of crayons. The hope is that the films won't be primitive for their own sake, but will seem enthusiastically primitive.

Cineaste: Do you usually have specific visual ideas in mind when working on your scripts?

Maddin: I always have a visual scheme in mind quite early in the project, but, mainly because of economic factors, it never works out in quite the way I had planned. Even in the early days when I made the sets myself, the fact is that I'm not a very good carpenter and things turned out differently. It's just like when you sit down to write—you never know exactly what you're going to say and one sentence leads to another. Things sort of evolve, and I often have a piece of music that I'm really determined to get into a movie. It's just so visually evocative, and strangely enough, every now and then, I'll shoot a whole scene with a piece of music and it doesn't fit. But I'll try the music in another part of the movie and it will fit perfectly. The way picture and music marry up is unpredictable—just as people's marriages are unpredictable. But it's very pleasing when it works. My short, *The Heart of the World*, is the only movie I've ever made which looked and felt exactly as I hoped it would. By some fluke, it turned out exactly as I had planned. Everything else has been very difficult to control. You just do damage control in terms of little nudges and steering along the way. I've used this comparison before, but I think of making a movie as being like trying to guide a missile while riding it bareback, using your thighs to change its direction. You can really only get it on target minimally. Once a movie is launched, a movie seems to be headed in one place and one place only. So it's up to you to aim it correctly in preproduction before you launch—i.e., considering the casting and the other details.

Cineaste: Although you mentioned that you're not fond of political satire, I suppose that there's a certain satirical point embedded in the fact that your Cagney/Warner Baxter figure is a Canadian. An impresario of this sort seems quintessentially American. Is he repressing his "Canadian-ness"?

Maddin: Well, there are so many Canadians who come down to America and are very successful. There are the secret tribe of Canadians who lived in Hollywood; Mary Pickford, for example. It's a certain kind of Canadian, the Canadian who turns his back on Canada. And then there's the kind of Canadian who embraces his heritage or ethnicity. There aren't many patriotic Canadians, but in Winnipeg there's a huge Ukrainian population. So someone named Danielle might adapt her Ukrainian name—Danishka. She might then start wearing traditional Ukrainian garb. You get a lot of that in Canada, much more than in America. America is called the "melting pot," while Canada is considered a "cultural mosaic." This sort of thing usually just emerges two or three generations into a family's stay in Canada. People who have never been to their ancestors' homeland are the most fiercely Serbian, Lithuanian, or Armenian. Good Armenian friends of mine, who have never been to Armenia, turn out to be the most intensely Armenian people. I'm not making fun of it in the film, that's just the way it is. It's a fairy tale structure, but there aren't three brothers as there are in most fairy tales. The father stands in for the third brother. He's a patriotic Canadian, although it's really hard to find patriotic Canadians. That's why he ends up being pretty doddering and foolish.

Cineaste: But you manage to get the Canadian flag into a few of your movies.

Maddin: Yeah, my version of it. Our current Canadian flag was designed in 1965 and it just looks so "sixties." I just thought it should have a little more tradition. The maple leaf has been our emblem forever. I felt a big, veiny expressionist maple leaf would look much better than that sort of sixties, Roy Lichtenstein flag we ended up with.

Cineaste: It's like a logo.

Maddin: Yeah, that's what it is. It's like an oil company logo. That's almost traitorous for me to say. I love the maple leaf. I just wish our flag had a few more veins in it! Less logo, more organic.

Cineaste: Did you find it farfetched when Jonathan Rosenbaum termed *Careful* a movie about Canadian repression?

Maddin: It probably isn't very farfetched. I sort of even had this in the back of my mind, even though the film never actually states what country it's set in. I guess I decided to make it when I'd been walking around in the Swiss Alps a bit and was reading some Robert Walser and other people who had taken a lot of mountain strolls. I've never spent that much time in those countries and I hate doing research. So it's a Canadian film, I'm a Canadian, and it's as Canadian as they come. It's about me, so I guess it's about Canada.

Cineaste: Was Leni Riefenstahl's *The Blue Light* an influence on *Careful*?

Maddin: I hadn't even seen it until I got this fan letter from Riefenstahl. She was very flirtatious. She sent me a photograph of herself taken many, many years earlier. Then some photos of some underage nude girls that she'd photographed—the Nuba. She said, "This is my little girl and it's from me." I was once in Munich, the city where she lived, at a film festival. I was there with an acquaintance of mine, George Hickenlooper. He was trying to get me to talk to her; "Wanna talk to Leni?" he'd say. I didn't want to; I just imagined her Teutonic thighs squeezing the brains out of my head. Sure enough, when I saw *The Wonderful, Horrible World of Leni Riefenstahl*, she had this sidekick—I think he was called Helmut—carrying around her oxygen tank. He seemed to be quite a whipped dog of a man; this ninety-eight-year-old woman ordering this guy into sexual service. I'm just as glad that I didn't get into that time machine! There's time travel and there's time travel. I never claimed that living that in the past would be better than living now. I like to look at certain women from the past in movies. And it's also a matter of their inaccessibility—the keyhole stuck in the door that's seven or eight decades thick makes them very alluring to me. But some periods are better not accessed. And, whatever prom of the mind Leni Riefenstahl evokes, I'm staying home!

Cineaste: How did you go from working in a bank to being a filmmaker?

Maddin: I just stumbled into this. It certainly wasn't part of a master plan. Like so many twenty-something slackers, I just knew that I didn't want to be working at a regular job. I was pretty lazy, but that banking job was not suited to my temperament. I spent a lot of time crying in the vault. Literally—I'd say, "I'm going into the vault," and would put my head in my hands and weep for twenty minutes. When I quit, it felt good. I didn't know I was going to start making films then. It was only the day I quit that I snuck into a very dark room at the university with a friend who said, "They play movies in here." I started watching films like Luis Buñuel's *L'Age d'or* and I was immediately hooked. I began to habitually sneak into movie screenings. I became a fixture and they eventually let me take the films home for the weekend so I could watch them on my projector. And eventually there were videos. Every now and then when I'm complaining a lot, I realize how lucky I am. It's really great. I meet so many people who are dreaming of working in film. They want to give me their scripts or tapes of films they've done. They remind me so much of myself when I was starting out. You just can't dismiss these people. You can watch their movies and then dismiss them. [Laughs.]

Cineaste: You really seemed to start from scratch with your first film, *The Dead Father*.

Maddin: Yeah, I didn't have a visual style at all in my first film. I just wanted to get some images on film and tell a story. I thought that if I had any strength at all, I'd be a primitive. Usually being a primitive is a weakness, because people try to make a certain kind of film and fail because they're not good enough yet. So I knew I wouldn't be good enough and thought that I'd make an intentionally primitive movie; I'll just make a kind of dream. I had this autobiographical feeling that I was trying to get at. My father had died a few years earlier, but he frequently revisited me in dreams. I thought I would get the dreams—these fragmented episodes that dreams resemble—down on film and hopefully create in the viewer the same feeling that I had as the dreamer. I failed, I think. But during the course of making that movie, I accidentally stumbled across a few visual tricks. I just started to learn a little more about what can be done with light and shadows, and accidents. Mostly accidents—I decided to make all of my technological accidents happy accidents. So very early on, I was congratulating myself for embracing the primitiveness that proved inevitable. Now I'm more stubbornly sticking to it. It's sort of like The Ramones. I just refuse to learn how to play my instrument. The Ramones will never go away, as far as I'm concerned. I work more slowly than they did, but I hope that by the time I go away I'll have a nice body of work.

Cineaste: At some point, you began to consciously smear Vaseline on the camera lens.

Maddin: I was using Vaseline just to blur out Winnipeg. [Laughs.] I didn't want anyone to see the world I lived in.

Cineaste: You don't see much of the actual Winnipeg in your movies.

Maddin: No. And then finally I made it a point to mythologize Winnipeg. But that meant that I had to build a Winnipeg because you still don't want to see the "real" Winnipeg. Other filmmakers are showing the real Winnipeg, including some friends of mine. Ed Lachman, the cinematographer, is shooting the real Winnipeg in his movie. It's going to look pretty amazing, so maybe we'll get that city the attention it doesn't deserve. [Laughs.]

Cineaste: Did you feel at one point that all of your films include variations on a few themes? Many of them include father figures, brothers, and scenarios involving two men in love with the same woman.

Maddin: Yeah, those are autobiographical themes. I don't know what it is with me. I was such a terrified child. I was always scared that my dad was just going to die on me. When he finally did, I was shocked that I wasn't hit with the tsunami of grief that I thought I would be. I wasn't even upset. I realized that some psychological mechanism had kicked in—the grief would overdraw me at the bank and I would have to pay on the installment plan. I make these weekly payments during my dreams, paying in tears for all of the loved ones I have lost. I don't get happy at the appropriate moments, or in my dreams either. My father's been dead longer than he was alive in my life. It's a literary theme and fathers mean so much. I'm beginning to get a better idea of how fathers resonate throughout literature: weak fathers, absent fathers, tyrannical fathers. So much of literature is just the family.

And then sexual jealousy is a constant theme. For the longest time—it's almost healed over now—there was a huge scar on my psyche from my very first love and all of the jealousy that sprang from it. Everyone was jealous. There were all kinds of infidelity, all of those great melodramatic operatic, almost homicidal incidents. This relationship reminded me of those operas where people were falling on daggers, poisoning each other, hiding behind curtains, and climbing on ledges. It was very traumatic. I feel that I won the war, but I definitely came out of it with a lot of shrapnel. I feel these big incidents from my life can be illustrated in a sort of melodramatic shorthand quickly. Everyone has been jealous about something at one time or another.

And then competitive brothers also involve melodramatic shorthand. I actually have no competition with my siblings at all.

When I was young, I began to understand some great works of literature by approaching them as fairy tales. There was a template placed upon literature by the Brothers Grimm and Victor Hugo. And then I started to understand Faulkner through these terms. Some authors are more approachable than others using these terms, but it was a way into certain moments in Faulkner. I began to understand more and more how he worked and discarded the fake fairy tale entrance. As a starting point for beginning a story, I'm just comforted by fairy tale structures. Maybe as I get a little bit older and more sophisticated, while maintaining "primitivity," I'll abandon the fairy tale structure and go for something a little more unpredictable. Like so many movies of the 1930s, *The Saddest Music in the World* has a fairy tale structure. Last year I borrowed the plot of Euripides' *Electra* for *Cowards Bend the Knee* and blended in elements from *The Hands of Orlac* and my own family. I just tried to use structures that are time-tested—and then messed with them so much that no one would give them a warrantee of more than a month. [Laughs.] You take this 2,500-year-old structure that served Euripides so durably and then break it down.

Cineaste: Why did you initially conceive *Cowards Bend the Knee* as a peep show installation?

Maddin: It was a commission. I kept things autobiographical; as a pre-adolescent, I spent a lot of time drilling holes in walls and staring at people. Little Brother is watching; my version of *1984*. I just thought that, to even the score, it was only fair to let the world look in a peephole and see me. It was a chance to be as honest as possible, and as cruel as possible to myself. That was cathartic for me. The only chance I had to make an installation interesting to another person was to be as lurid and self-flagellating, and self-pitying, as possible—all of those nauseating qualities.

Cineaste: It seems clear that you're as entranced with literature as with movies. You speak of your fondness for Nabokov in *From the Atelier Tovar*. Perhaps it wasn't conscious, but there appear to be a few echoes of Nabokov's *Glory* in *Archangel*—e.g. the references to the anti-Bolshevik fervor at the end of World War I. In addition, were you aware of Donald Barthelme's novella *The Dead Father* when you made your film of the same name?

Maddin: *Glory* may be the one Nabokov novel I haven't read. I have a copy of it that I purchased at a garage sale in the upstairs bedroom of my beach cottage. I intended to read it, but as I get older I spend less and less time at the lake—so I haven't had that summer of glory. My inspiration for *Archangel* came from one of my many muses, a real hardcore anachronist who loves early aviation and war stories. He told me about this place where there was a lot of fighting well after the end of the Great War, simply because people seemed to have forgotten that the war had ended. The only kind of soldiers that could be drummed up for these battles were amnesiacs, people with missing limbs, and soldiers crawling to the infirmary in various states of delirium. I also thought that *Archangel* was such a charming, mystical name—a name also taken by a heavy metal band.

As far as other literary preoccupations go, I really love the Polish writer Bruno Schulz, Osip Mandelstam, the Soviet poet sent to his death by Stalin, and, strangely enough, I really like John Cheever and Raymond Carver. I came quite late to reading. But Nabokov was really my first love; literally the first serious writer I read. There's something concrete in his language. So I didn't have to look for symbols, and I read interviews with him where he eschewed symbols and Freudian subtext—in fact almost all subtext. I loved how he unfurled these miraculous, unbelievably lengthy sentences. He got very top-heavy with specificity and you thought that there was no way he could end the sentence. He would somehow find just the right word at the end of a sentence to make it conclude with a powerful punch line. After a while, there's a cumulative dream effect that results from that super-specificity; he managed to be extremely concrete and vague at the same time. I then liked exploring the vaguer shores of literature exemplified by Robert Walser, Gerard de Nerval, and Robert Musil.

I was aware of Barthelme's *The Dead Father*. It was the very first book that I ever bought. Strangely enough, I bought it at a 7-Eleven. When I was considering titles for my first film, I couldn't think of any other title but *The Dead Father*. Someone told me that you couldn't copyright a title. But Barthelme's novel was a thrill for me. I was too intimidated by traditional literature; some bad teachers in high school spoiled it for me.

Cineaste: Why did you recently decide to make a movie in Spanish?
Maddin: Yeah. I just made a movie in Spanish, and I don't speak a word of that language. We were in Winnipeg, which doesn't have many Spanish-speaking people. But many people on this film spoke Spanish, and so did many of the crew members. So, I said, "Why don't we shoot this movie in both Spanish and English?" And I got tired after the first two shots of doing it in both languages. That's the way they used to do it in the old Hollywood days—they'd shoot an English version and than a Spanish and French version. And not only in Hollywood. Carl Dreyer's *Vampyr*, for example, was shot in Danish, German, French, and a bit of English. I gave up on that and said, "Let's just do the whole thing in

Spanish." And the performances seem really good. I have no idea what they're saying [laughs]. But, luckily, my editor's sister speaks Spanish, and she's making sure that no one's getting anything mischievous in and is giving us an idea of what the best takes are. We'll see. But I'm not going to even have English subtitles. I'm just going to release it in Spanish. It can pretty much exist as a silent movie anyway. So it will be in Spanish for Spanish-speaking people—and silent for English speakers. I'd love to go to France. In a way, I've got that little bit of mischief out of my system with the Spanish project. Although I haven't used Winnipeg up, I feel like I should live for one year in France, one year in New York, one year in London. And, of course, Italy.

Cineaste: You probably got a taste of that working with Isabella Rossellini.

Maddin: With Isabella I feel that I'm getting shortchanged because she has so many Scandinavian traits.

Cineaste: So her Italian aspects are at war with her Scandinavian traits.

Maddin: Yes, her reactions to her things are these huge Mediterranean gesticulations. But she's not kissy kissy. She's just as happy with a firm handshake. I like that about her. It's very Winnipeg, she fits right in there.

Cineaste: If I understand correctly, you started writing film criticism as a corrective to unsatisfying reviews you read in magazines and newspapers.

Maddin: It's hard writing on film, especially when you're given so many bad films to write on that are bad in the same way. No, I have too much respect for good writing to feel that I could come in and offer something new. I did it for the usual reason I do something—I was broke. [Laughs.] First, I phoned up Gavin Smith, the editor of *Film Comment*. He had programmed a couple of my short movies, and he gave me Dennis Lim's phone number at *The Village Voice*. Gavin was able to give me a $100 every three months. That didn't fix anything in a hurry, but Dennis Lim was very helpful. As a matter of fact, I feel that I should be easing off on my movie writing. I'm not an academic, although I feel that I have the occasional flippant piece in me and that's about it. I just couldn't do it on a weekly basis. I only have so many tricks up my sleeve and I've run out of them already.

Cineaste: And the *Voice* has recently been publishing your *Saddest Music* diaries.

Maddin: I recently wrote a little piece for *The Village Voice* just hoping to exploit the conflict of interest—to take advantage of my being both a filmmaker and a film reviewer at the same time—to get some publicity for my movie.
Cineaste: Since your diaries are so candid, do you now have mixed feelings about publishing them?
Maddin: My feelings aren't even mixed; it's almost complete regret. Like many things I've done, it was a snap decision and probably a foolish one. Someone just said to me, "Do you want to publish these diaries?" So I handed them to him, and he published them. That was a mistake.
Cineaste: Well, it's not a mistake for us. They're quite enjoyable. It's not easy being honest, I suppose.
Maddin: It's not easy being honest and doing the damage control that comes later.
Cineaste: Do you see any parallels between being a cinephile and a hockey fan? I find it interesting, for example, that you once compared Divine (the John Waters actor) to "one of those limited role-players on a Stanley Cup winning team that you need on the fourth line." Would you say that these two interests coalesce somewhat in *Cowards Bend the Knee*?
Maddin: There aren't many cases of great artists being hockey fans, although the novelist Mordecai Richler was a huge Montreal Canadiens fan. Baseball and football seem to benefit the most from writers; there's almost a whole genre of baseball writing. For me, what makes sports special and what makes film special are two different things. Re-viewing a film is great, but rewatching a videotape of a hockey game isn't. The game doesn't get better with each viewing! It's so in the moment. But a great movie and a great game will both give me goose bumps.

I want to correct myself about Divine, however. Having watched *Polyester* again since that book was published, I have to say that Divine carries the entire team on her back in that movie. Divine gets to be Jean Beliveau and Mario Lemieux wrapped into one. I won't give her any more left-handed compliments.

There are so many great baseball movies, or at least there are many that are near great and beloved. But there's only one great hockey movie—*Slap Shot*. It really nails seventies hockey quite nicely. I noticed a lot of still photos of thirties and forties hockey games taken with a flash bulb, so that most of the game, except for some details, just receded into the deepest, darkest John Alton–like shadows—complete blackness. When preparing *Cowards Bend the Knee*, I thought it would be fun to film a hockey noir where the players could literally skate off into complete, inky obscurity and then return in a puff of blackness. Everyone could operate under the same kind of murk and mire and eternal suspicion under which all people must be viewed, as in an old episode of *The Untouchables* or an old noir filmed by John Alton.

Cineaste: Perhaps you could do an *Umbrellas of Cherbourg* type musical set in an ice rink.

Maddin: It sounds like a lot of work, and I might end up marginalizing myself even further. [Laughs.] *The Umbrellas of Cherbourg* is sort of a miracle, because it's such a beautiful film, and it's wonderful that the movie has found its audience.

Cineaste: Although *The Heart of the World* seems to pay explicit tribute to (as well as parody) Soviet cinema, does it also pay equal homage to Abel Gance's editing?

Maddin: It's interesting that you mention Gance's editing style. I was totally inspired by just how far Gance was willing to go. Not only in *Napoleon*, but also more bravely in his previous films—*La Roue* and *J'accuse* where the shots are only one frame. I was determined to do that in *The Heart of the World*. Right at the moment when the heart of the world breaks, so do the hearts of the two sibling lovers; I kept increasing the cutting speed until it was one frame for each brother. It creates the effect of merging the two brothers into one broken entity, and it's an effect borrowed completely from Gance. It's something meant for silent film, because when you watch it, even without a sound track, the speed of cutting almost fills your ears with the sound of machine guns. You can derive from Gance an editing vocabulary, virtually a handbook, that's almost completely different from anything that's commonly used. It's not like anything you see in rock videos or other kinds of montage. Unlike Gance, however, I'm not interested in creating films in a medium like "Polyvision" that can't be viewed anywhere. But he was a cocaine-fueled megalomaniac—and I love him for that.

Cineaste: You're fond of certain formats such as Super 8. But would you ever want to shoot on DV à la Lars von Trier?

Maddin: Yeah, I would. I've been watching von Trier's *Medea* a lot lately, a film of his from the eighties. He did a beautiful job with it, and I don't have any mixed feelings about that medium. It's great. I haven't found the right project for DV, but I'm thinking about it a lot. If I'm lucky enough to be making films twenty years from now, I probably will have to make my own film stock. So I better start planning to shoot on DV.

Cineaste: For some viewers, your films might be reminiscent of the self-contained worlds of Joseph Cornell boxes. Can you comment on the influence of Cornell on your work, if you think there is any?

Maddin: It's nice of you to say that; I love the idea of Cornell boxes, although I've never seen one in person. I love where he cuts in his film *Rose Hobart*; he cuts in the oddest places. Starting with *The Heart of the World*, I tried to get cuts that went on a frame too long. It was hard to do in a movie that had to be so tight, though. By the time I did a fine cut, all those Cornell cuts were missing. I really got a feeling for them, that fake randomness he had when the shots stayed on a smidgen too long. There's a genius in how he got the blue tint in *Rose Hobart* by projecting it in through the bottom of an empty jar of Noxzema (or whatever he did). It's very exciting; it's the movie that launched a million found footage movies. I love watching found footage movies, I can watch them forever. I love Arthur Lipsett, Matthias Muller, and Martin Arnold. I don't know what kind of influence Cornell has had on my work. I'm such a dilettante that maybe my knowledge will never get past the fact that he hung out with his mother quite a bit and had good proper obsessions with pretty girls. He also had a quaking, ersatz consummation with a poor man's Yoko Ono. That's good enough for me.

Cineaste: In your diaries, you speculate on reassembling *Undercover Brother* in the manner of *Rose Hobart* and give a place of pride to the Denise Richards sequences.

Maddin: I was flipping a coin back and forth. I didn't know whether to talk about Denise Richards as the Rose Hobart of our day or Alyssa Milano. My heart told me Alyssa Milano, because I did have an obsession with her at one time, and I've never been obsessed with Denise Richards. That's why I think I went with Denise Richards, in a rare moment of concealment rather than candor. Like one of those Proust tricks, where he substituted female names for male names in his autobiographical novel, I just put a harmless Denise Richards in there instead of Alyssa Milano—the most important actress of the last fifty years. [Laughs.] To be serious, I guess that's the most important Cornell influence—to become pathological about someone's image. And what's more fun—as long as you stay at least a hundred yards away from the actual person.

Cineaste: We've only seen only one example of your acting on screen—a scene with a bag over your head included in Noam Gonick's documentary on your work, *Waiting for Twilight*. Are you ever tempted to act more? Most of the films have some sort of "Guy Maddin" character, don't they?

Maddin: No, I'm not tempted to act more, I'm a terrible actor. Not only that, I can't stand looking at myself. So if I acted in one of my own movies, it would mean that I couldn't look at them. I'm happy to make movies with slimmer, younger, hairier versions of myself. They kind of act like I do—Kyle McCulloch in some of the earlier films, Darcy Fehr in *Cowards Bend the Knee*. They're basically just imitating me.

Cineaste: Although you weren't a particular fan of *Dracula* before filming *Pages from a Virgin's Diary*, did the use of dance give you some necessary distance from the material? Are there any resemblances between how Transylvania functions in *Dracula* and how you view Winnipeg?

Maddin: That's an interesting question. Dance probably gave me some necessary distance because I would never have been talked into it if it was just another adaptation. It's been done so many times. The fact that it was dance made it a huge challenge to me. When I began, I was pretty much resigned to the fact that it would be unwatchable. But I thought that I'd at least earn a paycheck and learn a lot of about filming big, swooping arcs of motion that the dancers give you and is really hard to capture. It's usually hard to give it any personality, since the camera has to be so far back. It was a coincidence that I was able to find some interesting elements in the Bram Stoker original and inject those into this very tired tale. I don't really treat Transylvania much in the movie; it's just featured in a castle included in a micro-montage. It's supposedly a place where Dracula came back and hoarded British money and money from other countries. I guess it was tied to some sort of anti-Semitic paranoia that had either Stoker, or his redneck vampire hunters, believe such a thing. I do feel a bit like Dracula in Winnipeg. I'm safe, but can travel abroad and suck up all sorts of ideas from other filmmakers—both dead and undead. Then I can come back here and hoard these tropes and cinematic devices. Gance's editing style is one example. And I sit here in almost eternal darkness all winter long and try to make these dead things live.

Cineaste: It was unusual to see a dance film where the director was in such close proximity to the dancers.

Maddin: Yeah, and the dancers love it. Dancers never get closeups and they love that. If dancers had their way, there would probably be a big "Jumbotron" like you have in football stadiums. It would be just above the stage where opera surtitles usually are. Dancers do a lot of work with their faces. They're silent movie actors, and they deserve their closeups just like everyone else.

Cineaste: Since you sometimes write of imaginary movies, what would be your dream cast?

Maddin: I actually don't like movies that have too many stars. So I'd have to have a core cast of about four people. I like those Ernst Lubitsch movies with three or four strong characters. And I'd also have to have a lot of strong character actors. Choosing from that pool, I'd take Franklin Pangborn, Eric Blore, and Edward Everett Horton. They could be my queer Greek chorus. I could throw Gary Cooper and Eddie Bracken into the mix, but that would be a horrible hodgepodge. I couldn't have Marlene Dietrich in there, because Eddie Bracken and Marlene Dietrich in the same frame would cause the audience to break into hives or puke. How about Betty Hutton, Greta Garbo, Eddie Bracken, and Gary Cooper? I haven't chosen too many contemporary actors, have I? Better throw Sean Penn in there too. [Laughs.] I'd like to see a scene between Sean Penn and Franklin Pangborn; that's for sure. Just to continue: Sean Penn and Gary Cooper would have to have a fist fight—each using the fist-fighting styles of their respective eras.

Dissecting the Branded Brain: An Interview with Guy Maddin

David Church/2006

From *Offscreen.com*, January 31, 2006. Reprinted by permission of the publisher.

The films of Guy Maddin are an uncanny amalgamation of personal obsessions and private memories made public. Maddin's fears and desires sparkle forth amid melodramatic tropes so winkingly heightened and bizarre that every new convolution begs for laughter. Filled with death, psychosexual deviancy, and familial strife, his pictures recall the unlikely history of Winnipeg's foremost native son of the cinema. Born in February 1956 to a family of Icelandic descent, young Maddin's formative years were split between the beauty shop where his mother Herdis and aunt Lil worked (directly adjacent to the Maddin family home), and the smoky realm of the cavernous Winnipeg Arena, home of the Winnipeg Maroons, the hockey team for whom Maddin's father Chas was manager. Maddin fondly remembers being lulled to sleep at night by detuned radio shows, tucked in by blankets of static fuzz as the broadcasts struggled their way across Manitoba's icebound prairie.

But not all was fond childhood memories for Maddin. His teenage brother Cameron killed himself upon the grave of a recently deceased girlfriend, and his father died suddenly some years later. In his published journals, Maddin has described sex and amnesia as two different anesthetics for the pain of loss. Amnesia is a constant state for us all, he believes, for it allows one to disavow the pains caused and incurred in everyday life—though Guy clearly has not entirely forgotten his own wounds. His early traumas surface repeatedly in his films like so much scar tissue, but he is no miserablist. A strong sense of gallows humor permeates the masochistic, almost incestuous revisitation of such old injuries.

Perhaps it is amnesia that allows him to create the way he does. He lovingly cannibalizes the visual styles and methods of archaic films, infusing his wildly surreal melodramas with a boldly postmodern (though he would not use that word) gaze into the dusty corners of cinema's past. From his memories of old radio shows to his encyclopedic (and largely self-taught) knowledge of classic film, he layers his tableaux with the grain and grime of decades long gone, evoking a time when movies were still developing anew and taking on strange lateral developments. With the help of longtime writing collaborator George Toles, Maddin makes the sort of pictures that he wishes (or literally dreams) had been made by directors both great and forgotten, but in doing so, he creates something distinctly his own—and paradoxically, something strikingly original and new in modern cinema. Along with David Cronenberg, he is perhaps the greatest and most vital of Canadian auteurs, handcrafting something fresh (and, he hopes, emotionally eviscerating) from so much artifice and potential camp.

Working almost exclusively out of Winnipeg, Maddin began filmmaking as part of the Winnipeg Film Group with his 1985 short *The Dead Father*, the story of a son revisited by the eponymous family member, and the start of a long filmic obsession with fathers both deceased and cowardly. (Maddin somehow suspected that his own father had not really died, but had gone to live with another family out of cowardice). His first feature, filmed over eighteen months, was *Tales from the Gimli Hospital* (1988), an "Icelandic folktale" of madness and necrophilia set during a smallpox epidemic within the Icelandic immigrant population of Gimli, Manitoba. This very tongue-in-cheek parody of Maddin's own cultural heritage succeeded as a midnight movie and paved the way for his second feature, *Archangel* (1990), another black-and-white part-talkie. Inspired by World War I propaganda films, it was a melodrama in an amnesia-infested outpost on the Russian frontier where no one had bothered to tell the troops that the Great War had ended. This was followed by *Careful* (1992), Maddin's first melodrama in color and his humorously pro-incest, pro-repression ode to the German mountain film.

Several years followed, during which Maddin produced a number of short films. (He routinely makes shorts between feature films, threatened all the while to be sucked back into the terminal laziness that affects him during unproductive periods.) His next feature was *Twilight of the Ice Nymphs* (1997), a 35mm big-screen fantasy that misfired in a big way for Maddin, despite its strikingly beautiful French Symbolistinspired visual style. Maddin followed the *Ice Nymphs* debacle with another series of short films, gradually building up the confidence and acclaim needed to helm another feature. Among these shorts was the frenzied mini-epic *The Heart of the World* (2000), Maddin's most fully realized homage to the Soviet school of montage.

2001–2003 was a watershed period for Maddin, who directed and released three feature films in succession—no laziness there! The first, *Dracula: Pages from a Virgin's Diary* (2002), was a filmic version of the Royal Winnipeg Ballet's *Dracula*; although Maddin says that male jealousy was the story's driving factor, his film also emphasizes the xenophobia at the heart of Bram Stoker's novel in a way lacking from all other film adaptations. *The Saddest Music in the World* (2003), starring Isabella Rossellini, was Maddin's largest production to date and perhaps his most critically lauded feature. This vividly elaborate melodrama about a search for the world's saddest music took on a politically allegorical dimension not seen in his earlier films. He concurrently directed *Cowards Bend the Knee* (2003), a heavily autobiographical peepshow installation subsequently released as a feature; it told of Winnipeg Maroon "Guy Maddin" and his descent into cowardice and mass murderdom at the hands of a woman obsessed with her dead father.

With his visual, storytelling, and editing techniques now matured from their somewhat shaky beginnings, Maddin seems poised to continue his quiet coup d'cinema. He recently finished filming his latest feature, *The Brand Upon the Brain!*, a companion piece to *Cowards Bend the Knee* shot in Seattle for the Film Company. Several months ago he premiered his most recent short film, *My Dad Is 100 Years Old*, a cinematic love letter to director Roberto Rossellini, written by and starring Isabella Rossellini.

I had the opportunity to speak with Maddin from his office in Winnipeg on December 15, 2005. He shed new light on his recent work, his upcoming projects, his theories on melodrama, his reflections on a career in progress, and thoughts on some of the strange (but aren't they all!) entries in his filmography.

Offscreen: I'd like to start with *My Dad Is 100 Years Old*, your most recently premiered short. The apparent clash between Roberto Rossellini's neorealist visual style and your own very antirealistic style comes up often in discussions of the picture, despite the fact that both of you essentially make melodramas. You've remarked elsewhere that irony and

melodrama are not mutually exclusive in your movies, that the heavily ironic, self-consciously "archaic" aspects of your visual style coexist with the melodramatic sincerity of the subject matter in your films. Would you say that this compensates for the seeming clash of visual styles?
Maddin: Yeah, I've done a lot of thinking about it and I've always thought of movies as another species of bedtime story or campfire story or tall tale or dream. There's no obligation to being literally realistic anywhere. These are storytelling techniques and then photography was first invented. There were a lot of people that tried to enslave it to document the world literally—and other people tried to manipulate it to convey a truth through more artificial means. So I just don't see why melodrama and irony, or melodrama and neorealism, would be mutually exclusive. It's all just ingredients in a recipe and some recipes are better than others. In this case, I did think long and hard before tackling the Rossellini project about how the film should look. I thought for a while that I could make it look sort of like my own movies without any difficulty— that'd be easy. Or I could set out to study Rossellini's more famous neorealist works and try to imitate that look. But that didn't even seem like a valid thing to do, even if I could do it, because he actually also made a lot of movies that didn't look that way and I wanted to respect those. To imitate one of his styles and omit his other styles seemed to be as insulting to him as the general public is, because he's really largely only remembered for his black-and-white neorealist movies, when in fact he was ready to move on from that stuff just as the world was getting excited about it. It seemed wrong to try to imitate it for a number of reasons: A) it was insulting to him, B) I probably couldn't have done it anyway. So it made sense that the movie should have its own style that was neither mine nor his.

I found that Isabella's writing voice was so strong that it seemed to suggest a style that was neither her father's nor mine, but neither inimical to either. She's the one who pointed out to me that her father and I actually have a lot in common. We're both going to just shoot things whether we have enough money or not. We have a sort of "can-do" spirit, so if someone says it can't be done, we'll just go home and shoot it behind the producer's back, even in our own kitchen, if necessary. We talked about shooting much of this movie in my kitchen, literally, in the spirit of paying tribute to her father properly (but we didn't end up shooting any of it in the kitchen).

I wanted it to feel kind of dark and lonely and gloomy, so a blown-out deserted movie theatre seemed to suggest itself—we have so many of them in Winnipeg anyway! We needed a meeting place for all of these movie immortals to convene in the film to debate Roberto's final place in the firmament (they're all played by Isabella), and so a forgotten, dusty old movie theatre seemed to be the best setting for all these characters. Then there was the problem of how to, on a really small budget, show Isabella three or four times in the same frame without using massive digital effects, which would've been cost-prohibitive. I just used some really dirt-cheap (free, as a matter of fact) old Alfred Hitchcock-caliber rear screen projections to layer up the number of Isabellas in the frame. In that way it was sort of giving a little nod to the horrendously artificial rear screen that appears in Ingrid [Bergman]'s *Notorious* appearances. She and Cary Grant are strolling in front of a glaringly flapping rear screen projection of Argentina in *Notorious*.

Anyway, somehow rear screen seemed to be the most organic and complimentary solution to the problem, as there's a level of artifice in the degree of convincingness of the impersonations—after all, Isabella can only be so convincing as Alfred Hitchcock, as Charlie Chaplin, as Federico Fellini. We kept it so that each one of her characterizations was at least still 50 percent Isabella and 50 percent the person she was trying to do. And even when she does her own father's voice, with technology I could have just turned a dial and pitched her voice down so she could have sounded like Paul Robeson or Bluto and sounded like a man, and even though that wouldn't have cost anything more, I resisted the temptation because I wanted her to sound like a little girl, a daughter trying to imitate her father's voice. So it's just a matter of making the right decisions with all of the artifice at your disposal, and a style kind of just emerged, kind of the way letters somehow end up getting pointed out by an Ouija board if you just let go. We just sort of let ourselves go and made the movie and a style just spelled out for us and remained with us for the duration of the shoot.

Offscreen: And yet both of you also draw upon memories of dead fathers in similar ways for subject matter.

Maddin: Before I'd ever met Isabella, I quickly read her autobiography, and that's when I knew we'd have something to talk about, because she seemed to have some unfinished business with her dead father, as did I for the longest time. And we did hit it off instantly, not on that subject necessarily, but on the million-and-one other subjects that we both share an affection for. So there's something I understand—this sort of Hamletism that we both have where we've maybe overvalued our fathers, but we seem to feel that the world should be reminded of their existence, and that we should at least remind ourselves of their existence for a little longer than what is perhaps healthy. At least in this case Isabella has her father's centennial as an excuse—and the guy is a titan of film history and everybody deserves to be reminded of Roberto Rossellini.

Offscreen: Do you find your films being appreciated by audiences more for their ironic and archaic visual aspects or for the melodramatic core of their stories?

Maddin: I wish it was the latter, but I'm not sure. When I first started out, I know that the few people that seemed to be paying attention to the movies just seemed to like the fact that they had no narrative, even though I was trying my hardest to really make the melodramas pay off but wasn't doing such a good job of it evidently. They seemed to also remark that the visual atmospheres were something they liked, but I think the melodrama is starting to win a slightly more respectable place in the balance and taking on its proper weight. I'd be happy with a 50/50 split there. I'm just delighted by Douglas Sirk's greatest works, by the artifice, the visuals, the acting styles, the mannerisms—everything that seems unprecedented in film, and yet there's just something as ancient as Euripides' Greek tragedies in the actual stories that are both delightfully ludicrous and powerfully human and tragic at the same time. I couldn't be more delighted when there is that mix of seemingly mutually exclusive feelings going on inside me simultaneously when I'm watching. I get that same feeling from Josef von Sternberg as well, and not that many other directors. So that hybrid feeling of being hit with a wrecking ball while being tickled with a feather really delights me.

Offscreen: Much of your audience consists of art house patrons, film festival attendees, and other members of the educated middle-class—precisely the audience that has learned to scoff at melodrama and other emotionally manipulative material. Does this complicate the intended effect of your films?

Maddin: Are you saying that most savvy modern audiences resent being manipulated? Yeah, it's unfortunate, but that's just a trend and I'm willing to wait until long after I'm dead. I'm a patient man! People will come to understand someday that it's all manipulation. They're just cognizant of a certain level of it, and soon enough they'll just give into it. It's just the way long hair for everybody went out of style at one point and then it became more acceptable to wear your hair at any length you wanted—it's just hemlines. I'm fine with it. People don't understand how easily manipulated they are. They're delightfully stupid—and I include myself among that. I must've watched reality shows for a few seasons before I realized I was watching the most primitive melodramas yet. Almost everything that's unscripted is scripted melodrama; if it's not the producers putting people up to do things to create a little conflict, it's the editors manipulating the footage to create melodramatic conflict. And it's done with the way the news is packaged at night, and obviously Michael Moore will tell you that news is always packaged to be as frightening as possible, so these elements—rife with villains—are the basic ingredients of melodrama. Everyone is manipulated into reacting in a certain way, and as long as you're aware of it, I'd say that's great.

I've always heard people complaining to film students who are making their movies that "You broke dramatic illusion" somehow, but do you think a little child getting told a bedtime story has forgotten that he or she is in bed? No, dramatic illusion can be broken a million times but you can still be completely under the spell of a story. You can be watching *Fantasia* and watching dancing hippos, or you can be having an Old Testament bible story read to you, or listening to C. B. DeMille narrating an old radio play, or watching the news, or talking to your own friends at recess, but you're always being manipulated and you might as well just enjoy it.

So I'd say it's a problem, but too bad for me and too bad for the people that are letting such ridiculous pride stand in the way of their full enjoyment of art. I have a very smart friend who was devastated by the movie *Forbidden Games*, one of the great movies of all time, and he said that he resented the tears that he cried at the end because they were manipulated out of him. Yeah, by real life! By the truth that the movie is presenting in one form or another—so having feelings is nothing to be ashamed of.

Offscreen: Do you think the archaic visuals and acting styles that you employ somehow make it safer for those audiences to engage the heightened melodrama on a more emotional level?

Maddin: I think people have always kind of resented the melodrama. It's been at least a century since the word "melodrama" has fallen into disrepute, and to be called "melodramatic" has been an insult for at least a century. I think people have always resented those things, and probably a lot of men didn't like watching women's pictures, like Joan Crawford and Bette Davis pictures. I think maybe if they're watching by themselves they'll let themselves go a bit more, and home video makes it more possible to make movie viewing more like the experience of reading a book, so what you lose by sharing emotions with a big room with people in the dark, you gain by getting the privacy of a book reader's experience and you can let yourself go a bit more perhaps.

Offscreen: Some have described you as a "cult" director, and you certainly seem to have some sort of cult audience. How do you respond to that?

Maddin: I'm happy with any audience! Once again, I'd be happy if people could keep watching my movies for a few years after I die. I think it was the writer Cyril Connolly who picked some arbitrary number—I think he wanted to be read for two generations after his death, that's all—and he felt that was the most immortality he could ask for in his wildest dreams. And I think that'd be pretty wonderful. So if it's just a narrow cult demographic, I know within there are people who, on a strange night watching a movie for all the wrong reasons with all the wrong attitudes, will still be sideswiped by something now and then and might see something that even I didn't know was in my pictures.

I had an experience watching *Written on the Wind* one night—and I've seen that movie about twelve times, but on about time number six I was feeling kind of vulnerable and I think I finally accepted the artifice of a 1956 equivalent of a Euripidean stage tragedy, and somehow my sympathies lay on that night almost entirely with Robert Stack, more than any other character, whereas usually they're spread around a bit differently. At about the twenty-minute mark I got filled to the brim with dread for the poor guy, and the dread didn't stop until the movie ended, at which time I nearly collapsed on the floor, completely wrung out by the experience (more like the experience that *Imitation of Life* leaves you with), devastated by it. And I haven't had a viewing like that since, and I've tried to recreate the attitude that I had going in, but it just caught me by surprise—sideswiped, T-boned by this thing—and I don't know how often that's happened with viewers of that movie because still all the while I was delighted at the ridiculousness that Sirk managed to pull off.

So I would be very happy if someone could promise me on my deathbed that there'd be a handful of people that had an experience like that with one of my films. Now, I've never made a movie that's that emotional, but if they could just somehow have some kind of unearthly experience where they're suddenly channeling the director's most desperate hopes and actually projecting them and feeling them, that would be pretty wonderful, and I think you've got a chance to do that every now and then.

I finally saw the Kuchar Brothers' movie *Sins of the Fleshapoids* the other day, which just got released on DVD not too long ago for the very first time, and that is a really low, low, low, lowest budget possible biblical epic kind of movie, and for some reason even that hit me pretty hard, and I was thinking, "Man, the Kuchars would be pretty pleased if they got the odd viewing like that from people," because most of the stuff that's dismissed as "cult fluff" every now and then hits you just right. And I don't mean to sound so self-congratulatory, but I've just watched enough movies that every now and then I'll be caught off-guard by the way that it's entering me.

In other words, I'd be thrilled if people just keep watching me, even if it's as a cult phenomenon, because then there's a chance that someone—maybe someone really smart—will write about it and give it a couple more years of immortality. Like renting a grave at Père Lachaise, I could rest comfortably for a couple more years if someone really bright has some kind of divine experience with my work . . . you know, before changing the channel to something else.

Offscreen: On the *Cowards Bend the Knee* DVD, there were excerpts from a 1997 feature called *Love-Chaunt in the Chimney*, which was apparently destroyed by a fire in your garage. Could you explain a bit about that feature? I imagine it was produced after *Twilight of the Ice Nymphs*?

Maddin: Just after. I decided to make it as a sort of antidote to that whole experience because I didn't enjoy making [*Ice Nymphs*], didn't enjoy the producer or anything. So in this case, I self-produced and did it really on the cheap, didn't pay anybody; everyone just sort of got together in this big sort of utopian experiment, and I didn't even shell out for insurance. We built some sets in my garage, some in the Winnipeg Film Group studio, shot some things outside in the winter, and I had reams of stuff. I don't even know how long that movie was going to be. It was real low budget, but it still might have been three hours long for all I know! It was a really nicely dovetailed amalgamation of Herman Melville short stories stuck together by my friend George Toles. I really liked the way they worked together, and I just shot the shit out of it, covered it from every different way and did a lot of improvisation for the first time. Then I started working on improvising with editing (the first time I did it) because I had so much footage that it was more like a ratio typical of a documentary where shooting ratios are like 100 to 1 instead of 10 to 1. So I started riffing with an editor friend John Gurdebeke who had a computer, and we started editing through stepprinting, slowing things down, speeding things up, reversing them now and then, duplicating shots—more or less as a way of fetishizing the frames. We were just getting started; we did it with a bunch of other stuff too, but that got lost, alas, as well. And so this is all that remains, other than a few seconds of stuff that wasn't cut (maybe about four minutes' worth of stuff that wasn't worth including as a bonus, wasn't manipulated at all).

Offscreen: Various portions of the surviving footage bear strong resemblances to different short films: for example, the *Zookeeper's Workbook* recalls *Maldoror: Tygers*, and another segment recalls *The Cock Crew* (which also went by the name *Love-Chaunt in the Chimney*). Could you explain the relation between what appears on the DVD and the short films that were finally completed in 1999?

Maddin: I shot those [shorts] at the same time, so in some of the scenes I used the same costumes—the same actors even—and some of the sets (not in their entirety, but they overlapped a little bit). That was just part of the spirit of making *Love-Chaunt in the Chimney* on the absolute lowest budget possible. I think I've always liked the story about how RKO recycled those *Magnificent Ambersons* stairs so much that they appeared in *Cat People*, *Curse of the Cat People*, and countless other movies. I just like the idea of having sets used over and over again, but in Winnipeg I don't own a studio so I can't afford to keep sets all the time. As soon as you finish a movie you've got to tear them down and throw them out or store them somewhere. I just wanted to shoot as much as possible to get the taste of *Twilight of the Ice Nymphs* out of my mouth. The money for *Maldoror: Tygers* and *The Cock Crew* was raised through a different source so I had to keep separate books on those.

Offscreen: How many of these unproduced feature film projects do you have waiting in the wings?

Maddin: *The Brand Upon the Brain!* might turn into one of them if I don't finish editing it! It's still not cut because I've been busy ever since shooting it, working on the Isabella thing, and I'm in preproduction on a feature right now. I've got a few things. George has written a feature script—

Offscreen: *Edison and Neemo*?

Maddin: A remake of *Svengali*. *Edison and Neemo* is being made right now, but not by me. George wrote that and it's being produced as an animation out of Vancouver, even though that'll be a few years down the road, but it's going to be good. I'm going to be involved in making a film-within-the-film. I've got some unproduced scripts, but whether I'll ever film them, I don't know. They're unproduced for a reason and a lot of times I've given up on them because the window closed a while back.

Offscreen: Like *The Dikemaster's Daughter*, for example?

Maddin: Yeah, that one needs to be rewritten to bring it up to speed with where I am right now. I was really lucky that it never got made. It just would've been a disaster. I like the basic idea of it, but rather than shooting it, I think I'd rather just make *Svengali*. That'll be something that I'm actually shooting at about this time next year. It's been a while since I've planned anything in my life, but I'm trying to plan ahead, so I have a movie I'm in preproduction on now that's going to be shot in February, and then maybe something shot next fall or early winter—*Svengali* perhaps. Maybe something else will come up in the meantime. We'll see.

Offscreen: I recall you did have that Svengali-like figure who mesmerized the character of Veronkha in *Archangel*.

Maddin: Yes, Ihor Procak is a real life Svengali, a sort of hypnotist who actually hypnotized Dorothy Stratten in a movie [*Autumn Born*] made in Winnipeg. Dorothy Stratten was the famous *Playboy* Playmate of the Year in 1980 who was murdered by her estranged husband because he was jealous of her involvement with Peter Bogdanovich. But Dorothy came up to Winnipeg and made a movie shortly before her death, and Ihor had a great big part in it, and it was his idea to wind up a little squeaky mouse toy to hypnotize her with or something. Anyway, he's an evil man and I always try to keep my girlfriend away from him.

Offscreen: Many of your short films are not in circulation but you've mentioned that they may someday appear in some form. Have you considered compiling a DVD of your complete short films or is such a thing already in the works?

Maddin: No, it's not in the works, but I'd like to when I get around to finishing them. In some cases I'd have to either pay for the rights to some music, recut them to fit another piece of music, or get some original music made. It's not something that can be solved inexpensively or overnight, so I just need a little bit of time to get that all straightened away. I was talking to Gus Van Sant about his first feature film [*Mala Noche*], which he's hoping will be released soon, and he's having exactly the same problem. He just used too much music that he couldn't clear, so he's taking care of that—either writing a new score or paying for it, I'm not sure which. So it'll eventually come out; I haven't seen it, but it's apparently really good.

So in some cases there's that problem, and in other cases there's the fact that I haven't quite finished them but I too hastily put them on my filmography early on in my career when I was beginning to feel sensitive about some inactive periods, so I started including things that were sort of stillborn projects and maybe those shouldn't be finished. But they'll surface eventually, even if only as fragments. My willingness to put those fragments on the *Cowards Bend the Knee* disc indicates that I have no shame and will put anything on!

Offscreen: In recent years you've expressed some ambivalence about using digital video, despite owning a number of DV cameras. With people like David Lynch moving to video (for his upcoming feature), do you ever see yourself making the switch?

Maddin: I do. I was just testing one three minutes before you called. I'm trying to decide whether to shoot in video or film. I actually want to shoot in video, but I just want to make sure I get a look that I like for this film that I'm shooting this winter, which is a documentary on the city of Winnipeg for the Documentary Channel here in Canada. It's a "docu-fantasia-mentary" or whatever you want to call it. I'd like to shoot in video, but there are reasons for shooting it in film, and I guess I'll decide sometime in the next month, maybe in the next week.

Offscreen: Have you been experimenting with the sort of filters that can be applied digitally in postproduction to make regular DV look more like film?

Maddin: I'm just going to start experimenting. There's one thing that these two clever boys at the Seattle Film Company were cooking up, a little device which seems to turn regular digital video into 1950s television kinescope. So I'm working with them through emails and video cameras and things. I'm hoping to get this device here so I can run a bunch of tests—so it's still in its early stages, but if I'm happy with the look, I'll go for it.

Offscreen: At least it should make for cheaper productions.

Maddin: Yeah, although I'm no expert on budgets, but it's easy to forget that the most expensive element in filmmaking is time if you're paying everybody. But I think it's got to be a little bit cheaper to use video. At least you can tape over it or something like that, although I don't think you're supposed to. More and more I like the look of it for certain subjects. When you're making a documentary of a city, Winnipeg looks ugliest on video, and that might be the way to go.

Offscreen: You seem to currently have a workload pretty comparable to what you had in 2001–2003 when you were in production on three features in succession.

Maddin: I love being busy, I really do. I've been a lazy person for so long in my life. It feels good to lick it for a while. I know I could slide back at any second like an alcoholic can start drinking or a smoker could light up again; I feel like I could just fall back on a couch and never get up, at a moment's notice. So I really love the feeling that putting in consecutive days, months, and years of productive time gives me.

Offscreen: Of those three features you directed in 2001–2003, *The Saddest Music in the World* was probably your largest and widest released film to date. Has its success increased your renown as a director and created new filmmaking possibilities for you?

Maddin: Yeah, it has. I'm pleased. It's going right according to plan. I never really had a plan for world dominance. I don't even know how Peter Jackson can make his movies. I don't even understand the process . . . something about "green screens" or something! I don't even get it, you know, and I love the guy but I haven't got ambitions to be that kind of filmmaker. I want to be more like Buñuel or a low budget Von Sternberg. Those are the people I'd give pounds of flesh to be. It's not like I want to be so popular that all the doors in the world would suddenly fly open for me or that every phone call be returned, but I've noticed that more and more phone calls get returned now and the level of recognition has ratcheted up a little bit—nothing ridiculous, but it's a pleasant feeling to be recognized now and then and especially within the industry—so it's had its desired effect. Isabella Rossellini, even though she hasn't been that active in the film world in recent years, is just a celebrity for so many reasons; just being associated with her really helped for some reason. It seemed to help me more than it's helped anybody else who have worked with her, for some reason. Maybe those other people didn't need so much help, I don't know! Richard Avedon didn't need much help and David Lynch didn't need much help, but it really seemed to help me nicely, so I'm really grateful for our friendship.

Offscreen: *The Saddest Music in the World* was a relatively large production with well-known actors and fairly wide distribution, but *Cowards Bend the Knee* was a much smaller, more intensely personal picture. Which was more personally rewarding and valuable for you to make?
Maddin: Making them at the same time like I did kind of makes it impossible to separate them. There are times where, perhaps out of sheer perversity, I'm way more proud of *Cowards Bend the Knee* because it cost so little and it was made clandestinely. Certainly odd circumstances under which to make a movie—sneaking off from one studio to a smaller one a few blocks away in preproduction. I wasn't shooting them simultaneously—that would've been too much! But I would just get away from my office in one building for a few days at a time, basically just disappear and make up a bunch of excuses and then shoot this movie. So it felt pretty good but it really was a script that came 100 percent from me. George and I are so much alike that I can't even remember half the time what he came up with and what I came up with in our collaborations, but I know that this one came from my own bilious broodings about how hard done by I'd been in my life.

I spent many hours daydreaming while swimming. Swimming requires a lot of patience and I'd swim for about an hour a day and just daydream about this movie and about things that have happened to me and how to fit it into templates established by maybe *Electra* or *The Hands of Orlac*—only to be astonished, after the swimming pool water had made my entire body as wrinkly as a prune, that all those stories somehow fit together. Maybe the soaking in the water really helped all those stories fit together; Euripides, *Orlac*, and my own autobiography were all the same story somehow and I got a sort of chlorine delirium everyday. The script was really written over probably about a one year period, the most I've ever spent on anything—and then after I wrote the script, I probably ignored it and just picked up a camera and shot it, kind of from memory—just gathered all the actors together and had them act out my life as I remembered it through a haze of chlorine and amnesia. I would shout out orders, directing while operating the camera so I could make instantaneous judgments in my head. It was a real pleasure and really strange. It felt like I was making a movie with methods unlike those used by anybody else ever. It was similar to old silent movie methods, but moving far more briskly. I hired a pianist and violinist to accompany the actors, but I found that I was moving far too quickly and talking far too much for them to be of any use. I was always leaving them behind, so they were told to go home after the first half-day. They were just too much trouble.

It felt really good to make the movie in a way that fit my story perfectly, so not only did everything in the story seem to fit together very satisfactorily, but even the way of making it fit the story like a glove. It almost seems like now you're talking about the way a painter might approach a subject, sometimes using bigger schema or bigger brushes or flinging the paint onto the canvas depending on the subject matter. Why shouldn't there be a different approach technically to the movie canvas depending on the subject matter? So I became very pleased that I'd found exactly the right way to make this movie, the way that suited the story just right. And if you think I'm into process, I'm not. I hate people who get high on the process of making things; I just want to get it made. But I found a way that was the most practical and tricksy, and also temperamentally the best way to make it. I guess all in all I'm more self-satisfied with the way that *Cowards Bend the Knee* turned out, but I'm also pretty proud of *The Saddest Music in the World* and grateful for the way it's really gotten out there a bit more, sending my name into a few more households.

Offscreen: When collaborating on a script with George Toles, how does he accommodate the more personal details of your own life that you might include in the story?

Maddin: Well, he knows them all for one thing, so sometimes he just puts them in there! We really are best friends and I don't keep any secrets from George. Sometimes he sneaks them in so that I don't even recognize them until much later; not until editing do I realize what he's getting at. A lot of times I give him a little "shopping list" or a wish list of things or elements or tones or flavors or directions that I would like the story to go in, and he just goes off and writes it. Every summer he goes back to his hometown of Hamburg, New York, a suburb of Buffalo, and he spends a month there in his mother's house. I think he does his old childhood paper route or something in the morning, and then writes scripts in the afternoon. Every year he comes back with a couple of major academic essays and a feature film script. So I like alternating little shorts written by me or him, and features written by him. Svengali will be a hybrid dance film and horror film—not like my *Dracula*, which was like 70 percent dance and 30 percent pantomime—but this will be more like 70 percent talking Universal horror film and 30 percent

dance. That one has a third collaborator: a choreographer, the guy that choreographed *Dracula* [Mark Godden].
Offscreen: Are you still hoping for your latest feature, *The Brand Upon the Brain!*, to be finished by September 2006?
Maddin: Yeah, that's the goal. I'm really hoping that it plays at the Toronto International Film Festival with a live orchestra and two live foley sound effects people also working in the orchestra pit or on either side of the stage, supplying footstep sound effects or smashing glass or foghorns—things that the orchestra can't do. I really wanted to have music and effects, and I think it would be charming. I think it would be kind of fun peeking down from the movie every now and then to watch them—and if you hate the movie, you can at least watch the foley artists. They're fascinating people to watch—the big, burly, hairy guy putting on a pair of women's pumps, getting in anticipation of the staircase a woman will have to climb in the upcoming scene. That might add elements of suspense, mystery, and intrigue that aren't otherwise in the movie! So that's my dream and I'm cautiously optimistic that my dream will come true.
Offscreen: It was originally planned as a short film but expanded into a feature—how did that come about?
Maddin: It got expanded pretty quickly. They approached me to make a short film, and I told them I didn't have enough time. I was teaching full time at the University of Manitoba here, and it just didn't seem worth it for me to go to Seattle to make a short in the middle of another job. But when I asked them what amount of film and processing they could come up with, they told me they could come up with ten hours worth, and I suddenly decided I had time to make a feature. That's enough film footage to make a feature, so I thought, "Well, I'll take a week off of school. If I leave immediately after one class and come back just before another, I'll be able to get in thirteen and a half days of work on the movie," so I agreed. So it was maybe by the second phone call that it had gone from a short to a feature.
Offscreen: One of the working titles for *Edison and Neemo* was *The Brand Upon the Brain!* Is there any relation between the two projects or did you just use the title?
Maddin: I've always liked the title and I just wanted to use it. When *Edison and Neemo* went into preproduction as *Edison and Neemo*, *Brand Upon the Brain!* came back to me. *Cowards Bend the Knee* was a title that

I was always kicking around long before the movie, and that title would indirectly apply to almost any movie I've made anyway. I just liked the titles. They seemed kind of muscular and old fashioned and just kind of evocative of some other era. They seemed to speak to me directly. I thought they were the titles of old movies, but I've done research on the Internet Movie Database and everywhere else and I can't find anything with those titles, so I think I dreamt them, strangely enough. *Sissy-Boy Slap-Party*, I've often said, was the only movie that existed as a title first, whereas *Cowards Bend the Knee* and *Brand Upon the Brain!* were titles long before I had the script ideas. They didn't instantly suggest the actual story, but with *Sissy-Boy Slap-Party*, the instant I had that title, I had the actual script as well—the title is the script! So I guess that's still more true than not true.

Offscreen: You've described *The Brand Upon the Brain!* as a companion piece to *Cowards Bend the Knee*.

Maddin: I still haven't decided whether or not to call the protagonist "Guy Maddin." In the script he's got a different name, and I don't think I'd have to literally call him Guy Maddin, but I might. I don't know. We'll see how confusing the experience is to a test audience or something, and maybe it's just simpler to call the characters "Mom," "Dad," "Guy" and "Sis," or I can give them the more baroque names that the script I wrote gave them. But it is a companion, not just because it's direct autobiography, but because it was shot using the same cameras and kind of the same attitude.

Although I've made a big point about how my technique to shooting *Cowards Bend the Knee* was a perfect fit for it, when I tried to use that exact same technique for *Brand Upon the Brain!*, I found the movie resisting it a little bit, and that's when I realized that for all the congratulations I'd been giving myself for finding a perfect fit, it was a bit presumptuous of me to assume that it would be a perfect fit again. The script is a little bit different temperamentally and needed a slightly different approach, and so I've found that one too. I think I'm pretty happy with the footage, but as we speak right now it's not cut, and I'm trying to find a cutting style that will be the perfect fit as well. If I don't find it, the movie will be a big mess.

Offscreen: The film is supposedly based primarily upon your own remembered early life—in this case the conflict between your mother and your teenage sister Janet during the period in which your sister became a local track star while your father's celebrity as a hockey manager was waning.

Maddin: Where did you find that out?
Offscreen: It was in the extras on the *Cowards Bend the Knee* DVD.
Maddin: Oh, right. Yeah, I haven't watched that thing. Yeah, it is. I don't know how thrilled to hear that my mom and sister will be, but they had some fights that are probably pretty typical of a mother and a teenage daughter. Nothing too exotic or rarified, but I was seven years younger than my sister. Maybe I was seven or eight years old, ten years old, when the fights really got big. They seemed big to me, anyway. I won't play the self-pity card too much, but they were kind of traumatizing little things. I'm not saying so out of self-pity; to make sense of them, they seemed really melodramatic in everyone's sense of the word when they think of melodrama as completely uninhibited expressions of emotion. These fights had a lot of fireworks, and they got pretty surreal. So I was cast into the role of an unlikely mediator trying to bring peace; I just wanted people to quit fighting. I still don't really like fights that much. And so it really did feel kind of odd, and it really made me understand the Jekyll and Hyde myth and the werewolf myth, the way people can transform from serene, beautiful creatures into monsters in a matter of seconds. It seemed like every day was a full moon in my house at that age.

Given the opportunity to make this movie on such short notice, I thought I'd best dip into autobiography for material because I didn't have time to go swimming for a year to daydream about how all these things would fit into Euripides and into other things—so I just took episodes way more literally than I did with *Cowards Bend the Knee* and maybe only had time to go swimming a couple times to sort of wrinkle up and soften the skin so that all the characters could be packed closer together into a ninety-minute show.

Offscreen: This is your first film shot outside of Winnipeg, and you've described it as your first "foreign" film.
Maddin: It felt great to hop off an airplane, be driven straight to a movie studio, and be all of a sudden present while actors and actresses are dressing and undressing for you, being given a tour of all the sets that were built in your absence. It reminded me of the way old studio directors must have worked back in the day when they would shoot back-to-back-to-back movies and just sort of show up and go, "Okay, where's my megaphone? Where's the first set? Let's go!"

It felt really exciting for me and it was my first job anywhere outside of my hometown, so I really felt like a grownup there briefly—though all feelings of being a grownup leave you once you pick up a little dinky

Super-8 camera! Size does seem to matter when you're at least posing for production stills. You should really have a fake camera, a gigantic one, to stand behind for production stills! But you really do feel like a kid when you start playing around, and the first weekend I shot with a bunch of little "orphans," and I had to fire them up and get them excited, and I had to really reach back because it's been a long time since I've played with children. So all those feelings of being a grownup on the road, a warrior having parachuted into enemy soil to work clandestinely—all those feelings disappeared when I just realized that I was basically making mud pies with kids again for the first time in forty years.

Offscreen: Was it at all difficult to set such an autobiographical story outside of familiar settings, with a brand new cast and crew that you've never worked with before?

Maddin: No, it wasn't. I was a little worried that it would be, but they were all very keen to help and adept readers of my wishes. A few times the actors even managed to create, in a few reductive melodramatic brushstrokes, exactly a memory as I remembered it, and a couple times I was astonished to find myself overwhelmed, and I would have to leave the set to go collect myself. As mannered and as strange and as odd and as fake as the movie looks—and it looks every bit as fake as *Cowards Bend the Knee*—a couple times I was literally rendered speechless. It was very embarrassing with people I'd only known for two days to suddenly squirt tears on their astonished faces instead of words coming out of my face. They were very thoughtful people; they managed to let me collect my dignity a lot sooner than I normally would have, so they're pretty sweet people to work with.

Offscreen: In your plainly autobiographical film treatment *The Child Without Qualities*, you mention a memorable trip to the 1962 Seattle World's Fair, the last trip your whole family took together. Did you draw upon those memories at all for filming such a personal picture in Seattle?

Maddin: That's right! It did really feel like there was some kind of weird closure of fate. Of all the cities in the world to invite me to make a movie, it had to be Seattle, the last place where my family was together all at once. And it did seem odd to see the Space Needle—of which I have such kind of seminal, primal memories of my brother, who died shortly after—to see it breaking through the clouds as I was landing in the plane was pretty chilling. You see it wherever you go in the city, and I was shooting lots of locations, so it really felt like this little thing was watching me. I say it's "little" because I've lived in Toronto and the CN Tower is really big. But I love the Space Needle. I remember my brother throwing some money off the top of it somehow. It might not even be a real memory because maybe the windows couldn't even be opened back then in '62, but I remember him taking a big fistful of dollar bills and throwing them off the top in a kind of weird, troubling gesture. I think he was angry about something, or just wanted to waste money and see what it looked like fluttering down to the World's Fair stands below. So it was a city that was already a little bit preloaded for me; it felt prehistorically full of "me" anyhow, so it was a good place. Maybe if I went to Minneapolis or Spokane, it wouldn't have been the same.

Offscreen: You always use various filmic and literary sources as wellsprings of inspiration for your pictures. What did you draw upon for this latest one?

Maddin: I drew upon George almost immediately because I told him I was panicking a bit. I had used, as an encourager, *Electra* and *The Hands of Orlac* for *Cowards Bend the Knee*, but I just kept asking George if there was something that he could suggest on such short notice. I wanted something in a hurry, and I didn't have time to read all of Euripides. He suggested I read *The Bacchae*, and I read it and the overall structure didn't send me, but I liked the way that it honored the savagery of the gods and the irrationality of love and the way in which we'll never understand how brutally we love. That wasn't a very good summary of what it's up to—but I wanted something at a more sort of "plagiarizable" level and it wasn't it, so he just fired off a bunch of suggestions. Seattle immediately put me in mind of lighthouses, and I remembered some old Grand Guignol plays from a collection that George had that were set in lighthouses. Lighthouses are obviously sort of claustrophobic, lonely, phallic places, so I told him I wanted something in a lighthouse. He suggested an unscrupulous orphanage used for organ harvesting or something like that, and then he set up some big melodrama involving a bunch of . . . I've got it written down somewhere.

I kept about half of it for my original treatment, and then in the act of grafting on the story of my sister and mother, some of his suggestions fell away as beside the point and others fit in perfectly. So it was kind of an act of fiction for a while, and then I realized that the untrue half was easily made completely true if I just tweaked what happened a little bit, and it suddenly just became my autobiography, but fit snugly into a lighthouse on the West Coast. So in very short order I had something that felt as real as *Cowards Bend the Knee*, without all those long swims. So there weren't any real filmic or even literary sources this time. It was just me taking a huge shortcut through my usual process, skipping the look of the film this time, with a lot of help from George to get the courage to start up.

Offscreen: You've been making films for about twenty years now.

Maddin: Yeah, I can't believe it but I have.

Offscreen: And you turn fifty next year.

Maddin: In about three months.

Offscreen: At this point in your career, which of your films are you most proud of?

Maddin: God, I wish I had a few more titles in there, but I'm going to keep going. The one movie I made that turned out exactly as I planned was *The Heart of the World*. I think *Cowards Bend the Knee* turned out better than I thought it would. And I think the first movie that I was genuinely terrified of going into, and really fought while making but was pretty pleased with the outcome, was *Careful*. I'd never worked in color before; things like that felt like I was really growing by leaps and bounds each time out.

I'll partially retract my answer, because I honestly don't really think about it that often. I can't really watch any of my movies. I remember reading in a Buñuel interview that he only watched his movies once, maybe twice, and then never watched them again. And I couldn't believe it because I'd just finished watching his *L'Age d'or* fifty times already and I thought, "Man, Luis, you've got to watch your movies more often. They're great!" But he knew what he'd made and had to move on, and I understand that now because I'm always just stinging at the end of a movie with regret and second guesses and desires to reshoot things and redo things, which you can't do. So I'm always thinking of what to do next. I guess that would be my official answer—I guess I'm not really proud of any of them, and I'm still hoping to make a really good one someday.

Offscreen: Although I suppose you're not willing to burn all of your negatives like Buñuel was.

Maddin: Yeah, did he really do that? He couldn't have!

Offscreen: He said in his autobiography that he'd be happy to do that, as some sort of final surrealist act.

Maddin: Well, he is an atheist supposedly, so what difference would it make to him?

Offscreen: You've said that Canadian cinema has arguably produced only a handful of great movies and the rest were relative failures. Do you see any of your own films within that small pantheon?
Maddin: Well, I'm using the word "great" in its toughest sense. No, I don't think any of my movies are great. On a good day, when I'm in a good mood or something, a couple of them may be approaching "okay." I believe I have a great movie in me and that's what keeps me going, but I need to do that yet.
Offscreen: Does the technique of willfully creating cinematic "artifacts" leave you with doubts about their worth, or do you think your use of pastiche in visual style and content improves upon what could've been accomplished by filmmakers in the past?
Maddin: It's all just a matter of what you do with what you've got. I don't think I'm fooling anybody, not people who really watch movies. I think people can tell what year more or less my movies are made in. I just want to create an atmosphere and a sense of fun, but certainly atmosphere and a sense of fun aren't necessarily obstacles to achieving an end in filmmaking. So I just recruit those elements and try to put on a nice watchable show and just free up some break time for myself to indulge the film in some other agenda that maybe I can sneak past the viewer.
Offscreen: You've spoken elsewhere of a personal project to reinvent cinema for yourself by shooting your way through its history. Is that still an ongoing project?
Maddin: I think I might have given up on that one a long time ago—maybe twenty years ago! So I was probably a bit impatient because there's certain eras that I wouldn't want to live through, and obviously if I had any hope of doing it in twenty or thirty years I'd have to go at it in an accelerated pace. I also didn't want to spend too much time at the *Great Train Robbery* level, as charming as those movies are—and I must say I haven't seen a Lumière Brothers movie I haven't adored. And gosh, I do wish I'd been one of the filmmakers who was invited to participate in that centennial project [Lumière and Company] back in 1995.

But I think it was something that, once said, was as good as done. I've got to just let my direction determine itself one picture at a time and sort of see what's got me fired up. The most frightening feeling, and I know this firsthand because I've gone through this in the late-1990s, is not really having anything fire me up, and it's a bad, bad feeling not finding yourself daydreaming about making movies at all. So as long as I'm fired up about something, even if it's surface values or something buried far beneath the surface, as long as I can be excited about it, I'm more or less confident that I can trick myself into making another movie.

Offscreen: For *Tales from the Gimli Hospital*, you used Kyle McCulloch as a black-faced minstrel and another white actor to portray a First Nations member. You've said that this was done intentionally to complicate the nostalgia of an archaic film. What ways have you complicated the nostalgia in your later features?

Maddin: There it was a pretty conspicuous one, and I wasn't sure I wanted to do it. It was Kyle who really argued long and hard about being able to do the blackface. I was being kind of chicken; I really didn't want to hurt anyone. But by the same token, I knew he was right, that it kind of had to be done. I had a clear conscience about it; I just didn't want to hurt anybody who took it the wrong way, that's all. He said, "Well, it will make for interesting dialogue and people can talk their way through it." And then he said, "Come on, just do it!" and I think he just put on some burnt cork and said, "Well, we can just shoot it but not include it." Then it just seemed right, so I put it in and I'm glad I did. I've had less comfortable fits, it seems, repeating African American stereotypes in films. I just didn't want to do that anymore. I felt it was so glaring there that it served its purpose comfortably enough, but when intentions became more ambiguous, I wasn't interested in risking hurting people, because you don't even find out most of the time when you've hurt people.

Other times of mixing up nostalgia? Yeah, I don't know. I operate now so instinctively. I've promised myself never to think about any one decision for more than about three seconds, and I can't even remember what I've done, but I'm pretty sure I've done it and just can't remember.

Offscreen: Missing limbs and other sorts of physical impairments are common in your pictures. Is this to help provide a visual shortcut to melodramatic effect or are there deeper matters at work, such as the way disabilities are used to signify fears of death or loss?

Maddin: It's mostly the former—just a shortcut. And once again, the more realistically and then dismissively that you treat such things at the same time, you're getting pretty insensitive and mean-spirited. So not all people with a limp are impotent, you know? People with disfigured faces aren't evil and scary. But this is just Brothers Grimm, Lon Chaney, Tod Browning country, where an outward injury is the visual artifact of some sort of emotional injury. It's just something people can see from the cheap seats. A profound limp, a missing something or other, is a spiritual limp, something missing, an injury incurred in childhood or something like that. It's a real old melodramatic device, and it can be chillingly effective like Ahab in *Moby Dick* or it can be more off-the-rack corny, as in an eye patch for the leader of SPECTRE in James Bond! But it's definitely something on the palette. I guess I'm running the risk of overusing it, but we'll see. There's always a new illness. I really like the neurological illnesses that writer and neurologist Oliver Sacks describes in his books. Those seem to be made up specifically to describe the human condition, fairy tale-style, but they're real neurological cases and his way of describing them makes him sort of a twentieth-century Brothers Grimm.

Offscreen: So you don't, either as an artist or on a more personal level, feel a particular identification with persons who are disabled or missing limbs? It's just a device?

Maddin: Yeah, it's just a device to help pinpoint feelings that you and I have both had at one time or another. If you didn't get any dates in high school, you get to end up with an amputated leg!

Offscreen: You've said that we all live in a state of amnesia that allows us to forget painful memories—but doesn't forgetting things like traumatic events or acts of cowardice just allow a person to constantly revisit and repeat those things in the future—for example, the recurring themes of dead fathers and cowardice in your films?

Maddin: Yeah, I don't have a lot of confidence in people to improve or to fail to repeat mistakes. I feel kind of Buñuelian in that way. He's a big left-winger, but like in *Viridiana* when the beggars, the starving people, the lumpen proletariat finally get the house and some food and some wealth, they don't even know what to do with it. They just trash the joint and become a bunch of gross pigs. I just feel it's such an old, broad-stroked, and cruel way of showing us what we're really like. And he's described as a humanist, but not an idealist humanist. He's a realist humanist or a practical humanist. It's really wonderful—there's so much truth possible in that kind of cruel surrealism that I don't even consider it surrealism.

Offscreen: You've said that your films are a way of coping with grief or the pains of everyday life—for example, you felt that the process of writing *Cowards Bend the Knee* made you less of a coward.

Maddin: Yeah, for about six months it made me less of a coward. I'm every bit the coward I always was, but for a while I was pretty good there. Actually, I always sort of suspected it was temporary. But I learned to confront people. I'm not so cowardly on the movie set, but in my day-to-day life I'm every bit as bad as Edward VII, the one-time king pussy-whipped into exile and oblivion and a bad liver.

Offscreen: How much do you think your films have helped shape you as a person in the twenty years that you've been making them, and do you think they will ever help provide solace for the biggest traumas in your life?

Maddin: I think I've recovered from all the traumas in my life . . . except for not having a girlfriend in high school. I don't know if they've shaped me at all, but they've at least enabled me to take some pride in what I do. For the longest time, in my twenties, it just wasn't shaping up like I was going to have a career, or even a part-time job. I was pretty depressed. So it's nice to just have something to do and not be alienated from my labor (to speak in old Marxist terms). I am what I'm making, and I'm making what I am, and it feels pretty good. There's got to be an audience, there's got to be someone giving me the money to do it, but it's just allowed me to be in the shape that I could've been in had I the ambition and foresight to plan a career in my teens and twenties (but I didn't). So it's just facilitated my entering into regular society.

I don't think it's changed what I potentially was, and it hasn't shaped me in any odd way. It sounds so self-centered, but it's enabled me to continually think of people and myself, and how I'm just regular like everyone else. It's a pleasure to be able to think of art a lot. I guess I'm really lucky that way because a lot of people who work in other fields don't have the time to think about that stuff, or the inclination, and they get kind of shriveled up in places as a result.

Offscreen: Your father has seemed to have the greatest formative impact upon your life. You've achieved some local, if not international, celebrity, not unlike him. Aside from the obvious associations that come up in your work (such as cowardice and death), how much do you either fear or desire becoming like him?

Maddin: I'm probably like him already. I tried Googling him the other day and there was virtually nothing. It saddens me, but I guess he just died in the pre-Google era and not much of his stuff has been retroactively posted. But maybe I should just devote some time to getting some crap of his on there, just so that he can exist in Googleland. It's not like "If you post it, they will come" or anything like that, but maybe someone will accidentally chance upon things. Who knows how you stumble upon things in E-world?

But I think about him often. I usually compare myself to him at whatever age I'm at. I remember when I turned thirty-eight, I was cutting the lawn and saying to myself, "This is how old he was when I was born." And when I was forty-five, I said, "This is how old he was when he lost his son." And right now I'm at the age he was when he had his first heart attack and things pretty much declined very rapidly from there. I'm still not sure about his life. One day a woman and a girl from Germany arrived at our door, rang the doorbell, and I realized later that I was probably staring at an illegitimate half-sister. And now I sort of have to add, "And this is the age my dad was when he fathered a child in Germany"! Sometimes I can say, "Jeez, I'm doing better than my dad right now. I'm getting out more." But then again my dad maybe fathered this kid in Germany, and I've got my work cut out for me there.

I just want to be happier than he was, because temperamentally I feel like I'm the same person, with a deadly strain of my mother mixed in (which I'd like to get rid of completely). Not a happy strain. And I'm not picking sides; she's just not always happy, and when I'm unhappy, it's in a way that my mom's unhappy and I don't like that. But I kind of like walking around as the embodiment of him. It feels healthier than what I did until I was about twenty. I walked around as the living ambassador of my dead brother, as this living ambassador of suicide, and that wasn't always a good feeling. So this one at least feels more warm and more like an ongoing tribute . . . kind of nice. And I'm not as crazed as Hamlet or anything. It's just a quiet unhealthiness that, except for the fact that I talk about it like this every now and then, no one would ever know about. That and I make movies about it!

When in Winnipeg

José Teodoro/2007

> From *Stop Smiling*, January, 2007. Reprinted by permission of the Stop Smiling Media, LLC.

For as long as he can remember, Guy Maddin wanted to make movies that look like movies from eighty years ago. He's a lifelong inhabitant of Winnipeg, an ice-encrusted, gloriously decrepit city on the terrifyingly vast Canadian prairie—an area that just happens to be the nation's secret cultural wellspring. As evidenced in his comparatively luxuriously budgeted *The Saddest Music in the World* (2003), which starred Isabella Rossellini as an amputee beer baroness, Maddin favors primitivism, melodrama, and the haunting artifice of early cinema, while complicating cozy nostalgia with frenzied editing, anachronisms, and bizarre, highly neurotic subject matter. His personal life is often an inspiration, but distorted and absurdly mythologized through the morbid imaginations of Maddin himself and longtime writing partner George Toles.

Maddin's silent feature *Brand Upon the Brain!* had its premiere at the 2006 Toronto International Film Festival with full orchestra, live Foley artists, and live narration. Like *Cowards Bend the Knee* (2003)—a love triangle involving abortion and obsession, hockey and hand transplants—it features a protagonist named Guy Maddin and is riddled with guilt, fearful slips into shadowy memories, and unresolved confusion over desire and identity, all played out on an island of orphans driven to emancipation by a hot teenage detective. The morning after the film's triumphant debut, Maddin's obvious glee was pushed to greater heights when he sweet-talked the armed officer rather ominously monitoring our talk into letting us fondle his machine gun and examine his hollow-tipped bullets.

Stop Smiling: An unusual and complicated strain of autobiography runs through your work. Why so many characters named Guy?
Guy Maddin: If you're being as transparently dishonest as most filmmakers—you know, Martin Scorsese having a taller alter ego in Robert De Niro—you might as well just come out and say who it is. Besides, you have to be pretty sure that your alter ego, if he isn't named after you, is doing pretty interesting, compelling things, whereas I feel like you're buying a little extra goodwill from the audience by naming the character after yourself. It's tricky, of course. You're all of a sudden engaging yourself in an act of masochism if you're making yourself look bad. You're really indulging yourself in self-pity if you're depicting your horrible childhood, and that can only be withstood by an audience for a few minutes before they hurl. So it's strangely liberating just being up-front about it, saying, "This is me," because every character in the movie is me anyway. All I can go by is what I myself would do in a certain situation.
SS: You've said somewhere that the "Guy Maddin" in *Cowards Bend the Knee* was actually less representative of you than another character in the film.
GM: Yeah, it was the girl that Guy went out with, this character named Meta. At some point I realized I was just as much her as I was myself. Not that I'm a girl. But a lot of her petulance and stubbornness and hysteria seemed to resonate. I remember Ingmar Bergman saying that in a film like *Persona* both of the women would be him, but two different aspects of him—that it's pure autobiography up there, not on a point-by-point basis, but as spiritual autobiography or whatever. That lit the way for me and was something I remembered for a long time: that different characters could simultaneously represent you, just not on a surface level. It's not whether your dad was really exhumed that matters, but the feelings that exhumation would produce in you, if you're being honest about things and putting them up on the screen. By breaking yourself up and spreading yourself around a bit, you can indirectly get at something you really felt.
SS: Your characters have qualities you've often attributed to yourself, such as cowardice, lust, guilt, and the desire to please.
GM: Oh, yes. I'm about as cowardly as they come. I don't know what happened to my lust. It's been replaced by gluttony.
SS: Is this an attempt at personal exorcism?

GM: Nah, I like myself enough. I mean, don't worry, I have self-loathing too, but I don't need to get rid of any demons. I kind of like them. I'd be sad if they were gone. That's one of the problems with making a movie on any subject. For instance, I made an alpine mountain drama once [*Careful*], researching everything I could about the genre, and by the time I was finished I didn't ever want to see a mountain again. I made one about the Great War [*Archangel*], which used to be my favorite war, and then used it up. So it's possible that by using myself as a subject I'll become very weary of myself—and maybe that's better for everybody else. I don't know if it's therapeutic or just a process of exhaustion, of attrition really, where you just grind your interest in a subject out of yourself.

SS: Since it also deals with a child Guy, has *Brand Upon the Brain!* caused you to lose interest in your unrealized project, *The Child Without Qualities*?

GM: I don't know if that'll ever get made. I wrote that so long ago, and I don't think it's filmable anyway. Maybe I'll just borrow chapters and feelings from it.

SS: Or at least the setting, because I think you could go even deeper into the Winnipeg Arena.

GM: Yeah, I'd really like to get that right. I did shoot a documentary about it, though I haven't cut it yet. The Winnipeg Arena was torn down last winter, and I got to go inside it during that process. I took the last pee in the men's room at the north end zone stands. While a wrecking ball was literally hitting the outside of it, I snuck in with my hardhat on and a camera and tripod, and I videotaped myself peeing into the urinal. Plaster was falling down just as I ran out of there. I was willing to die in there if I had to. I love that building. It really upset me that they tore it down. It was just some typical city council, land-grubbing, conflict-of-interest deal. It's a parking lot now. But I got in there. So I'm not quite through with the Winnipeg Arena.

SS: In your published journals, *From the Atelier Tovar*, it's clear you've spent a lot of time around old people, particularly old ladies. Has hanging out with an older crowd affected how you think creatively?

GM: When I was a teenager, all of my drinking buddies down at the lake were my friends' parents, these weekend drunks, some doctors and lawyers. They had great wine cellars, great beer, and their doors were always open. It was great hanging out with people that had been war veterans, who were really smart and read lots of books. When they went to bed or passed out, I'd go to bush parties with my teenage friends, but I hung out with many people far older than me. As a result, most of my best friends from my teenage years have just died of natural causes. But I always liked infiltrating the world of the grownup, which somehow kept me childlike. I'm fifty now, so I can no longer get away with behaving childishly.

SS: Did being around older people stir your interest in early film?

GM: No, they didn't really give a shit about early film. That was something I came across myself. But maybe both my interest in early film and my desire to hang out with these older people are symptoms of some other pathology.

SS: When you were at university, you were able to get your hands on a lot of actual prints of early films.

GM: Yeah, I'd already graduated with a useless BA in economics. But in my early twenties I'd befriended some film professors, and I'd always encourage them to bring me prints. Once I got my hands on the secret list of these bootleg 16mm prints the university library had, I was able to bring movies home every weekend.

SS: Did watching these early films in such a concentrated period affect your dreams? Do your dreams inform your work?

GM: When I was watching these movies, especially the really early, primitive ones, like the experimental films of Dalí, they emboldened me to hold onto dreams as plausible material for movies. I knew I could never be a slick filmmaker—it was already too late. I was in my mid-twenties, and I never went to film school. That would have involved work. So I thought maybe I could make primitive things, the filmic equivalent of a basement band, doing something very rough and ragged but still taking that direct route to the heart somehow.

SS: Do your dreams resemble film?

GM: No, almost never. Every now and then I have a dream that I'm watching one of my own movies, and it becomes much better than it really is, and I realize that I should have been a little more daring, or a little more ambitious. There'll be long tracking shots, and I have no idea where they're going to go. It'll be really intriguing and the curiosity mounts, and then there's a great payoff. Rarely when you wake up can you write it down and then act on it, of course. But these dreams remind me to try harder, work harder. I have this longstanding battle with my ambition. Sometimes I get really lazy. It usually helps to have a filmmaking rival that you can compete with.

SS: But you don't really have one, do you?

GM: No, I don't really. I used to try to make Atom Egoyan into a rival, but he's too nice and makes completely different kinds of films.

SS: Is it fair to call your work a manifestation of private fantasies?

GM: Not so much fantasies as secrets. I think if I really had a choice of what I'd be instead of a filmmaker, I'd be a writer, but I'm just not good enough to write a great novel. I always see it as a writer's job to be completely honest—even self-flagellating, if necessary—in the service of the novel. I guess the poet has the same obligation. Maybe all artists do. I see film that way too. Unless you're making a pure entertainment, you need to work to get as much readily recognizable human behavior out there. So it's not like a fantasy that I'm dying to see come true so much as something that already secretly exists.

SS: Carefully selected or totally invented paraphernalia is heavily strewn all through your work. Do you consider your films fetishistic, like Buñuel's or Hitchcock's?

GM: I try to fetishize things through editing, you know, instant replays of things you really like. Like with a great goal in hockey or a real tape-measure shot or a home run trot, you want to watch certain things again and again. So I try to get those moments, those little things that really taste good, and blatantly fetishize them. Sometimes they're intentionally goofy fetishizations. I don't actually feel like kissing shoes. But obviously it's a pretty prostrating thing to do, to kiss someone's feet. That's why I was so happy to get a castrato to sing in *Brand Upon the Brain!*, because the level of self-castration going on in this thing is just ridiculous.

SS: And yet characters aren't generally able to indulge freely in any sort of healthy or truly satisfying erotic fulfillment in your films. There are a lot of barriers, real and imagined, surrounding people's hands, for example. But these also instill an erotic charge through displacement and delayed gratification.

GM: That's something I learned from Buñuel. He almost never allows people to consummate. Even when Gaston Modot and Lya Lys in *L'Âge d'or*, who have been lusting after each other the entire film, are finally alone in a garden, they somehow contrive to prevent themselves from getting together. Buñuel also never has people successfully eat anything. They're always just raising the food to their mouths and then something interrupts them.

You realize that's the difference between film and pornography. In

porn, the payoff is so easily come by. It serves its purpose. But in whatever sort of nonpornographic storytelling, you gotta hold back, otherwise everyone is satisfied and wants to just roll over and have a nap.
SS: Your co-writer George Toles has a special interest in object-heavy films. Do objects play a large role in shaping the stories you two create?
GM: George does like objects. Like many Hitchcock scholars, he's noticed that Hitchcock's scripts are often built around an object. There was a great exhibition on Hitchcock a few years ago, in which they chose one object from each of his movies that the story rotated around, like the lighter from *Strangers on a Train* or the monogrammed pillowcase from *Rebecca*, that proved the point beautifully. George is always trying to think up things like that. I'm too busy trying to copy other directors' tricks.
SS: How about the connection between objects and memory? Objects, and places too, emphasize this idea of eternal return in *Brand Upon the Brain!* I'm thinking of the adult Guy and his paintbrush, for example. The way he returns home and begins painting the old lighthouse. It renders the brush as an unsettling sort of regressive tool.
GM: That's true. There's the paintbrush, certainly. I've spent a lot of time painting, and it seemed like, with every stroke, instead of covering something up I was uncovering some memory, because I just spend a lot of time brooding and daydreaming while painting. It's an irony that struck me hard enough to want to include it in the film. It's always nice to discover that some banal practice can be cinematic, can lead somewhere fruitful. House painting gets its due, finally!

Interview with . . . Guy Maddin

D. K. Holm/ 2007

From *Independent Cinema*, Kamera Books. Reprinted by permission of the publisher, www.kamerabooks.com.

D. K. Holm: How do you fund your films, broadly speaking? As I understand it, Canada has much more inclusive state grants than the United States (one more reason to move there?).
Guy Maddin: If a producer is lucky, he can get the state to cover half the budget with a loan, but not everyone is so lucky. For shorts and really low-budget affairs, Canada Council grants of up to $50,000 are awarded to a few applicants annually. I received a few of these over the years, but I don't think I've ever asked for the maximum amount. Our Manitoba Arts Council in my home province has been healthier than councils elsewhere in the country the last ten years, and that's made for a friendly filmmaking environment here in Winnipeg, but I try not to apply to it very often—I feel it's for artists either just starting out or those without any recourse to larger-budgeted affairs.
DKH: Do you have a convenient definition of "independent" cinema?
GM: Not a very good one. I feel independent, but I'm sure many people working for the man feel okay, too.
DKH: Would you even call yourself an independent filmmaker? Or, if you have to have a label at all, would you call yourself something else: maverick, maudit, experimental?
GM: *Regie maudit* would be romantic. I don't know what an experimental filmmaker is—something to do with shooting blobs of paint floating on oil?
DKH: Do you *want* money for films, or is there a certain dignity and purity in keeping the budgets low?
GM: Trying to raise money is time-consuming and humiliating. I'd rather shoot the precise moment I have just enough dough. That

moment varies from project to project, although I'm getting more and more impatient as I age and find myself happy to locate that moment sooner and sooner.

DKH: According to the IMDB, *Saddest Music* cost $3.5 million dollars Canadian. Is it terrifying to deal with such huge sums? Or is it peanuts, given that a movie such as *Narnia* costs $180 million dollars?

GM: It still felt like peanuts, because it was.

DKH: As your projects increase in complexity and expense, how do you manage to retain "control" of a film? Or have you redefined for yourself the role of director?

GM: I have as much control as I want or I don't make the picture. I've enjoyed tackling assignments where my job is to please my boss, but I've always managed to serve my own purposes simultaneously. I've been lucky that way. The only project where I had little control was *Twilight of the Ice Nymphs*, where my producer broke his word to me and made unilateral decisions designed to serve himself. I was forced to shoot in 35mm when the script was a 16mm script and the production design was a 16mm production design and even the performances were 16mm. I was completely sucker-punched and had no idea how to get my footing back. He betrayed me at too many turns to count.

DKH: What are the differences in life on the set between mainstream movies, as you have experienced them in Winnipeg, and low budget or indie films?

GM: It's all very similar the world over I bet.

DKH: What changes in presentation or marketing, if any, do you anticipate with the advent of digitalized content and downloading capabilities on the Internet?

GM: I embrace the future, believe it or not, but I am especially incapable of predicting it. Obviously big changes are afoot. As an old movie buff, I acknowledge that each change to cinema brought about by technological advances or social upheaval has been *very exciting*. I expect nothing less in the future.

Talking with Winnipeg's Remarkably Well-Adjusted Guy Maddin

Aaron Hillis/2008

From *The Village Voice*, April 22, 2008. Reprinted by permission of the author.

My Winnipeg—Canadian hyper-fabulist Guy Maddin's time-out-of-mind "docu-fantasia" about his provincial hometown—makes its U.S. premiere at Tribeca before seeing a wider release in June. Maddin spoke by phone about his ingeniously madcap and heartfelt pseudo-documentary.

Aaron Hillis: When the Documentary Channel approached you to make a nonfiction film, what were they expecting?
Guy Maddin: I wanted to make a documentary, but [the Documentary Channel's] Michael Burns is the one who suggested Winnipeg: "Enchant me with it. Don't give me the frozen hellhole everyone thinks Winnipeg is." So it was an assigned propaganda project, but I viewed it more as a documentary of my feelings, as ambiguous as they may be. I probably used, as a model, the writings of W. G. Sebald and those little peregrinations. He goes for these long walks, daydreams and digresses in the pages of his books, and ends up with something that feels psychologically, poetically true.
Aaron Hillis: Why do you think people are so obsessed with delineating fact from fiction in cinema?
Guy Maddin: I don't know—because it's a pretty literal-minded approach, which robs you of a lot of pleasure . . . if a movie is obliged to be a perfect representation of the real world. We can see that already, or we can watch security-camera tape if we want to see unbroken representation. It's been axiomatic that documentaries are incapable of presenting

the entire truth since the Lumière brothers first pointed a camera at workers leaving a factory, then got them to leave all over again for a second take.

Aaron Hillis: You've toyed with the line between autobiography and quasi-doc before in *Cowards Bend the Knee* and *Brand Upon the Brain!* What attracted you again to mythologizing pseudo-reality?

Guy Maddin: Canadians, especially Winnipeggers, are lousy self-mythologizers—pathologically so. I think it's because we're sitting next to a country that's so great at it. I decided, while I'm living here, I should try my best to bring Winnipeg at least up to speed with Cleveland on this sort of thing. I know we'll never be New York, but I wanted to preserve, sort of can the city's status. Kansas City is known for the blues, say, and I want Winnipeg to be known for one or two things—a shorthand version of itself, a distillation. Then my work on this earth—this Winnipeg earth, which is strewn with recently thawed- out cigarette butts—is done.

Aaron Hillis: Your films frequently thrive on self-consciousness and Freudian fixations. Are you as neurotic in your daily life?

Guy Maddin: Filmmaking is good for me because I'm becoming less and less neurotic, which is probably a boring answer. Since the last few films I've made have been so outrageously, self-indulgently autobiographical, they've amounted to an accumulation of things that have tired me out about myself—a form of aversion therapy. It's made me a lot healthier, somehow; I'm a lot more grounded, and I find myself doing a lot less cowardly things—filing my income tax on time, walking the dog when it needs to be walked. But somewhere along the line, a three-by-six-foot rectangle of soil opened up and yawned its gravy breath at me, and I realized I'm going to slide into the open mauve cemetery sometime in the next few years. [Laughs.] For the first time in my life, I'm fearing death a little bit—but other than that, I've got my sea legs and I'm ready for anything.

Interview with Guy Maddin, Director of *My Winnipeg*

James Nadeau/2008

From *Big Red and Shiny*, July 13, 2008. Reprinted by permission of the author.

Back in April I had the chance to interview Canadian filmmaker Guy Maddin. He was in town for the Independent Film Festival of Boston to screen his new film *My Winnipeg*. Guy Maddin has been making experimental films since the early eighties and is often referred to as the "Canadian David Lynch." He was the youngest recipient of the Lifetime Achievement Award at the Telluride Film Festival way back in 1995. He currently teaches film at the University of Winnipeg. *My Winnipeg* won the award for Best Canadian Feature at the 2007 Toronto International Film Festival, and it won the audience award at the IFFB here in Boston. It opened at the Kendal Cinema on Friday, July 11.

James Nadeau: One of the things I have found interesting about your film is that it prompts a lot of questions.
Guy Maddin: The biggest one that comes up all the time is "how much is that true?"
JN: That is one of the things that I really loved about the film, that it really plays with the notion of the truth or even about personal history. It walks that line between being a document and being a false document where ultimately it doesn't even matter.
GM: I don't think it really matters, but for the record it is true. The movie is equal parts fact, opinion—I make no bones about it being my opinion, I write things self-pityingly—and then legend. It's a fact that this is a local legend that some people either believe and (well, I don't believe in the paranormal personally) a lot more people in Winnipeg

do than in most other cities. And a lot of people buy into the fact that because it's this mystical connection of river forks and [Winnipeg being] the actual geographical center of the continent where if God were bored with himself and just spinning North America on the tip of his finger we'd all be sitting on God's cuticle. And we all sort of walk around as if God's cuticle is being shoved up our asses. Anyway, so Winnipeg has this temperament and I have this particular temperament and I don't know . . . I was commissioned to make a movie about *my* Winnipeg, not just Winnipeg. So I quickly realized that it was meant to be personal.

The Documentary Channel wanted my Winnipeg, the Guy Maddin tour. Although you know, the first year, when I made my first super-8 feature, Neil Young [also from Winnipeg] made *Greendale* (2003), a super-8 feature and I'm going, "Damn, I didn't even make the most famous super-8 feature from Winnipeg!" But anyway what was I getting at? Just, well, I realized that if I was to make my Winnipeg that what makes Winnipeg special to me is that it is my home, and then I realized that what makes it my home is that it is my childhood home. Which is so important to me. And it was there and what's a building without the family members in it, so my actual family and so they're all inseparable. And so I couldn't just stop at the city. I therefore I had to include all these things, and I had to include opinions and legends too. You know when you are talking about your own family it is more emotional facts that matter more then real ones. It's the myths. There is virtually no mythology about Canada or Winnipeg. And so when I was asked to make this documentary, I thought here is a chance for me to fill a void. Meanwhile every family though has its own myths. You can't escape that. So here I got a chance to sort of vivisect my family and look back at people living and dead and do my city and country [by extension] and my family and myself all at once. It is a historical, mythological look. And when I say mythological, I don't mean it's not true. I just mean it has been processed by the passage of time.

JN: So more the act of then?

GM: Yeah, and mythic truth is more important that facts anyway.

JN: I thought it was great that there are these two narrative lines. And it's like you are looking at the macro and the micro of family and family spaces alongside the citizen/public "personal" space. And you speak about how people inhabit private homes but also public spaces and make them identity-based spaces.

GM: Yeah, yeah. I'm glad you say that.

JN: There is the part about deconstructing that big store (I'm drawing a blank on the name) . . .

GM: Eaton's.

JN: Yes. And how the central loss that occurs is that how timeless that space is. Because once the building is gone it is almost like people don't even remember what was there.

GM: Um, yeah. Amnesia and demolition are our growth industries in Winnipeg. [Laughs] Home is really haunting to me. I literally do have dreams about my childhood home all the time. I guess I was hoping with the movie to be so specifically Winnipeg that I would actually push through that hazy specificity. And by some miracle reach some kind of universality that people from Boston or Cleveland or Timbuktu might be able to find themselves in. Somehow, even though they have no intention of ever going to Winnipeg. I've saved them the trouble.

JN: Well, I had several moments while watching the film where I asked myself if this was even a real place. Does Winnipeg really exist?

GM: Sometimes it does feel like a bit of a dream. I often think about the ideal poster, what it should be, and IFC [Independent Film Channel] is doing a great job and they have cooked up some poster that's beautiful, but I'm just thinking that some sort of icy, metropolis, just a dazzling sort of fairy land would have been nice.

JN: Like a fortress of solitude?

GM: Yeah like some sort of ectoplasm, and it would be expensive to print, but if the ectoplasm could somehow rise off of the pagers of the poster. Like a frosty breath. That would be the ultimate poster for it. It is an intoxicating thing. Especially in January. That is when Winnipeg is special. People say, "you should come and visit in the summer, that's when it is pretty," but then it is just like Milwaukee. But in the winter, that is when it is special. That's when it's as cold a city there is. Except for Ulan Bator [in Mongolia] now. I got one fact wrong in the movie. It's not the coldest city in the world. Thanks to global warming Ulan Bator has shuffled up ahead of us. But no, it is really special. And the place just seems sugar coated. And it is so cold your nostrils feel like they are being turned inside out with pliers.

JN: Can you talk about the film from a process perspective? Because the film is such a mélange of technologies. From super-8 to super-16 to HD [High Definition], mini-DV and is this . . .

GM: Plus cell phone.

JN: [laughs]

GM: You know I didn't use Fisher Price Pixelvision. I'm kicking myself.

JN: So is this multiplicity of medium just methodology for you? Or perhaps a way to break out of the confines of each technology?

GM: I was hoping this movie would help me break into digital technology. So I bought these HD cameras. I thought that maybe I can get comfortable, the way David Lynch really got comfortable in Inland Empire with this new technology. Maybe I can. The subject matter didn't quite allow as much HD to be used as possible. I shot a lot on HD. Some of it I incorporated into the rear screen projection, which was then later shot on film. Some of it was actually incorporated into the movie but never quite sat well, so I projected the edited sequences, the finished sequences, right on to my fridge and just reshot them with a film camera to embed them. You know it just finally seemed to make sense. The simple approach—the past is shot on film and the present was shot on video—it just seemed quite simple and . . . there was no point in trying to confound people on that level.

JN: 'Cause it does seem kind of counter to your aesthetic to have this fine, super high pixel HD image.

GM: Yeah, yeah, and I don't know how to mess with . . . basically I had to learn how to unlearn cameras. I have gotten most of my atmospheric effects through screw-ups on my camera. But I haven't, these new HD cameras are kind of screw-up proof. So I have chanced upon . . . you actually have to master them to get good effects where I was just screwing up to get good effects before. So it's not user friendly that way. I'm not getting the love back from these cameras. Nothing special happened so not much video made it in. I'm just going to keep some video diaries and keep breaking the camera in until something good comes out of it.

JN: It's interesting in that with this film the role that the super-8 and the super-16 play, not so much with the narrative itself but within the form of the film itself, is that is helps to pull in these historical moments. And it seems integral to the film to have this flicker and have the tone . . .

GM: Well, you know when you are talking about mythic things it seems like they should be halfway biodegraded already somehow. Not necessarily through trumped up aging but just, they should be less explicit. They should be more archetypal, more murky. A little less razor sharp revealing that's all. So I'm not trying to imitate old movies so much as removing color that has no point to make. What difference does it make? It's winter! It's light, sky, and snow. And any other color is beside the point. There's no good reason to shoot in color. As a matter of fact I am presenting the movie as a propaganda piece. I was commissioned to enchant the executive producer. He said, literally, "I want you to make a documentary that's about your Winnipeg and enchant me." I was basically given this Leni Riefenstahl-ian task of enchanting him, and so whenever I think of propaganda I think in black and white terms. Winnipeg is black and white, my task was black and white, and I wanted to make a snow noir. Winnipeg deserves a snow noir. So that is what I made.

JN: Did you set out to have a narrative arc at all?

GM: I did. We had to shift around the order of the anecdotes, that's all. And then about a year after I shot I had a little daydream that resulted in me having a train interior set built. And I came up with this narrative grout. This, sort of, train set and the idea . . . I was able to link the anecdotes together by train and since the city was built on rail . . . the rail industry . . . it seemed like the perfect solution. I love train movies and I love the sleepy, womb-like rocking that a train car gives.

JN: And some of those scenes are the most vivid and grounding of the film.

GM: It felt really good to shoot them. I was able to use a handheld camera again. 'Cause for rear screen projection filming you are almost always locked down to a tripod so I was able to get organic and move the lights around a lot and go in and out of focus. And just deal with spaces again. I just like closeups more then anything else.

JN: How crucial was the voiceover aspect for you?

GM: I really don't like the sound of my own voice that much. Well, I didn't at the time. Most people aren't comfortable with it. And so I really wanted Lorne Greene to do it. But he's dead. Especially since I lost my virginity to Lorne Greene narrating *Lorne Greene's Nature Wildlife Theatre*. He's got such a great voice and he's Canadian and everything. So I really wanted someone like that. But my producers finally just said, look, no one is going to believe what's in this movie anyway, you've got to be you. Use your own voice whether you like it or not. So I was ordered by Michael Burns, at the Documentary Channel, and Jody Shapiro, my producer, to use my own voice. I had my editor cut it into like a radio show, and he treated the narration like editors usually treat temp music. So, instead of cutting to music to get the rhythm of the film, he cut to my narration.

JN: . . . and you do the voiceover live at some screenings, don't you?

GM: I have done it live. I did it in New York at Tribeca, I did it in Berlin and Toronto, and I am going to be doing it at the screenings in Sydney and London. I can't wipe the smile off my face thinking of these live presentations. It was a gala presentation at the Film Forum at the Berlinale. I could not get the smile off my face. I hate performing but it was so worth it. I got to do a travelogue on Winnipeg.

JN: So to finish up, your filmmaking style has been referred to as "Postmodern Expressionism" and links it back to the German Expressionism. Do you feel that is appropriate?

GM: I like the idea of expressionism, the simple definition, you know, just an interior landscape expressed in the exterior. It seemed simple enough to me. It gave me a really simple strategy for set design.

JN: Lots of shadows?

GM: Yeah! Shadows are cheap and they produce a lot of atmosphere. You know, you can't afford more décor, then let's add more shadows! Unplug another light. I like the economy, the atmosphere, and it also gives you permission to manner your performances closer to dance or opera. I'm comfortable with it. And you know I had to have someone define just what postmodern was, and it seems that is just isn't a term that is relevant anymore.

"So, this was our first full talkie. And how"

Guy Maddin and George Toles/2009

Extract transcribed from the audio commentary track of *Careful*, published on March 24, 2009 by Zeitgeist Video. Reprinted by permission of the publisher.

George Toles: So, this was our first full talkie. And how. And I wonder what your recollection of the avalanche of voiceover commentary, at the beginning of this decision. I recall being mightily influenced and impressed by Linda's voiceover in *Days of Heaven*. At least a permission to try something with voiceover. I also remember Vic Cowie having the most magnificent reading voice for Shakespeare which he—
Guy Maddin: Yeah, Vic, there he was. (Oh, there's the Seven Ages of Bondage.) Well, I loved Vic Cowie's voice, and he did a little bit of voiceover in *Archangel*, and I idolized him as an actor and as a professor and just as a roué. Well, for people interested in such things, I have it on record that you write every word of dialogue in all the movies, and I love the dialogue, but I needed to find my way into the movie and sort of set the tone for myself to make it, and it was kind of fun to sit down and just sort of poke . . . make an attempt at the voiceover myself for awhile, just to get all the elements—to kind of consider it an overture—and to get all the visual and vocal elements in place early on. But just knowing it would be spoken by Vic really helped.
George Toles: We were both steeped in German Romanticism—reading—at that time—
Guy Maddin:—and its kissing cousins in England.
George Toles: Yeah, I mean, Theodor Storm, and Hoffmann and Kleist, and, well, Hoffmann's *Mines of Falun*—and Hawthorne; American offshoots of romanticism. I think there were lots of threads, and of course the more than thread of Robert Walser's *Jakob von Gunten*—but I mean

it's just suffused, not only with mountain film references, but German romantic flavorings.

Guy Maddin: Yeah, for me it felt very mischievous just being so new to reading and especially reading that stuff. To be able to grab, collage, steal, mutate all these canonical and almost canonical literary masterpieces and stick them into an underground film, or at least the flavor of them or what I processed the flavor of them into these things. There's also a lot of John Ruskin. I just couldn't believe reading John Ruskin's description of mountains how he managed to get so much pedophilia into them and there just seemed to be so much mischief in that stuff. And then later I read *Pierre*, Melville's *Pierre*, a favorite of yours, of course, and realized just how much of the spirit of that was in your dialogue.

George Toles: I wanted, yes, to somehow approximate that fervid stretch beyond strain quality of the language which is both effusive and artificial but somehow drenched in some genuine thing.

Guy Maddin: And of course Mann's *Holy Sinner*, I'd just read, and that does the same thing as Walser's.

George Toles: So do you want to say something about the color in this section because it seems to me if you're going to love *Careful* this is your litmus test. I adore the—

Guy Maddin: Yeah, I was just going to say something about it because it comes out of all those literary sources. I needed that supersaturated effulgence that those writers wielded and yet the themes of the story—to be cautious, to be careful—led me to suppress those very colors after I had painted all the sets with as much saturation as possible. So Mike Marshall, my DOP, and I did these experiments where we overexposed the film various numbers of stops and then printed it back and ended up with a kind of Represso-Vision where the colors seem to be very saturated but then repressed and then seem quivering to get out, and I was quite pleased. This was my first color movie. I was ordered to make the movie in color and never have been more glad—and I've been glad many times—to be ordered around.

George Toles: So how much of the two color Technicolor effect determined the way in which you worked the colors in this.

Guy Maddin: I was really in awe of color films, and scared of them.

George Toles: Careful, Guy.

Guy Maddin: Yes, I know, I thought it was best to take a very cautious approach to color in the film, appropriately enough. A color movie I'd been watching a lot of around this time was *The King of Jazz*, that revue featuring Bing Crosby and the Rhythm Boys, Paul Whiteman, and some unbelievably gorgeous two-strip Technicolor color stuff. Now that stuff really quivers. There's a robin's egg blue that seems to be quivering with the pecking of infant birdies just behind it, and that's just amazing, so I remember writing a post-it note to myself to actually waver the aperture on this so that—in every shot—so that the color saturation would flicker, quiver, or tremble. And I forgot to do it and it's perhaps good luck that I did. It probably would have become a gimmick that would have worn thin.

Guy Maddin

Isabella Rossellini/2009

This interview was commissioned by and first published in *BOMB Magazine*, Issue #109, Summer 2009, pp. 52–59. © *Bomb Magazine*, New Art Publications, and its Contributors. All rights reserved. The *BOMB* Archive can be viewed at www.bombsite.com.

A cinephile would have to delve deep into the industry vaults of spooled monochrome to find a more beautiful ongoing collaboration than that developed by director Guy Maddin and actress Isabella Rossellini. The best comparisons would, no doubt, include the sensual ennui of Monica Vitti reified through the lens of Antonioni or the baroque stare of Liv Ullmann captured in the snow-globe world of Bergman. Few images are more exciting or iconographic than the female form, frenzied or subdued. While this cinematic tradition has been explored in Roland Barthes's ode to the face of Garbo—which he compares to "mystical feelings of perdition"—it is Jean-Luc Godard's glib observation that is the most quotable: "The history of cinema is boys photographing girls."

In contrast to the patriarchal tradition that enjoined the elder, virile artist with his female ingénues, the Maddin/Rossellini relationship is a thoroughly postcoital affair. From their first collaboration in *The Saddest Music in the World* (2003) to their most recent loop *Send Me to the 'Lectric Chair* (2009), they have consistently traded gendered representations of masculine power for a bunco scam of sexual aporias. As a director and an actress whose bond might very well be called "epicene," resistant to the psychology of the domineering male *artiste* but also shedding the habiliments of dowager feminism, their creative romance resides in androgyny.

But sexual transgression is only half of the story. In the Maddin/Rossellini world, sexual identity can never be separated from genealogical identity, conjugal pleasures from the congenital curse. If Rossellini's artistic passions toward the world at large have always appeared as heirlooms of a visionary father, director Roberto Rossellini, then Maddin's visions of the world in miniature have equally proceeded from an impassioned and overbearing mother. In the 2005 Maddin film My *Dad Is 100 Years Old*—scripted entirely by Rossellini—the actress lovingly narrates her father's artistic heritage as she is shadowed by his omnipresent naked belly. Maddin's subsequent films, *Brand Upon the Brain!* (2006) and *My Winnipeg* (2007) have, in turn, featured "Mother" as their central character. Conceiving of elaborate paeans to domesticity with dramatizations of Oedipal longing, Maddin designs beautiful, bleary netherworld—often silent, sometimes surreal, always melodramatic—from the Vaseline-smudged chiaroscuro of his camera eye.

When Maddin and Rossellini produce something together upon the screen, they appear rarely as two separate artists but much more like atmospheres. Hers is the scorched radiance of the sun, and his is the crenellated chill of a snowdrift.

—Erik Morse

Isabella Rossellini: So, Mr. Maddin, I have you in my interrogation chamber!

Guy Maddin: Yes, Isabella. I remember getting to interview you a few years back. I know this is your chance for revenge, but please, no hooding or forced nudity. Remember there are protocols against that now.

IR: I'll let you remind me of that if it comes up. In the meantime, I've been thinking lately of how we met, in Central Park, way back in 2002. Did you set that up? It sure seems convenient for you how it all worked out.

GM: I swear I set up nothing. How could I? I was merely strolling through the park when I saw you petting that big Labrador. It was natural that I would start petting it too.

IR: You didn't hire the Labrador for the occasion?

GM: That's something Fred Astaire would do to meet Ginger Rogers. I wish I were that smart. No. Its master was simply taking it for a walk, and you were talking to its owner, a man who remains only a mustache in my memory, and the dog was holding your hand in its mouth. I do remember pretending not to recognize you. I struck up a chat with you and the mustache and slipped my own hand inside that same Labrador mouth, the one that held your hand.

IR: That was a sneaky move. The men back in Rome would never stoop so low.

GM: I couldn't care less. I was happy. I remember the dog's tongue, which seemed as long as a hall runner, had wrapped itself in between and around all your fingers, and mine too, and then the dog and mustache at some point went away, and we were left crouching on the walk, our fingers all tangled up and glistening with drool.

IR: That's when you mentioned you had written a script for me!

GM: And you ended up working on the picture *The Saddest Music in the World*. Couldn't have worked out better if I'd hired a skywriter! Strange how someone else's dog brought us together, considering how important dogs are to you, how many you have, and how often you've walked your own in Central Park.

IR: Yes, I've always had my own dogs and, more recently, puppies that I help train for the Guide Dog Foundation. Every June the foundation sends me a pregnant dog and I act as midwife to the litter—I keep one puppy and ready it for service. I have one named Jamal right now. He's doing just fine.

GM: Do these puppies ever remind you of your own childhood? I know your parents split up when you were just five, and off you went to live in a Paris hotel, right? That's a change every bit as sudden as being sent off to guide dog college.

IR: Yes, we three kids went to live with my mother in the Hotel Raphael in Paris, but since she had to work in movies, we were often with our nanny. After a year my siblings and I were sent off to Rome to live with my aunt. There I saw my father at least every weekend and my mother whenever she wasn't working on a picture. We were happy puppies.

GM: Long before I met you I'd read your memoir *Some of Me*. I was struck by how frankly you spoke of your love for your father. Your writing voice is unique. I know a ghostwriter was initially hired to compose this book, but then let go after the editor read your superb notes. As a writer you are sometimes still a young daughter; sometimes the worldly sophisticate people expect you to be; sometimes you're as bawdy or clinical as a sailor or scientist—and frequently you're all of these things simultaneously. The real revelation for me was when I read that almost three decades after your father's death you still thought often and tenderly of him. He died way back in June of 1977, exactly three weeks before my own father. That made a temperamental connection with me; I felt we would understand each other.

IR: There was certainly something that clicked between us right away. I'd like to think it was more than our dead fathers. I know we are both comfortable with watching melodrama—perhaps that's your Icelandic heritage. Your motherland has all those sagas that are told in broad, violent strokes. I'm Scanditalian, a perfect mix of Ibsen and opera! We both watch melodrama without cringing, and see the world as melodrama. I've seen you behave very melodramatically, especially on set.

GM: Yes, the first movie we watched together, before you signed on to *Saddest Music*, was *The Unknown*, with Lon Chaney—we both loved it. Lon plays a man in love with a woman who has been traumatized by the groping hands of too many men, so he has his arms amputated in a miscalculated attempt to please her. Very self-castrating! Pure Grand Guignol melodrama! Opera without singing! It's like that movie was shot where Iceland and Italy intersect. I've since watched the movie with other people and never got the same feeling from them. That movie went down so easily for you—it was like watching you drink a glass of water.

So few people understand what melodrama is. It's not real life exaggerated, as so many people feel. It's not the truth exaggerated. Exaggerating the truth would deform it, make the art dishonest. Really good melodrama is the truth *uninhibited*. In our dreams, where our emotions are uninhibited, if we are lucky, we get to do and experience all the things we repress during civilized waking hours. In our dreams we get to possess the one after whom we lust, strike the one we hate, steal, wail out loud, and remove our clothes—all in front of a public which wouldn't tolerate this unrestrained behavior in the daylight world. In our sleep thoughts we get to be as childish as we long to be! We dream the truth about our feelings, sometimes in a discombobulated way, but these are real feelings churning themselves up. In a good melodrama the same disinhibition occurs. You see, these are not *exaggerated* feelings, they are *repressed feelings liberated*. There's a big difference! If you look at melodrama in this light you won't cringe.

IR: I know from watching the films you make that violence is not what holds your interest, though. People and things that are no longer here haunt you; you want to put the feelings they produce in you up on the screen. You thought I was just as haunted as you when we first met, but I'm not. I believe some people are just born haunted—you are one such person. I don't mean to belittle your ghosts. It's a good thing to be so in touch with the past, with your place in the grand flow of time. I've never met anyone more obsessed with calculating his precise position in some big, abstract arc. It's kind of sweet.

GM: By day I'm just following through on a bunch of questions of intense love and longing that are raised in my dreams almost every night. But, oh, Isabella, it's not so sweet. I think there's something wrong with me. It's true. I can't stop thinking of the unstoppable tide of time. It's practically made me a necrophiliac. Let's say I pick up an old baseball card. I read on it that Yogi Berra was born in 1925. I instantly know that that was the year of Babe Ruth's big bellyache; the year my Aunt Lil worked as a chambermaid while my mother was nine and still on the farm; I'll realize that Berra is eighty-four now and that when my grandmother was eighty-four, I was seven—which is when my brother died! My musing always brings me back to some death or sudden removal, someone or something I loved that is no longer with me. No matter what I pick up—be it a baseball card, a paperback, or even dog droppings—I'm always back in this sad, but sweet, state of recollection. It is way more sweet than sad, by the way.

I just assumed that since you too had had this sudden removal at such a young age, you were wired the same way. My long-gone brother remains a mystery to me, but I feel I've somehow gotten to know my father better through all the dreams I've had of him since he died. I'm no mystic; it's possible that I have just started to get to know him through the better access to memory that dreaming sometimes offers. Do you ever dream of your parents, now that they're both not only divorced from each other, but dead? Wait, the idea of Isabella Rossellini dreaming of Roberto Rossellini and Ingrid Bergman makes for quite the star-encrusted dream program.

IR: I think the dream paparazzi might be very disappointed by the unsexy inventory of maiden aunts, old school teachers, Starbucks baristas, and vacuum-cleaner salesmen that people the dreams of their favorite stars. There are not many conventional tabloid photo ops in the subconscious. You or David Cronenberg might like to lug your cameras around in my nightscape, though.

I had a series of dreams about my father for about seven nights in a row shortly after he died. He was so alive and talking to me in them, but every night he was a little worse off. On the first night he was very tired, on the second night he was bluish in color, on the third night he was starting to decay. He wanted to borrow some of my perfume to cover the smell of his rotting. With each passing night his ridiculous condition worsened, yet he also became more stubborn, more reluctant to die. In the end he died in my dreams just as he had died in life. Over the years, my father has returned in occasional dreams, but with his health restored. Once I dreamt that he had not died at all, but had gone to live with a family he liked better than ours. I hated the feelings I was left with all day after having these dreams.

With my mother, the dreams are completely different. She had cancer for nine years before she finally died. In my dreams I approach her, a figure reclining on a couch or bed. She is in her forties and very beautiful. She is healthy, but always half-asleep and so languid. She opens her eyes with great effort, begging to be left alone, only to shut them again. She literally fights through her sleep to say, "I want to be alone," just like Garbo. Then she returns to sleep.

GM: That's uncanny! Have you ever seen *Necrologue* by Matthias Müller? It has exactly the same sad and weighty tone as your dream of your mother; shockingly, the film even stars your mother! The filmmaker takes a shot of Ingrid from *Under Capricorn* and ever so slowly, by step printing the clip into the slowest of slow motion, he opens her eyes, awakens her from sleep, and then just as slowly returns her to it—it takes about five minutes. So strange to hear you describe your mom in the same way Müller presents her.

IR: That's so odd. I must see it.

GM: I'll send you a copy. I've had it for a few years but I thought you might be too uncomfortable looking at your mother represented this way until I just heard your account of that dream. Such a strange coincidence! Speaking of which, as with your later dream of Roberto, where he has found a more suitable family for himself, as a child I found out my father really had one of these secret families, another whole life. A real-life character out of *Wakefield*, but with kids. I spied on them through the window as they dined, marveling at their familial harmony. Then I discovered, with horror, that my mother had the same secret family. Not just one but both of my parents had parallel lives elsewhere, together, with happier and better kids: a Mr. and Mrs. Wakefield, although I don't think Nathaniel Hawthorne had this in mind when he wrote that great tale of deadbeat paternity. Both my mom and dad were much happier one block away. Still, they had to return regularly and grudgingly look after us, their dreary, inferior children. Or, at least, they did in my dreams, for this scenario wasn't really a part of the waking world, but a recurring dream of mine that perplexed me for many adolescent years.

IR: Are these perplexed feelings the kind you are trying to reproduce in your movies? For all their bizarreness, they do orbit around loss and betrayal, things all of us have felt at one time or another.

GM: Yes, it's strange. When I started making movies, I was in my late twenties and thought I was making really hip stuff. It was cheeky and looked underground. But, the more I think of it, I was writing stuff that would more naturally come out of a much older man, an elderly man contemplating all the things that have gone before which he can only revisit through sudden accesses of lucid memory, Proust-like! Admittedly, this older man was a very horny one, and his boner seemed to be the divining rod that found the narrative thread for the director whenever he lost it. But there was definitely a delirious representation of loss in the movies. It was so obsessively represented, in fact, it was almost a celebration.

Now that I've finally finished the book version of *My Winnipeg* and gotten it into stores, now that I'm done with all this self-indulgent consideration, I think I see what I've been up to all along. It's positively puerile in a way. When my brother Cameron passed away, I remember asking my other brother Ross if Cam was going to come back to life. He didn't know what to say, so he just told me, "Yes, he's coming back." I ran upstairs to console my mother with the news that her son would soon be coming back, and alive, too. She corrected me, though I don't think I've ever been able to let go of this childish notion of resurrection. I'm not religious, so it's a secular resurrection. I find it in my movies all the time. People forgetting their loved ones are dead, people forgetting they've been dumped, people going back home again after a long absence—these are all forms of resurrection, ways of reviving feelings for people and places that matter most.

With the film *My Winnipeg* I even became obsessed with casting Ann Savage, the long-retired film noir femme fatale whose ferocity seemed to push through all the decades of her inactivity. She lived and breathed fire for me whenever I watched her in *Detour*, made way back in 1945. I lured her up to my hometown and put her on screen as my mother. I was working with the same mad zeal that possesses Dr. Frankenstein in his lab, except I was godlessly trying to resurrect Ann Savage. She's much more gorgeous than Karloff. In the film I also attempt to raise buildings that have been demolished, to reoccupy my childhood home, to shame the city of Winnipeg for changing even a single thing since my childhood. The whole thing is one big wish fulfilled for a very young child! Except that when you think back to our working definition of melodrama, you realize the movie is actually a melodramatic documentary. Everything I describe in the city is done so with childish, uninhibited feeling. These are my unrepressed longings brought to light and packed into eighty minutes, except in a documentary form, but using the same methods as the director of a good melodrama might.

IR: I love My *Winnipeg*, but I've never thought of it as a melodrama. That's interesting.

GM: I think I'm just developing these takes as I go, but I'm pleased with them. Why shouldn't there be a place for a documentary that eschews objectivity and inhibition and just lets desire flap in the breeze like a giant flag at Perkins? The movie would seem as large a distortion of Direct Cinema's old correlatives as the most heinous propaganda, but unlike propaganda it would be, at heart, completely true!

IR: Well, armed with this new clarity of purpose, what are you up to now? What's your next project?

GM: I want to get back to dramatic fiction and make a feature film. I'm describing this next movie to myself as an autobiography of a house. It might even be narrated by a house, who knows? I want to embed within a story of a large family the powerful feelings held latently within the architecture of a home. Everybody's home, if he or she is lucky enough to have one, is jam-packed with powerful emotional signifiers. Even a homeless person, shuddering beneath a cardboard lean-to, has a perception of that shelter as a home—at least that's what Gaston Bachelard, the author of that postwar philosophical bestseller, *The Poetics of Space*, would assert. I want to expose for the viewer, using melodramatic implements of excavation similar to Bachelard's philosophic ones, the overwhelming and mysterious values both active and dormant in each room of this giant house. Film and philosophy don't always mix so easily, although they obviously can, but the home is a locus of pure feeling and I'm happy to let philosophy stand aside and let classical drama take over. After all, it's as ancient as philosophy, and as durable. If you read Euripides's plays now, over 2,500 years after they were written, they are as easy to ingest as soap operas, and they're beautifully composed and tell us all about our families now. I'm hoping you'll star in the film, Isabella. I think you'd make a great Medea! I know in real life you are the most wonderful mother, but you have to admit you'd be one sexy monster of a mother on screen! You have that Scanditalian edge on Joan Crawford!

IR: I just played a mother in a film. Joaquin Phoenix is my son in *Two Lovers*!
GM: That picture is destined to be a classic. And it's Joaquin's last film, if you're gullible enough to believe what you hear of his retirement.
IR: He is so sweet! One of the great impostors of Hollywood! A very nice man to work with.
GM: So I need you to play another kind of mother in this autobiography of a house. It's called *Keyhole*. It's actually a crime film about a family of gangsters holed up in a big house, but there's been a fissure along gender lines and everyone trembles in fear and loathing within a house divided. In the backstory, you'd be the adoptive mother of an Amazon warrior. I want to adapt Kleist's *Penthesilea* of the '30s, an incredibly intense play about the literal battle of the sexes, between the armies of the ancient Greeks and the Amazons. The beautiful Penthesilea and Achilles hate each other so much they transmute the hatred into lust, naturally. They are constantly tearing away at each other's flesh but don't know why, or to what end, whether mortal or sexual. The lust is almost entomological—it's almost as crazy as with the insects you portray in your *Green Porno* films! I want to borrow all the mad love from Kleist and those amazing shorts of yours and weave them somehow onto this philosophical text. I still find myself wishing that my undergrad philosophy courses had more crazy sex in them. You have more *Green Porno* films coming out, don't you?
IR: Yes, some just came out this spring; they're up on the Sundance Channel site. Four more are coming out this fall.
GM: I just adore them! Everyone should be exposed to your *Green Porno*, from kindergarten kids to debauched old men. They're under a minute in many cases, but they're packed with so much erotic allegory. When you chose the sex lives of insects for your subject, you had yourself a wild frontier of moviemaking. Insects mate so savagely, sometimes so counterintuitively. At times they remind you of the mad love of humans, and at others they are just inexplicably alien. I've always identified with your male black widow spider. You are almost always the male in these sexual reenactments, by the way—I love the joy you put into all that masculine humping! Except with this spider there is no humping. The female spider is too terrifying, so the male collects his sperm on his, well, sort-of hands, and speeds past the female in a cowardly dash, smearing his seed on the female before she suspects anything. I've often

felt like that's what we men are basically doing out here in the great mating ritual marshland. Your little sexual lessons are as cruel as real life, and hilarious too.

IR: I've never thought of them as allegories. I just read up on all these fascinating ways that insects mate. Now, with the latest batch, I've done sea creatures as well. There are so many ways to mate and they're all so much fun! I try to distill what charms or intrigues me about each and then try to personify it. I dress up in a stylized mantis or squid costume and go at it. I've been lucky that people like them so much. You've always bemoaned what a late starter you are, Guy, but I too have always been a late starter. I started modeling at twenty-eight, I started acting in my thirties, writing in my forties, and now I'm directing in my late fifties. I love it. I'm even hoping to get my masters degree in biology in the next few years.

GM: I'm glad you love it, and seem to have no regrets. I still regret not learning to skate till I was eighteen. That kept me out of the National Hockey League. The shame of not skating as a child in Winnipeg—incredible! Is it true you were almost killed by an elephant seal while shooting the latest *Pornos*?

IR: Yes, I was standing in front of one and talking into the camera. This male weighed, I don't know how many tons. Apparently he spotted a female nearby and charged at it. I was standing with my back to this stampeding slab of muscle and had no idea it was coming. If you look carefully, you can see the cameraman reflected in my sunglasses, running for his life. The bull just charged right by me in his pursuit of a mate; he just missed me by what seemed a few inches!

GM: That's a thrill not many people can report having.

IR: It was over before I knew I was having it.

GM: Even that statement seems like a snippet of sexual allegory. Everything that comes out of your head, Isabella! You told me something else about these seals that I like. There is one dominant male who basks in the center of a veritable harem of females, and outside of this harem lie many "peripheral" males waiting for the sultan of the harem to leave or weaken for a second, so they can sneak in for their shot at copulating. I've always been one of these peripheral elephant seal males.

IR: There you go anthropomorphizing again. You're like Walt Disney and his ducks.

But you're not alone. We have a friend in common who couldn't get it out of his head that he was an anglerfish; or at least one as we portray

him in the *Green Porno* films. The male anglerfish attaches itself to the side of the female and slowly loses all his functions except the continual production of sperm. He is reduced to nothing but a set of genitals that impregnates the female whenever she desires it. Likewise, our friend feels he has no brain, no other organs but the One.
GM: These movies of yours really take you on a frightening ride of introspection. That's what I want to expose the kindergarten kids to; more children should be aware of the fathomless terrors of sex! Let's show the world together, Isabella, the plangent hauntings of every home and the empty, but horrifying, attics of sex!
IR: Okay, sign me up.
GM: So I can star you in *Keyhole?* And I want to get your friend Geraldine Chaplin in there, and her daughter Oona! And my new friend Luce Vigo, the daughter of Jean Vigo! Perhaps I can resurrect more than I can handle by engaging these mesmeric talents! I even know Judy Wyler now, daughter of William, though she's not an actress. I must be on the verge of some occult formula which will unleash memory upon itself and show us the unblinking eye of truth in cinema once and for all!
IR: Perhaps you've gone mad?
GM: I'll tell you how mad I am, how mad to resurrect: I have an unshakable fantasy of persuading the great Olivia de Havilland—who's ninety-two, just like my mother—to shoot an extra scene to be tacked on to the end of her 1949 masterpiece *The Heiress*. I would return to the still-surviving *Heiress* set on the Paramount lot in Hollywood and have her walk down the very stairs she climbed sixty years ago after bolting her front door to Montgomery Clift. After descending these steps, she would then unlock that front door and look outside for a second to see if, by some miracle, Monty is still there. Then she could climb the stairs all over again and go back to bed. This scene could be shot so simply! I must do it; if I don't I shall regret the missed opportunity forever. Talk about regrets! O, tortures!

Index

Achilles, 19
Ahab, 163
Ain't It Cool News, xv
Aldrich, Robert, 31
Alekan, Henri, 116
Alibi, 31
Alice, 31
Allan Cup, 68, 121
Almodóvar, Pedro, 59
Altman, Robert, 124
Alton, John, 136
amnesia, 140, 141, 163
amnesia films, 120
Anatomy of Melancholy, The, 123
Antonioni, Michelangelo, 86, 185
Applause, 34
Archangel, xii, 3, 4, 9–10, 11, 12, 13, 19, 22–25, 28, 45, 57, 63, 85–86, 89, 91, 95, 98, 112, 120, 132–33, 141, 150, 168, 181
Archangel (town), 10, 22
Arnold, Martin, 137
Astaire, Fred, 186
Asther, Nils, 32
Astin, John, 54
Atlantis Alliance, 55
Autumn Born, 150
Autumn Leaves, 31
Avalon Hotel, 110
Avedon, Richard, 152

Babes in Toyland, 31
Bacchae, The, 159
Bachelard, Gaston, 192
Bacon, Lloyd, 120
Bad Timing, 15

Bailey, Norma, 83
Bambi, 15
Bamboozled, 48
Banting, Frederick, 48
Barber, Dave, 16
Barrymore, John, 33
Barthelme, Donald, 132, 133
Barthes, Roland, 185
baseball, 135
Battleship Potemkin, 24
Baxter, Ted, 49
Baxter, Warner, 123, 128
Bay, Michael, 115
Bazenholtz, Ben, 23
Beardsley, Aubrey, 53
Beethoven, Ludwig van, 62
Beliveau, Jean, 135
Bennett, Compton, 36
Bergman, Ingmar, 167, 185
Bergman, Ingrid, 144, 189
Berkeley, Busby, 101
Berlin, Germany, 181
Berlin, Irving, 51
Berlinale, 181
Berra, Yogi, 189
Best, Charles, 48
Big Red Shiny, xiv
Birth of a Nation, 21
Birtwhistle, Tara, 69, 102
Bitter Tears of General Yen, The, xv, 32
Black Cat, The, 34
Black Narcissus, 26
Black Silhouette, the, 68
Blackmail, 32, 45, 126
Blore, Eric, 139

Blue Light, The, 32, 129
Bluto, 144
Bogdanovich, Peter, 150
Boles, John, 120
Bolivia, 123
Bollywood, 48
Bomb, xv
Bond, James, 163
Border Crossings, ix, xi
Borzage, Frank, 65
Boston, Massachusetts, 176, 178
Bowman, Scotty, 111
Bracken, Eddie, 139
Brand Upon the Brain!, xiii, 142, 149, 155, 156–58, 166, 168, 170, 171, 175, 186
Broadway, 119
Broken Blossoms, 21
Brooks, James, 121
"Brother, Can You Spare a Dime?," 101
Brothers Grimm, 131, 162, 163
Brown, Jim, 88
Browning, Tod, 34, 38, 64, 92, 162
Buffalo, New York, 154
Buñuel, Luis, 19, 34, 35, 49, 54, 62, 65, 80, 113, 129, 152, 160, 163, 170–71
Burns, Michael, 174, 180
Burton, Robert, 123
Burton, Tim, 19
Bussières, Pascale, 46

Cagney, James, 120, 128
Calgary, Canada, 94
Cameraman's Revenge, The, 32
Canada Council, 172
Canadian Broadcasting Company, 117
Canadian Film Foundation, 23
Canadian filmmaking, 29, 35
Cape Fear, 32
Cape Fear (Scorsese), 88
Capra, Frank, xv, 32, 33
Careful, xii, xv, 26, 27, 28, 42–44, 45–46, 57, 86–91, 92, 93, 95, 100, 106, 121, 122, 128, 129, 141, 160, 168, 182–84
Carrey, Jim, 54
Carver, Raymond, 133
Cashiers du Cinemart, xiii

Cassidy, Neil, 84
Cat People, 149
Celebrations: Islendigudaggurun, 32
Cell phone photography, 178
Central Park, 186, 187
Chaney, Lon, 92, 116, 162, 188
Chang, 32
Chaplin, Charlie, 144
Chaplin, Geraldine, 195
Chaplin, Oona, 195
Charlie's Angels: Full Throttle, 75, 113
Cheever, John, 133
Chekhov, Anton, 27
Chienne, La, 32–33
Child Without Qualities, The, 158, 168
Chronicles of Narnia, The (movie), 173
Church, David, xiv
Chute, David, xiii
Cineaste, 121
Cinemateque (Winnipeg), 16
City Girl, 33
City Streets, 34
Cleveland, Ohio, 175, 178
Clift, Montgomery, 195
Clive, Colin, 35
CN Tower, 159
Coach House Books, 77, 78
Cock Crew, The (*Love-Chaunt in the Chimney*), 148, 149
Cocteau, Jean, 19, 65
Cohan, George M., 123
Cohen, Ari, 23
Connolly, Cyril, 147
Connor, Shawna, 106–7
Conte, Richard, 38
Cooper, Gary, 139
Cooper, Merian C., 32
Cornell, Joseph, 36, 62, 137
Councillor at Law, 33
Cowards Bend the Knee, xiii, xiv, xv, 52, 58, 61, 63–64, 65, 66, 67–69, 79, 85, 97, 102, 106, 121, 132, 135, 136, 138, 142, 148, 151, 153, 154, 155, 156, 157, 158, 159, 160, 163, 166, 167, 175
Cowie, Victor, 68, 89–90, 182
Cox, Paul, 46, 87, 88, 89, 92

Crawford, Joan, 31, 36, 60, 147, 192
Cremaster Cycle, 62
Crime Wave, 81, 82
Cronenberg, David, xii, 23, 29, 36, 51, 141, 189
Crosby, Bing, xi; and the Rhythm Boys, 184
Cukor, George, 36
Curse of the Cat People, 149

Daffy Duck, 62
Dalí, Salvador, 80, 113, 169
David, Paul, 118
Davis, Bette, 147
Day of Wrath, 60, 123
Days of Heaven, 33, 182
Days of Wine and Roses, The, 33
de Havilland, Olivia, 195
de Medeiros, Maria, 58, 120
De Niro, Robert, 167
De Sica, Vittorio, 50
Dead Father, The, xi, 3, 8, 11, 12, 13, 14–15, 19, 51, 66, 79, 80–81, 83, 119, 121, 130, 132, 133, 141
Dead Father, The (Barthelme), 132, 133
Dedrick, Christopher, 104, 105
Dein, Edward, 35
Delvecchio, Alex, 111
DeMille, Cecil B., 25, 146
Design for Living, 33
Detour, 191
Detroit Red Wings, 111
Dietrich, Marlene, 139
Dikemaster's Daughter, The, xii, 29, 36, 47, 51, 92–93, 121, 150
Direct Cinema, 192
Dirigible, 33
Disney, Walt, 194
Divine, 135
D.O.A., 33
Dobrowolska, Gosia, 88
Documentary Channel, 151, 174, 177, 180
Dolby Stereo Surround, 90–91
Dominion Bridge factory, 119
Don't Look Now, 86
Douglas, Kirk, 54
Downtime, 38

Dr. Frankenstein, 191
Dr. Jekyll and Mr. Hyde, 33
Dr. Zhivago, 24
Dracula, 138
Dracula (Browning), 38, 64
Dracula (Coppola), 38
Dracula: Pages from a Virgin's Diary, xiii, xv, 47, 51–52, 59, 64, 65, 68, 69, 73, 79, 96, 101, 102, 107, 108, 117–18, 138, 142, 154, 155
Dreyer, Carl Theodor, x, xv, 38, 60, 61, 65, 66, 121, 123, 133
Drones, xi, 38–39, 47, 58
Duvall, Shelly, 46
DV, 136–37, 151
Dyck, Russ, 34

East of Borneo, 62
East Side, West Side, 34
Eastern Europe, 126
Eaton's, 178
Ebert, Roger, xvi
Ed Sullivan Show, The, 54
Edison, Thomas, 100
Edison and Neemo, 100, 150, 155
Edward VII, 163
Egoyan, Atom, xii, 29, 50, 51, 170
Eisenstein, Sergei, 19, 24, 37, 47, 65
El Salvador, 71
El Topo, 51
Electra, 52, 132, 153, 159
Emu (a Drone), 48
Enright, Robert, ix, xi
Epstein, Jean, 34
Eraserhead, xiv, 22, 28, 80, 81, 112–13
Erin Brockovich, 124
Eternal Sunshine of the Spotless Mind, 110
Ethiopia, 123
Euripides, 60, 132, 145, 147, 153, 157, 159, 192
Extra Large Pictures, xi
Eye Like a Strange Balloon Mounts Towards Infinity, The, 61, 66, 92, 107, 121
Eyolfson, Lil (aunt), 37, 64, 65, 67, 69, 94, 140, 189
Eyolfson, Ron (uncle), 32

fado, 71
Fall of the House of Usher, The, 34
Fantasia, 146
Far From Heaven, 124
father figures, 121
Faulkner, William, 131, 132
Faust (opera), 103
Fehr, Darcy, 68, 138
Fellini, Federico, 144
Fichman, Niv, 108, 125
Film Comment, 134
Film Company, The, 142, 151
Film Forum, 59, 97
Film Forum at the Berlinale, 181
film noir, 11, 59, 67
First Nations, 162
Fisher, Terence, 34
Fisher Price Pixelvision, 179
Flaming Creatures, 50
Flaubert, Gustave, 16
Foolish Wives, 47, 68
football, 135
Footlight Parade, 120, 123, 124
Forbidden Games, 146
Ford, John, 34
42nd Street, 123
Four Devils, 92
Fox, David, 110
Frampton, Peter, 122
France, 134
Frankenheimer, John, 33
Franklin, Chester M., 45
Free Design, The, 104
French Symbolism, 141
Fresh Air, xiii, 70, 72
Freud, Sigmund, 86, 117, 133, 175
Freund, Karl, 35
Friedrich, Caspar David, 61
Friesen, Melanie, 88
From the Atelier Tovar, 77, 87, 132, 168
From the House of the Dead, 103
Fuller, Dale, 47

Gance, Abel, 36, 66, 92, 136, 138
Garbo, Greta, 139, 185
Gardner, Katya, 91
Garfunkle, Art, 15
Garland, Judy, 36
George, Maude, 47
George Costanza, 62
German Expressionism, 12, 65, 96, 119, 181
German Romanticism, 182, 183
Gibbons, Cedric, 106
Gimli, 21, 44, 83, 141
Gimli Hospital, 17
Gimli Saga, xii, 8, 40
Gimli Theatre, 31
Glass, Philip, 34, 64
Gleason, Jackie, 33
"Gloomy Sunday," 123
Glory, 132
Godard, Jean-Luc, 185
Godden, Mark, 101, 155
Golden Braid, 88
Gonick, Noam, xii, xiii, 46, 82, 137–38
Gorshin, Frank, xv, 46, 53, 54, 92; as the Riddler, 54
Gottli, Michael, 20, 23, 25, 95
Gounod, Charles-François, 103
Goya, Francisco, 24
Grace Hospital (birthplace), 4
Grand Guignol, 159, 188
Grand Illusion (theater), 94
Grand Theft Canoe, 107
Grandmother, The, 80
Grant, Cary, 144
Gravina, Cesare, 47, 68
Great Depression, 70, 101, 119, 126
Great Train Robbery, The, 161
Greed, 68
Green Cine, xiv
Green Porno, 193–95
Greendale, 83, 177
Greene, Lorne, 180
Gretzky, Wayne, 31
Griffith, D. W., 21
Gross, Terry, xiii
Guide Dog Foundation, 187
Gurdebeke, John, 149

Hall, Monty, 83
Halloween, 83

Halperin, Victor, 38
Hamburg, New York, 154
Hamlet, 27, 60
Hammer Films, 15
Hammerstein, Oscar, 105
Handford, Ian, 32, 38
Hands of Ida, The, xii
Hands of Orlac, The, 35, 52, 96, 132, 153, 159, 160
Hanec, Greg, 38
Hanford, Dr. Cuthbert, 4
"Happy Birthday to You," 103, 104
"Happy Days Are Here Again," 101
Harvie, John, xi, 9, 32, 120, 132
Hatchet Man, The, 32
Hawks, Howard, 120
Hawthorne, Nathaniel, 182, 190
Haynes, Todd, 59
Hays Code, 125
HD-TV color and cameras, 107–8, 178, 179
Heart of the World, The, xiii, 35, 47, 61, 64, 79, 92, 95–96, 121, 127, 136, 137, 142, 160
Heath, Terry, 11
Heck, Angela, 18, 20, 91, 95
Heflin, Van, 34
Heimatfilm, 65
Heiress, The, 195
Hell's Angels, 126
Herrmann, Bernard, 90, 105
Hickenlooper, George, 129
Hill, George Roy, 38
Hillis, Aaron, xiv
Hitchcock, Alfred, 32, 45, 94, 126, 144, 170, 171
Hobart, Rose, 65
Hoberman, J., 77
hockey, xv, 64, 67, 76, 109, 110, 121, 136, 170
hockey film (unmade), 29–30
Hoffmann, E. T. A., 182
Hollywood, 79, 119
Holy Sinner, The, 183
Horror of Dracula, The, 34
Horton, Edward Everett, 139
Hospital Fragment, 35, 94–95

Hotel Raphael, 187
How Green Was My Valley, 34
Howe, Gordie, 31, 111
Hughes, Howard, 126
Hugo, Victor, 30, 131
Hull, Bobby, 87, 88
Hush, Hush Sweet Charlotte, 31
Hutton, Betty, 139

"I and My Chimney," 51
Ibsen, Henrik, 188
IFC Films, 97, 105
I'll Do Anything, 93, 121
"I'm in You," 122
Imitation of Life, xiv, 60, 122
"In Flander's Fields," 9
Independent Cinema, xiv
Independent Film Channel, 178
Inland Empire, 179
Institute Benjamenta, 87
Internationals, The, 82
Internet Movie Database, 156, 173
Interpretation of Dreams, The, 86
Ishiguro, Kazuo, 57, 65, 70, 99, 100, 122, 125, 126
Italy, 134
Ivan the Terrible, 96
Ivan the Terrible Part III, 37
Ivory Snow, 91

J'accuse, 136
Jackson, Peter, 152
Jacobs, Ken, 62
Jakob von Gunten, 87, 182
Janáček, Leos, 103
Jancsó, Miklós, 36
Jazz Singer, The, 21, 22
Jesus Christ, 95, 96
Jodorowsky, Alejandro, 51
Joe 90, 34
Johnny Guitar, 34
Jones, Alan, xiii
Jumbo Pictures, xi

Kansas City, Missouri, 175
Kansas City Confidential, 34

Karlson, Phil, 34
Kaufman, Boris, 37
Kaurismaki, Aki, 63
Keaton, Buster, 51, 61, 116
Kendal Cinema, 176
Kennedy, John F., Jr., 95
Kern, Jerome, 105, 122
Keyhole, 194, 195
Kid Brother, 43–44
Kill Bill Vol. 2, 110
Kinescope, 33
King Kong, 32, 91
King of Jazz, The, 42, 183–84
Kingston, Ontario, 40
Kino Delirium, xi, xv, 79, 92
"Kites Are Fun," 104
Klymkiw, Greg, 17, 38–39, 85, 88, 91
Klymkiw, Julian, 88
Korine, Harmony, 59
Korngold, Erich Wolfgang, 90
Kozak, John, 16
Kramer, Edith, 97
Krige, Alice, 46, 69, 106
Kuchar, George and Mike, 148
Kuleshov, Lev, 47
Kurosawa, Akira, 37

La Roue, 36, 66, 92, 136
Lachman, Ed, 124, 131
L'Age d'or, 62, 80, 113, 129, 160, 170
Lake Winnipeg, 17, 45
Lancaster, Burt, 54
Lang, Fritz, 11, 65, 66
Larionov, Igor, 111
Laurie, Piper, 33
Lauzon, Jean Claude, 35
Laxness, Halldor, 53
Le Roy, Mervyn, 34, 120
Lee, Christopher, 34
Lee, Rowland V., 39
Lee, Spike, 48, 49
Leech Woman, The, 35
Lemieux, Mario, 135
Leni, Paul, 68
Leolo, 35
Lewis, Dave, 111

Lewis, Joseph H., xv, 37
Lichtenstein, Roy, 128
Lifetime Achievement Award at the Telluride Film Festival, 176
Liliom, 65, 66
Lil's, 68
Lim, Dennis, 134
Lindsay, Ted, 111
Lipsett, Arthur, 137
Little Match Girl, The, 35
Little Nicky, 48
Lloyd, Harold, 43–44
Lola Montes, 36
London, 134, 181
London After Midnight, 92
Lord Dufferin, 8
Lorre, Peter, 35, 96
Losier, Marie, xii, xiv
Love Me Tonight, 33, 127
Love-Chaunt in the Chimney (The Cock Crew), 148, 149
Lubitsch, Ernst, 33–34, 38, 39, 139
Lumière, Auguste and Louis, 33, 161, 175
Lumière and Company Project, 161
Luna Park, 63
Lupino, Ida, 36
Lyceum Theater, 4
Lynch, David, xii, xiv, 19, 26, 58, 80–81, 112–13, 151, 152, 176, 179

M, 21
Mackendrick, Alexander, 37
MacMillan, Ross, 94
Mad Love, 35, 96
Maddin, Cameron (brother), xi, 73, 140
Maddin, Charles (father), xi, 4, 67, 140, 156
Maddin, Guy: on acting, 82, 138; on amnesia, 63, 74, 133, 163; on *Archangel*, 5, 9, 85–86; on *Archangel* as a real place, 9–10; on aspect ratios, 106; on autobiography, 63, 67, 74, 131, 132, 153, 157, 158, 167, 175; on ballet dancers, 101–2, 117, 138–39; on being a cult director, 148–49; on being famous, 83; on being a hockey fan, 135; on birthdays, 103–4; on blackface, 21–22, 48–49, 162; on budgets of

Archangel, 23; on budgets of *Gimli*, 23; on budgets of his film, 172; on budgets of *Saddest Music*, 58; on budgets of *Twilight*, 29, 92–93; on Buñuel, 163; on camerawork, 7, 9; on camp, 59, 124; on Canada as a melting pot, 128; on Canadian cinema, 50–51, 100, 116, 161, 175; on the Canadian flag, 128; on cannibalizing, 12; on car accidents in his movies, 73; on cartoons, 15; on chicken, 122; on childhood terrors, 5; on Christianity, 96; on Christmas, 35; on color films, 26, 42, 86, 183–84; on competitive brothers, 131; on Joseph Cornell, 137; on cowardice, 62, 67, 163–64, 167; on crowd scenes, 15; on *The Dead Father*, 8, 12, 14–15, 80–81; on dead fathers, 144–45; on decadence, 53; on dialog, 124, 125; on diaries, 117–18, 134–35; on digital video, 151–52; on directors of photography, 115; on dramatic illusion, 146; on dreams, 8, 17, 74, 81, 86, 130, 169, 178, 189; on Dreyer, 60–61; on DVD collection of all his short films, 150; on faces, 83; on fairy tales, 25, 59, 132; on families, 70; on fearing death, 175; on financing his films, 172; on fish in *Gimli*, 21; on forgetfulness, 10, 13, 25, 63; on Abel Gance, 136; on getting into movie making, 6–7; on ghosts, 111, 188; on Gimli, 17; on gluttony, 167; on "going Hollywood," 23, 27; on Googling his father's name, 164; on grief, 73, 74; on "Hamletism," 145, 165; on hands, 68; on his birth, 4; on his childhood, 5; on his childhood homes, 178; on his diaries, 77–79; on his editing style, 148–49; on his interest in war, 24; on his mother watching *The Dead Father*, 14; on his "re-creating film history film by film" project, 161; on honesty, 112; on horror movies, 4; on how his filmmaking career has changed him, 164–65; on humanism, 163; on hysteria, 43; on the idea of a Winnipeg film style, 7–8, 11; on independent cinema, 172; on installation art, 61; on the Jekyll and Hyde and werewolf myths, 157; on Kinescope, 33; on laziness, 9, 152; on lighthouses, 159; on lust, 167; on lying, 98; on David Lynch, 80–81; on Cameron Maddin, 75, 165, 189, 191; on Charles Maddin, 4, 74, 131, 164–65, 187, 189–90; on Herdis Maddin, 4, 165, 189, 191; on Kyle McCulloch, 84–85; on mediocre movies, 75; on meeting Isabella Rossellini, 186–87; on melodrama, 59, 60, 68, 70, 122, 131, 143, 146–47, 163, 188, 191; on memory, 75, 171; on minimalism, 21; on modernism, 21; on Murnau, 15; on music, 22; on musicals, 121–22; on myoclonus, 111; on mythmaking, 5–6, 63, 68, 114, 175, 177; on the narrative arc of *My Winnipeg*, 180; on necrophilia, 15, 114; on neorealism, 9; on nostalgia, 5; on objects in movies, 171; on old girlfriends, 89; on old people, 168–69; on opera directing, 103; on ostriches, 53; on painting and house painting, 171; on part-talkies, 21, 31, 32, 126–27; on passive narrative, 6; on passivity, 16; on pastiche, 124; on the phrase "heart attack," 74; on ping pong, 16, 18; on police movies, 11; on political satire, 123; on politics in his films, 11; on power, 18; on primitivism, 28, 47, 57, 62, 96, 113, 114, 127, 130, 132, 146, 169; on propaganda, 10–11; on realism in movies, 143; on reality TV shows, 146; on research, 48, 168; on Denise Richards and Alyssa Milano, 137; on *Rose Hobart*, 137; on sadness, 75; on Bruno Schultz, 80; on screenwriting, 9, 153; on self-loathing, 167–68; on self-pity, 70, 72, 73, 79; on sex in films, 16; on sexual jealousy, 131; on shooting schedules of *Archangel*, 23; on shooting schedules of *Gimli*, 23; on showbiz parents, 83–84; on silent cinema, 21, 24; on the similarities between Maddin and Roberto Rossellini, 143; on skating, 76, 194; on songwriting, 72; on the sound of his own voice, 180; on soundtrack music, 42–43, 64–65, 71–72, 90–91, 100–1, 103–5, 127; on Spanish, 133–34; on special

effects, 25, 29; on sports writing, 109; on spying, 61, 69; on stigma, missing limbs, and physical impairments, 162–63; on success, 16; on surrealism, 59, 81, 113, 163; on swimming, 153, 157; on swimming in Lake Winnipeg, 17–18; on *Tales of the Gimli Hospital*, 8–9, 13, 15, 16, 20–22; on television, 76; on titles for his movies, 155–56; on Tobey (childhood dog), 76; on George Toles, 99–100, 153, 154, 171; on truth in *My Winnipeg*, 176; on *Twilight of the Ice Nymphs*, 49–50; on *Twilight*'s dual lead actors, 54–55; on the two versions of *Sissy-Boy Slap-Party*, 94; on unplanned pregnancies, 81, 112; on unrequited love, 113; on the use of the word "tropes," 63; on vampires, 15; on virginity, 118; on von Stroheim, 47; on watching television, 4; on Winnipeg actors, 124; on the Winnipeg Arena being torn down, 168; on working in a bank, 129; on wrestling in *Gimli Hospital*, 14, 20; on writing film criticism, 134; on writing screenplays, 99
Maddin, Herdis Eyolfson (mother), xi, 4, 67, 69, 102, 140, 157
Maddin, Janet (sister), xi, 156, 157
Maddin, Ross, 191
Madison, Guy, ix, 4
Magnificent Ambersons, The, 149
Mahler, Gustave, 65, 101
Mala Noche, 151
Maldoror: Tigers, 95, 149
Malick, Terrence, 33
Mamoulian, Rouben, 33, 127
Man Who Laughs, The, 30, 68
Man Without a Past, 63
Mandelstam, Osip, 133
Manitoba, Canada, 21, 40, 45, 119, 141
Manitoba Arts Council, 7, 9, 23, 172
Mann, Thomas, 183
Mark of the Vampire, 92
Marlow, Jonathan, xiv
Maroons (Winnipeg hockey team), xi
Marshall, Mike, 183
Mary Tyler Moore Show, The, 49

Marykuca, Kathy, 23
Mason, James, 34, 36
Masquerade, 87
Master of the House, 65
Masterpiece Theater, 43
Mate, Rudolph, 33
Matisse, Henri, 127
Matrix Reloaded, The, 75
Mauve Decade, 30
Mayo, Archie, 37
McBride, Jason, 77
McCulloch, John, 90
McCulloch, Kyle, 8, 17, 20, 21, 22, 23, 45, 46, 84–85, 88, 89, 95, 138, 162
McDaniel, Hattie, 37
McKinney, Mark, 58, 104, 106, 110, 120, 123, 124
McMillan, Meg, 106
McMillan, Ross, 55, 110
Mechanical Infanta, The (*The Piano Tuner of Earthquakes*), 87
Medea, 41, 192
Medea (von Trier), 136
Meins, Gus, 31
Méliès, Georges, 33
Melodrama, 166
Melville, Herman, 43, 51, 148, 183
Memento, 63
Memorial Day Service, 9
Mexican genre cinema, 121
MGM Home Video, 106
Midsummer Night's Dream, A (movie), 29, 116
Mifune, Toshiro, 37
Milano, Alyssa, 137
Milestone, Lewis, 38
Milwaukee, Wisconsin, 178
Mines of Falun, 182
Mini-DV, 178
Minneapolis, Minnesota, 159
minstrelsy, 48–49
Miracle of Morgan's Creek, The, 35
Mitchum, Robert, 32
Moby Dick, 43, 51, 68, 163
Monk, Philip, 61
Montpellier, Luc, 115–16

Montreal Canadiens, 88, 135
Montreal Expos, 104
Montreal World Film Festival, 4
Moore, Michael, 146
Moscow, Russia, 71
Mr. Beaks (Jeremy Smith), xv
Muller, Matthias, 137, 190
Munich, Germany, 129
Munich International Film Festival, 3–4
Murnau, F. W., 15, 33, 65, 92
Museum of Modern Art, 122; "Canadian Front," 121
musicals, 79
Musil, Robert, 133
Muybridge, Eadweard, 63
My Dad Is 100 Years Old, 142, 143–45, 149, 186
My Winnipeg, xii, xiv, 151, 174, 176–79, 186, 191
My Winnipeg (book), 191

Nabokov, Vladimir, x, 99, 121, 132, 133
Nadeau, James, xiv
Napoleon, 136
National Hockey League, 88, 111, 194
National Society of Film Critics, 85
Nature Wildlife Theatre, 180
Neale, Brent, 46, 95
Necrologue, 190
Negin, Louis, 68
Negulesco, Jean, 36
Neorealism, 142–43
Nerval, Gerard de, 133
Neville, Sarah, 23, 45, 91
New Iceland, 40
New York City, 134, 175, 181
New York Yankees, 104
Night of the Hunter, 65
1979 Avco Cup, The, 31
Nolte, Nick, 93
Nosferatu, 15
Notorious, 144
Nuba, The, 129

O'Brien, Edmond, 33
Obsession of Billy Botski, The, 6

Oilers (hockey team), 31
Oland, Warner, 32
Oldman, Gary, 38
Olvidados, Los, 35
Olympia Film Festival, 87
Ono, Yoko, 137
Ophüls, Max, 35, 36
Ordet, 60, 61, 64, 66
Ottawa Senators, 111
Ozu, Yasujiro, 61

Pacific Film Archive, 97
Pageant 16mm projector, 47
Paizs, John, xi, 6, 81–82
Pangborn, Franklin, 139
Paramount, 195
Paris, France, 187
Passion of the Christ, The, 95
Payne, John, 34
Penn, Sean, 80, 139
Penthesilea, 193
Peranson, Mark, 120
Père Lachaise, 148
Perestroika, 126
Perfect Circle Productions, 100
Perkins's, 192
Persona, 167
Phantom Museum, The, 97
Phoenix, Joaquin, 193
Picasso, Pablo, 127
Pichel, Irving, 37
Pickford, Mary, 128
Pierre, 43, 183
Pinocchio, 84
Plaisir, Le, 35
Playboy Playmate of the Year, 150
Poetics of Space, The, 192
Polo, Malvina, 47
Poltergeist, 5
Polyester, 135
Pomps of Satan, The, 30
Porton, Richard, xii, xiv
Powell, Michael, 26
Power Plant Contemporary Art Gallery, 57, 58, 61, 67, 96–97
Primitivism, 166

Procak, Ihor, 150
Prokofiev, Sergei, 65
Proust, Marcel, 137, 191
Prussia, 45
Pudovkin, V. I., 37

Quad Cinema (New York City), 22
Quandt, James, xiv
Quay Brothers, 36, 58, 87, 97
Quick and the Dead, The, 36

Raiders of the Lost Ark, 80
Raimi, Sam, 36
Ramones, The, 121, 130
Random Harvest, 120
Ray, Nicholas, 34, 64
Raymond, Gene, 39
Reagan, Ronald, 39
Red and the White, The, 36
"Red Maple Leaves," 120
Redon, Odilon, 61
Reimer, Terry, 7, 35
Reinhardt, Max, 116
Remains of the Day, The (novel), 70
Renoir, Jean, 32, 35
Reykjavik Film Festival, 21
Richard, Maurice, 88
Richards, Denise, 137
Richler, Mordecai, 135
Riefenstahl, Leni, 32, 42, 48, 86, 88, 129, 180
Rimmer, Vince, 46
Rite of Spring, The, 90
RKO, 149
Road House, 36
Road to Glory, The, 120
Robertson, Cliff, 33
Robeson, Paul, 123, 144
Robinson, Edward G., 32
Rocky Horror Picture Show, The, 22
Roeg, Nicholas, 15
Rogers, Charles, 31
Rogers, Ginger, 186
Rome, 186, 187
Ronde, La, 36

Rose Hobart, 36, 62, 137
Rosenbaum, Jonathan, 128
Rossellini, Isabella, xv, 57, 58, 59, 69, 106, 110, 112, 120, 124, 125, 134, 142, 143–45, 149, 166, 186–95
Rossellini, Roberto, 59, 142–45, 152, 186, 189, 190
Rotterdam Film Festival, 58, 61
Rowan and Martin's Laugh In, 8–9
Royal Academy of Dramatic Arts, 94
Royal Winnipeg Ballet, xiii, 69, 142; *Dracula*, 142
Ruskin, John, 183
Russell, Michael, ix
Ruth, Babe, 189

Sacks, Oliver, 163
Saddest Music in the World, The, xiii, xv, 57, 58, 63, 65, 69, 70, 72, 74, 77, 89, 93, 94, 97, 98, 103, 104, 106, 107, 108, 110, 114, 116, 119–20, 121, 122, 123, 124, 125, 126, 132, 134, 142, 152, 153, 166, 173, 185, 187, 188
Salammbo, 16–17
San Francisco International Film Festival, 77, 98
Sanatorium Under the Sign of the Hourglass (Bruno Schultz), 79
Sandler, Adam, 48
"Santo" Mexican wrestling, 124
Saturday Night Fever, 4
Savage, Ann, 191
Scarecrow Video, 87
Scarlet Street, 32–33
Schoedsack, Ernest B., 32
Schroeter, Werner, 58
Schultz, Bruno, x, 80, 87, 133
Schumacher, Joel, 48
Scorsese, Martin, 87, 88, 167
Scotland, 71
Sea Beggars, 51
Seattle, Washington, 94, 142, 155, 158
Seattle World's Fair (1962), 158–59
Sebald, W. G., 174
Secretariat, 35

Seid, Steve, 97
Send Me to the 'Lectric Chair, 185
Serling, Rod, 33
Seventh Veil, The, 36
78 RPs, 101
Shakespeare, William, 182
Shapiro, Jody, 180
"Show Me the Way," 122
Signora di Tutti, La, 36
Silent cinema, 166
Simpson, O. J., 88
Sins of the Fleshapoids, 148
Sirk, Douglas, xiv, 60, 119, 122, 145
Sissy-Boy Slap-Party, 30, 51, 94, 97, 156
16 mm, 115
Slap Shot, 135
Smith, Gavin, 134
Snyder, Stephen, xi, 35
Some of Me, 187
"Song Is You, The," 105, 122
South Park, 84, 85
Soviet agitprop, 96
Soviet cinema, 136
Space Needle, 158–59
SPECTRE, 163
Spokane, Washington, 159
St. Laurent, Yves, 51
Stack, Robert, 60, 147
Stanley Cup, 110, 135
Star Is Born, A, 36
Starbucks baristas, 189
Starewicz, Wladyslaw, 32
Stewart, Amy, 69
Stockholm, Sweden, 71
Stoker, Bram, 64, 117, 138, 142
Stop Smiling, xiv
Storm, Theodor, 182
Storm Over Asia, 37
Stranger Than Paradise, 38
Stratten, Dorothy, 150
Stravinsky, Igor, 90
Street of Crocodiles, 87
Strike, 37
Sturges, Preston, 35
Sundance Channel, 193

Sundance Film Festival, 77
Sunrise, 33
Super-8, 96, 107, 115, 136, 158, 177, 178, 179
Super-16, 178, 179
Surrealism, 65
Svankmayer, Jan, 31
Svengali, 37, 150, 154
Sviridov, Georgi, 64
Sweet Smell of Success, The, 11, 37
Swiss Alps, 129
Sydney, 181

Tales from the Gimli Hospital, xii, xv, 3, 4, 6, 12, 13, 15, 16, 18, 19, 20–22, 23, 26, 28, 40–41, 45, 47, 57, 63, 64, 65, 82, 83, 85, 91, 94, 95, 100, 121, 141, 162
Technicolor, 45, 126, 183, 184
Telefilm Canada, 23, 93
Telluride Film Festival, xii, 29
Teodoro, José, xiv
Terminator 3, 113
Terror in a Texas Town, xv, 37
That Obscure Object of Desire, 55
Theron, Charlize, 91
They Won't Believe Me, 37
This Is Spinal Tap, 38
Thompson, J. Lee, 32
Three Songs About Lenin, 37
Three's Company, 61
Throne of Blood, 37
Tiefland, 86, 88, 94
Timbuktu, 178
Tin Pan Alley, 100–1
Tobey (childhood dog), xi
Toles, George, xi, xv, 6, 9, 10, 26, 50, 87, 99–100, 103, 124, 125, 141, 148, 149, 153, 154, 159, 166, 171, 182–84; on eavesdropping, 44; on his father's love of Frank Gorshin, 54
Toll of the Sea, The, 45
Toronto, Canada, 67, 77, 91, 96, 159, 181
Toronto Festival of Festivals (Toronto Film Festival), 4
Toronto International Film Festival, xiii, 47, 59, 105, 155, 166

Toronto Maple Leafs, 111
Traeger, Tracy, 91
Transylvania, Romania, 138
Tribeca Film Festival, 174, 181
Triumph of the Will, 11
Trouble in Paradise, 38
Tunes a Plenty, 38
Turchyn, Gerry, 7
Twilight of the Ice Nymphs, xii, xiii, xv, 28, 29, 35, 46, 49–50, 53–56, 57, 61, 65, 69, 87, 92–94, 95, 98, 106, 125, 141–42, 148, 149, 173
Two Lovers, 193

Ukrainian bandurists, 71
Ulan Bator, Mongolia, 178
Ullmann, Liv, 185
Ulmer, Edgar G., 34, 107
Umbrellas of Cherbourg, 136
Un Chien Andalou, 62, 80
Under Capricorn, 190
Undercover Brother, 137
Universal horror, 154
Universal Studios, 60
University of Manitoba, xi, 155
University of Winnipeg, xi, 176
Unknown, The, 38, 188
Untouchables, The, 136

Vampyr, xv, 38, 60, 133
Van Sant, Gus, 151
Vancouver, British Columbia, 77, 90, 100, 150
Vancouver International Film Festival, 88
Vatnsdal, Caelum, xi, xv, 79, 95, 96
Vertov, Dziga, 37
Vienna Film Festival, 58
Vigo, Jean, 195
Vigo, Luce, 195
Village Voice, xiv, 77, 134, 135
Virgin Suicides, The, 124
Viridiana, 163
Vitti, Monica, 185
von Helmolt, Vonnie, 107–8
von Kleist, Heinrich, 182, 193
von Sternberg, Joseph, 32, 145, 152

von Stroheim, Erich, 47, 51, 68
von Trier, Lars, 136

Wagner, Richard, 105
Waiting for Twilight, xii, 46, 49, 82, 137–38
Walk in the Sun, A, 38
Walser, Robert, x, 87, 129, 133, 182, 183
Walt Disney cartoons, 15
Warhol, Andy, 66
Warner Bros., 101
Waters, John, 135
Watson, J. S., 51
Wayne, John, 62
Webber, Melville, 51
Wedding of the Painted Doll, 126
Weinberg, Herman G., 33
Welk, Lawrence, 49–50
Welles, Orson, 65, 94
Wellman, William, 32, 101
"We're in the Money," 101
Wershler-Henry, Darren, 78
West, Roland, 31
West of Zanzibar, 103
White, Barry, 24
White, Mike, xiii
White Zombie, 38
Whiteman, Paul, 42, 184
Whitmey, Nigel, 46, 55, 94
Widmark, Richard, 36
Wild Boys of the Road, 101
Willow Island, 44
Willy Loman, 58
Winnipeg, Canada, 71, 83, 84, 88, 90, 91, 106, 119, 122, 124, 126, 128, 130–31, 133, 134, 138, 140, 141, 144, 149, 151, 152, 157, 166, 173, 174, 176–81, 191
Winnipeg Arena, 52, 67, 68, 140, 168; being torn down, 168
Winnipeg Film Group, xi, 4, 9, 12–13, 121, 141, 148
Winnipeg Folk Arts Council, 71
Winnipeg Jets (hockey team), 31, 39
Winnipeg Maroons, 67, 121, 140, 142
Winnipeg University, 21
Wonderful, Horrible World of Leni Riefenstahl, The, 129

Wood, Edward D., 11
World Hockey League, xv, 31
World of Henry Orient, The, 38
World War I, 120, 141, 168
Written on the Wind, 60, 147
Wuthering Heights, 73
Wyler, Judy, 195
Wyler, William, 33

Young, Neil, 83, 177
Young, Robert, 37, 195

Zabava, 38–39
Zeitgeist, 97
Ziegfeld, Flo, 126
Zoo in Budapest, 39
Zookeeper's Workbook, 149

www.ingramcontent.com/pod-product-compliance
Lightning Source LLC
Chambersburg PA
CBHW021839220426
43663CB00005B/311